W. Warren Bentley

Songs of the New Life

a Collection of gospel hymns and choicest music for use in gospel meetings,

devotional meetings, and the Sabbath-school

W. Warren Bentley

Songs of the New Life
a Collection of gospel hymns and choicest music for use in gospel meetings, devotional meetings, and the Sabbath-school

ISBN/EAN: 9783337265779

Printed in Europe, USA, Canada, Australia, Japan

Cover: Foto ©Lupo / pixelio.de

More available books at **www.hansebooks.com**

SONGS

OF THE

NEW LIFE:

A COLLECTION OF

Gospel Hymns and Choicest Music

FOR USE IN

GOSPEL MEETINGS, DEVOTIONAL MEETINGS, AND
THE SABBATH-SCHOOL,

BY

W. Warren Bentley.

Philadelphia: **JOHN J. HOOD,** 1018 Arch St.

COPYRIGHT, 1883, BY JOHN J. HOOD.

GREETING.

Go, precious work, and sweetly sing
   The pure, unchanging love
Of Him, our best and dearest Friend
   In earth or heaven above;
Go, precious work, a message bear
   To manhood, youth, and age;
Thy songs of joy, like crystal streams,
   Gush forth from every page.

Go, precious work, divinely blest,
   Oh, may thy mission be;
God grant that many, many souls
   May come to Him through thee;
Go, precious work, faith bids thee on,
   Her wings will speed thy flight;
Where sorrow dwells and darkness reigns,
   Go, scatter joy and light.

May they, whose Christian zeal combined
   Thy songs with greatest care,
And for the glory of their Lord
   Now send them forth with prayer,
May they behold their precious work
   Fast spreading far and wide,
And millions coming home to Him
   Who once for sinners died.

—FANNY J. CROSBY.

New York, Jan. 1, 1883.

SONGS OF THE NEW LIFE.

2. Are You Ready to go?

E. A. H. — "Watch therefore."—Matt. xxiv. 42. — Rev. E. A. Hoffman.

1. Are you ready to meet the Lord Should he suddenly come this way?
2. If the summons should greet thee now, Would your spirit be wash'd and white?
3. Follow, brother, your ris-en Lord; Pray, my brother, oh, watch and pray,

Could you welcome the blessed Christ, And be ready to go to-day?
And be fit-ted to dwell in heaven, In the palace of love and light?
At his coming be then prepared, And be ready to go each day.

CHORUS.

Are you read-y to go? Are you read-y to go? Are you read-y al-way, al-way? Are you read-y to go? Are you read-y to go? Are you read-y to go to-day?

4. Why not Come to Him Now?

Rev. A. S. Dobbs, D. D.   Heb. ii. 2.   W. Warren Bentley.

1. I now am so happy in Je - sus' love, No sorrow my song can control:
   I'm wash'd in the fountain which flows from his side, And Jesus speaks peace to my soul.
2. I know I'm a sinner, a sinner redeem'd, A brand taken out of the flame!
   I'll let my light shine so that others may see, And glorify Je - sus' name.

CHORUS.

Oh, why not come to him now? Oh, why not come to him now? He'll cleanse you, and save you, and fill you with joy: Oh, why not come to him now?

3 Oh, poor, wand'ring sinner, cast off by the way,
   And ready to perish and die,
   Believe, and accept him while mercy is near,
   For Jesus is now passing by.

4 The way is so simple the foolish may view,
   The lame and the blind may come, too;
   Though your sins are as crimson, he'll welcome you home,
   His blood can make whiter than snow.

DO RE MI FA SO LA SI

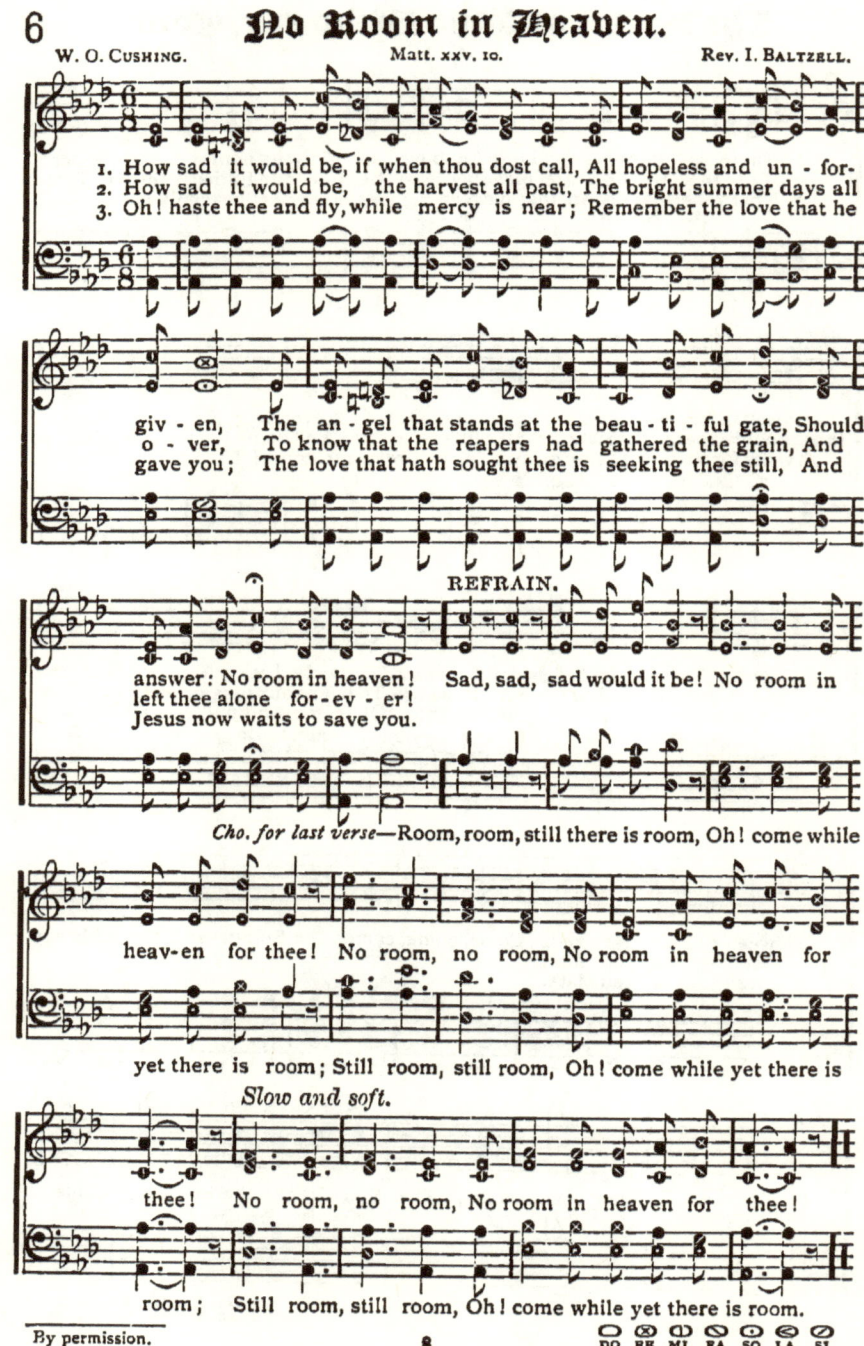

7. The Wondrous Story.

"For God so loved the world, that he gave his only begotten Son, that whosoever believeth in him, should not perish, but have everlasting life."—John. iii. 16.

J. E. H.   J. E. Hall.

1. Do you know the wondrous sto-ry? Have you ev-er heard it told?
2. Have you heard how much he suffered, Hanging on the cru-el tree?
3. Is it true that you have heard it? Have the tidings reached your ear?

How that Je-sus came from heaven, Seek-ing lost ones from the fold?
That we all might have sal-va-tion, And should live e-ter-nal-ly.
Then why not just now believe it, And find comfort, hope and cheer?

CHORUS.

Do you know the wondrous sto-ry? Have you ev-er heard it told?

Do you know the wondrous sto-ry, That with tell-ing ne'er grows old?

DO RE MI FA SO LA SI

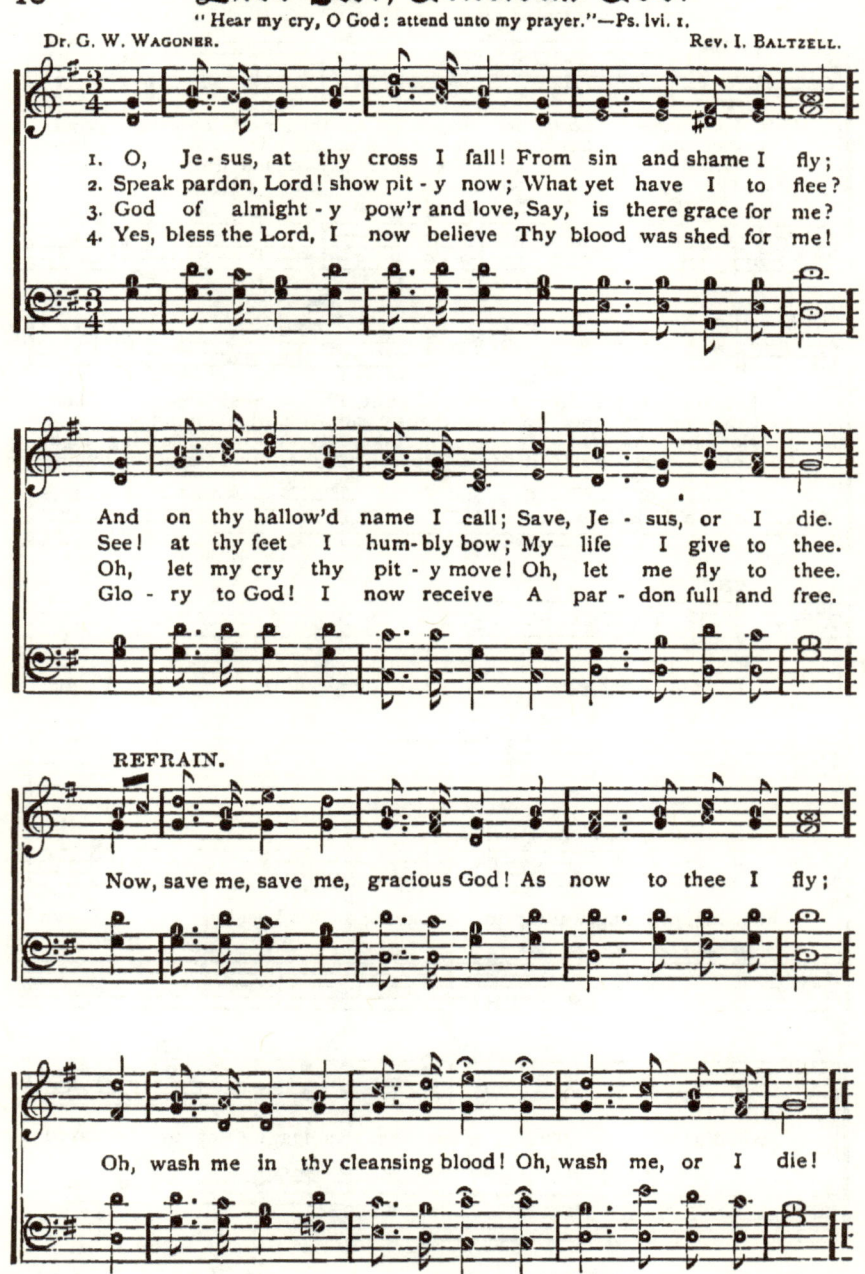

I am Saved by His Blood.—CONCLUDED.

Hal-le-lu-jah! hal-le-lu-jah! I am saved by his blood.
Hal-le-lu-jah! hal-le-lu-jah!

13. More Love to Thee.

"Continue ye in my love."—John xv. 9.

Mrs. Elizabeth P. Prentiss. W. Warren Bentley.

1. More love to thee, O Christ, More love to thee! Hear thou the
2. Once earth-ly joy I craved, Sought peace and rest; Now thee a-
3. Then shall my lat-est breath Whis-per thy praise; This be the

prayer I make, On bend-ed knee; This is my ear-nest plea,
lone I seek, Give what is best: This all my prayer shall be,
part-ing cry My heart shall raise, This still its prayer shall be,

More love, O Christ, to thee, More love, O Christ, to thee, More love to thee!

Copyright, 1883, by John J. Hood.

15

DO RE MI FA SO LA SI

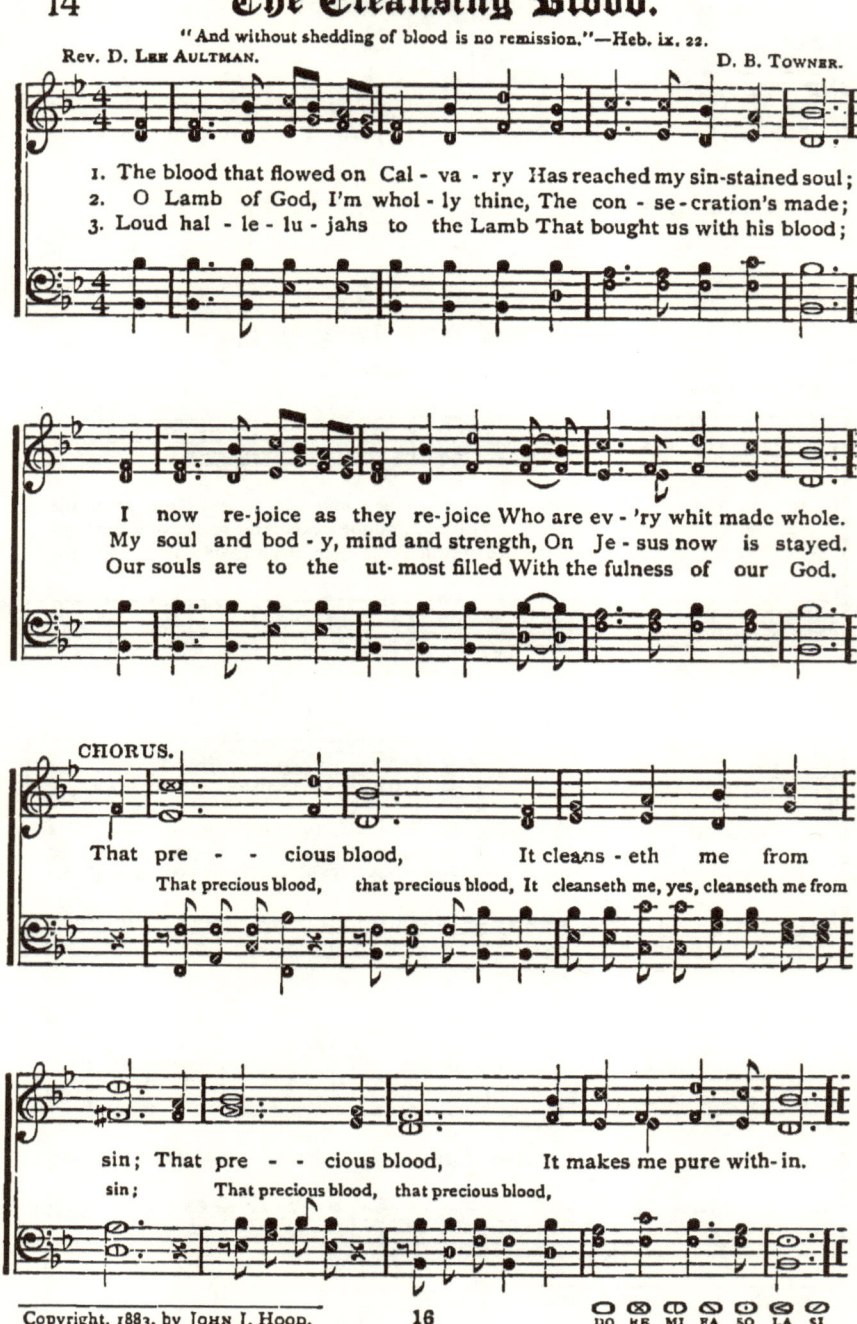

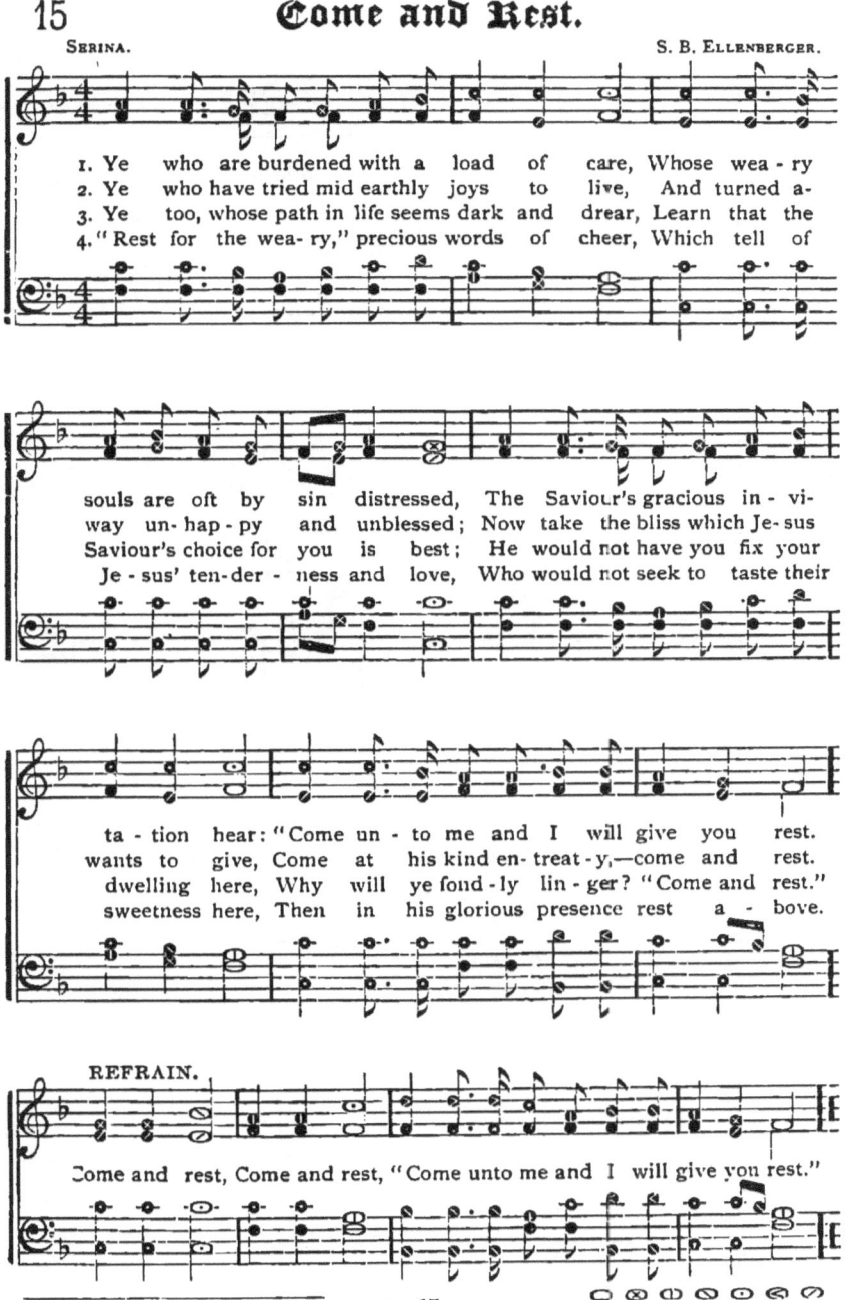

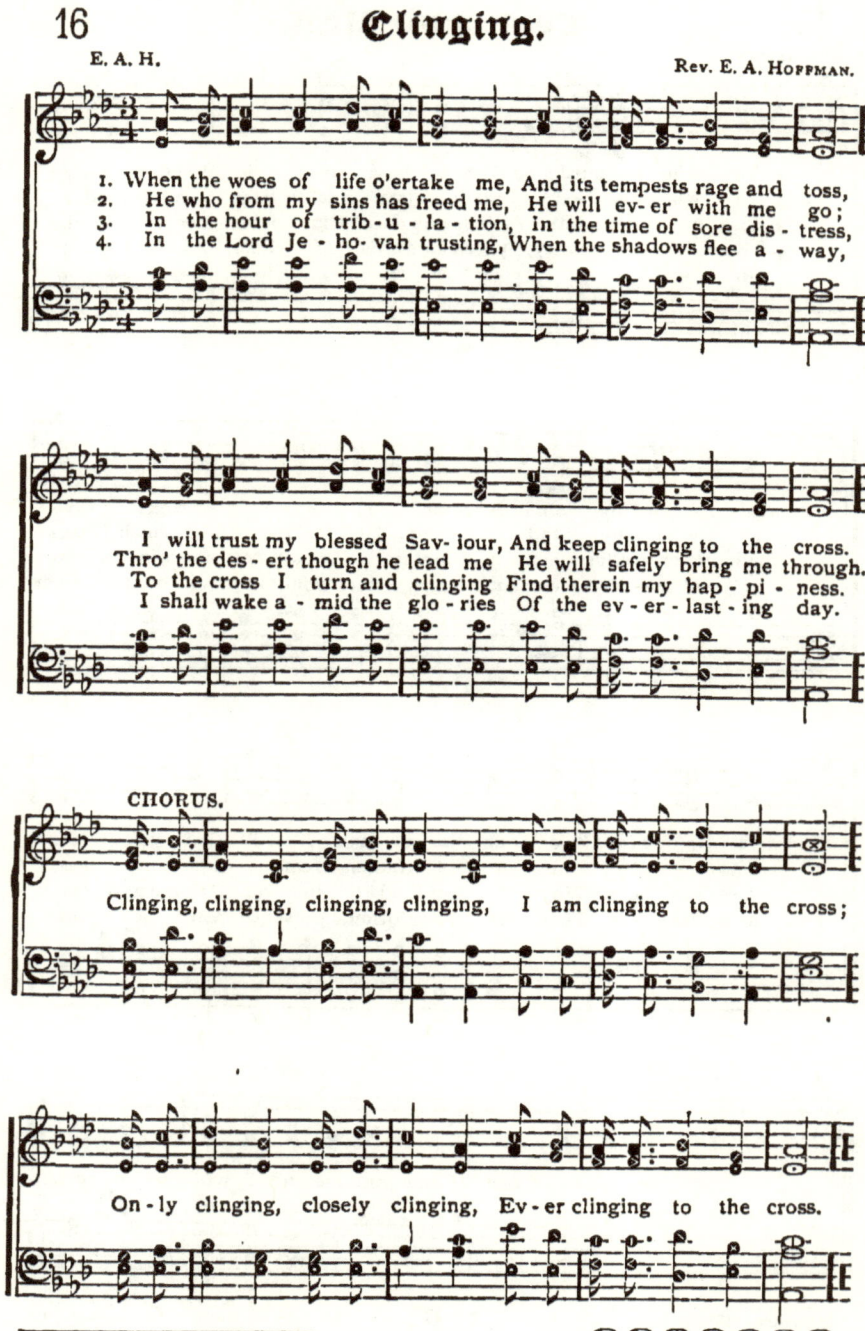

17. Close to Thee.

FANNY J. CROSBY.   W. WARREN BENTLEY.

1. Close to thee, O Lamb of God, May thy Spir-it hold me;
2. Close to thee when weak and faint, Du-ty's path pur-su-ing,
3. Close to thee, O Sav-iour mine, Near thy cross a-bid-ing;
4. Close to thee when earth-ly ties One by one are break-ing,

'Neath thy all-pro-tect-ing wings Let thy mer-cy fold me.
Let me feel thy circ-ling arm All my strength renew-ing.
I can brave the tempest's power, In thy love con-fid-ing.
When my soul to life a-new Glad and pure a-wak-ing.

REFRAIN.

Close to thee, close to thee, Keep thy child for-ev-er;
Anchored firm-ly on the Rock, Sin can harm me nev-er.

Copyright, 1883, by JOHN J. HOOD.

21. Each Day a Little Nearer.

"Draw nigh to God, and he will draw nigh to you." James iv. 8

FAITH WILLIAMS.   J. H. TENNEY.

1. Each day a lit-tle near-er To Je-sus would I rise,
And find his ser-vice ev-er A glad and sweet sur-prise;
Though what each day is bring-ing My soul may nev-er guess,
But to his cross I'm clinging, And on my way I press.

2. And day by day I'm learning That though my earth-ly way
Is oft through shadows winding, 'Twill lead to per-fect day;
Each day I know I'm near-ing His shelt-'ring, rest-ful arms,
My heart, this thought enfold-ing, Is safe from earth's a-larms.

3. So, trust-ing in his mer-cy And love so measure-less,
Each day my soul is ful-ler Of peace and joy-ful-ness;
Each day, while life is giv-en, Still near-er would I come,
Till from on high my Saviour Shall call me, Child, come home.

Copyright, 1883, by JOHN J. HOOD.

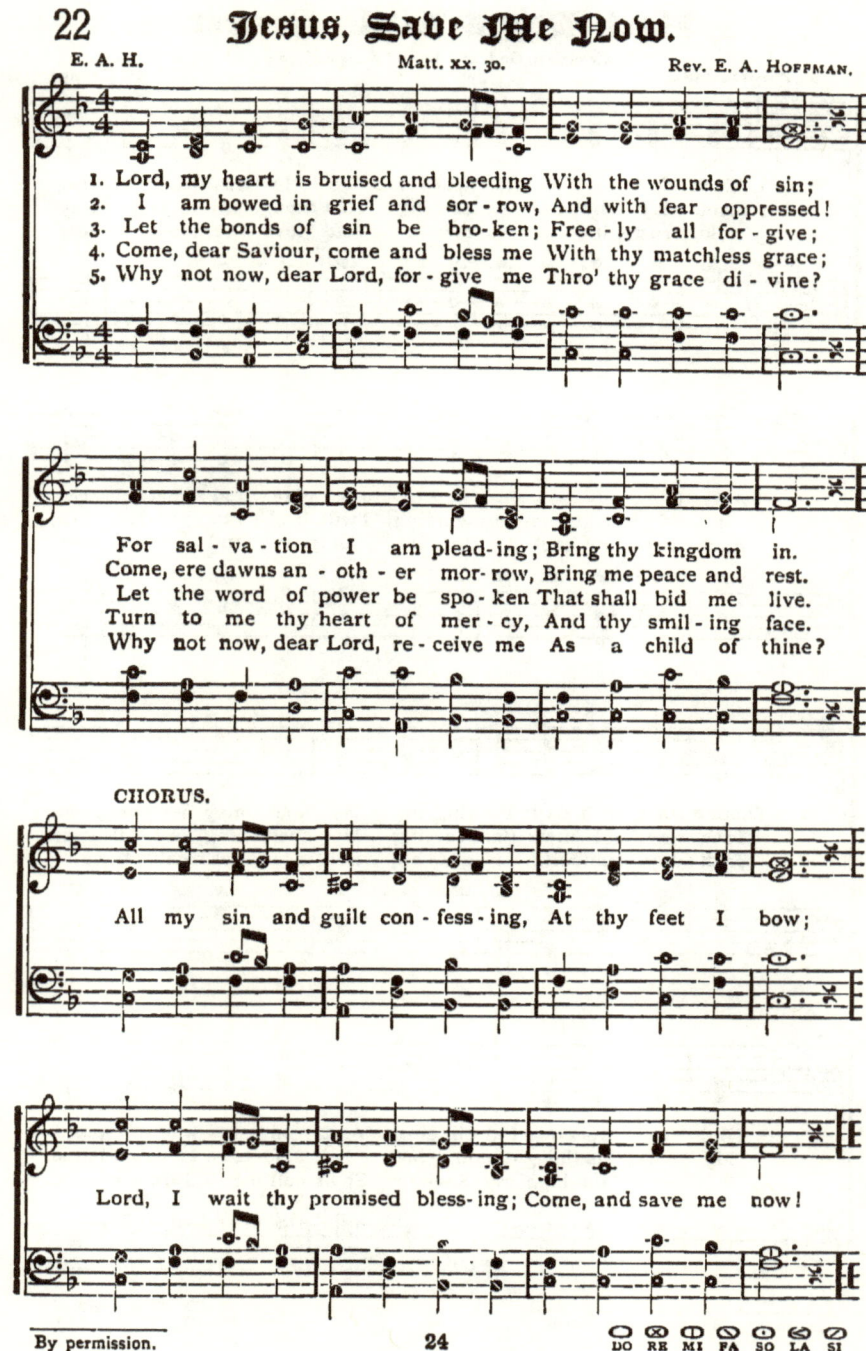

When the Sheaves, etc.—CONCLUDED.

How shall we make answer For the talents given, When the sheaves are gathered in.

33. "Jesus Wept."

Anon. John xi. 35. HARRY SANDERS.

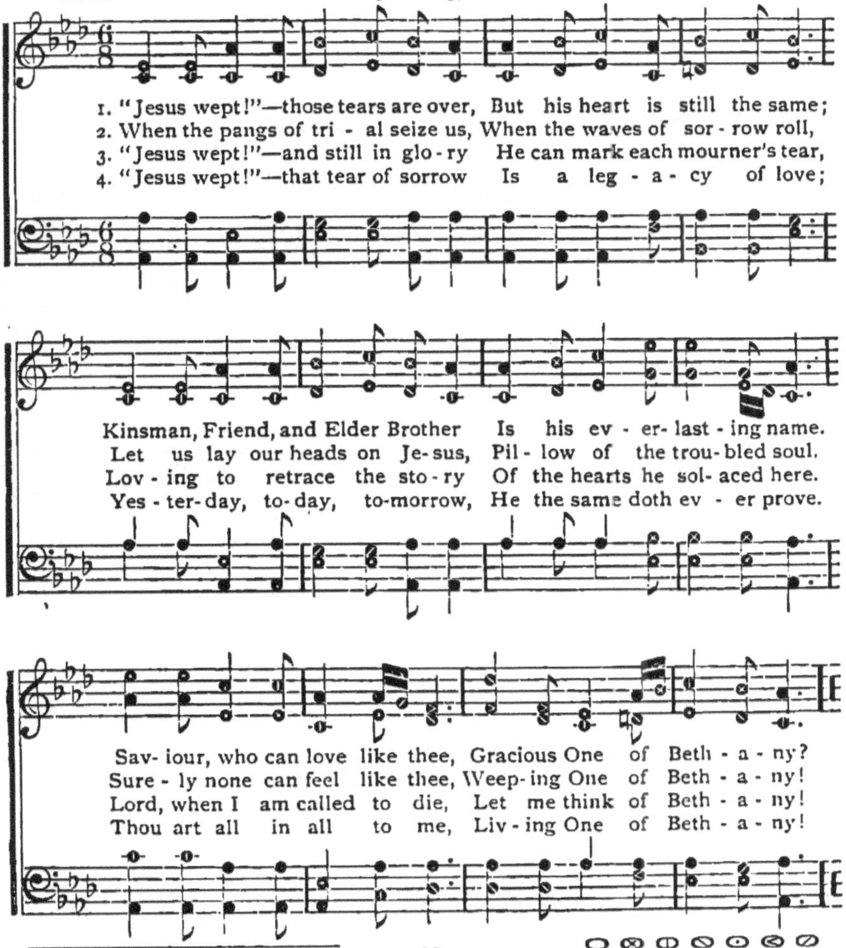

1. "Jesus wept!"—those tears are over, But his heart is still the same;
2. When the pangs of tri - al seize us, When the waves of sor - row roll,
3. "Jesus wept!"—and still in glo - ry He can mark each mourner's tear,
4. "Jesus wept!"—that tear of sorrow Is a leg - a - cy of love;

Kinsman, Friend, and Elder Brother Is his ev - er - last - ing name.
Let us lay our heads on Je - sus, Pil - low of the trou - bled soul.
Lov - ing to retrace the sto - ry Of the hearts he sol - aced here.
Yes - ter - day, to-day, to-morrow, He the same doth ev - er prove.

Sav - iour, who can love like thee, Gracious One of Beth - a - ny?
Sure - ly none can feel like thee, Weep - ing One of Beth - a - ny!
Lord, when I am called to die, Let me think of Beth - a - ny!
Thou art all in all to me, Liv - ing One of Beth - a - ny!

Copyright, 1883, by JOHN J. HOOD.

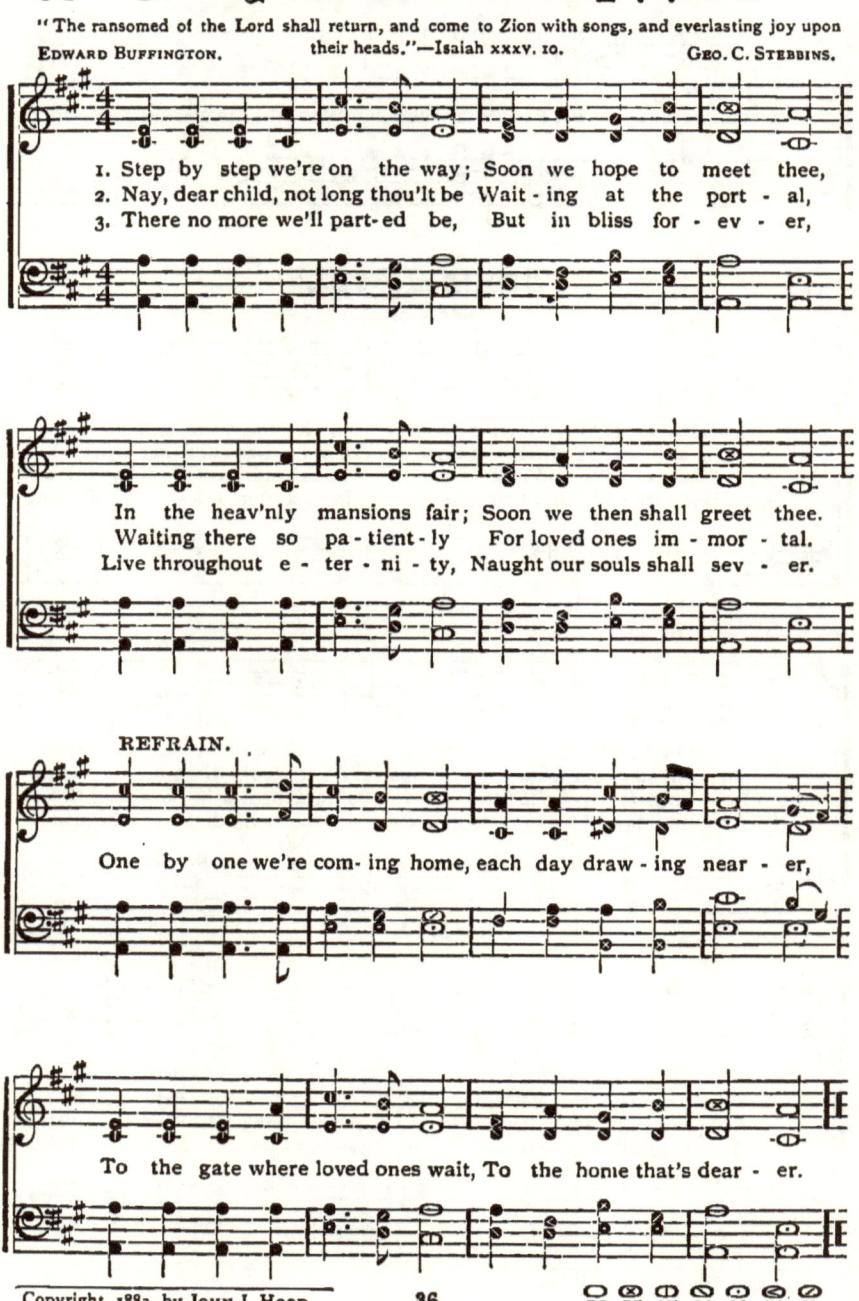

35. Trust thyself to Jesus.

Anon.
W. Warren Bentley.

1. Oh, trust thy-self to Je - sus When conscious of thy sin,—
2. Oh, trust thy-self to Je - sus When tempted to trans-gress,
3. Oh, trust thy-self to Je - sus When dai - ly cares per - plex,
4. Oh, trust thy-self to Je - sus As thy spir - it takes its flight,

Its hea - vy weight up - on thee, Its might - y power with - in:
By hast - y word, or an - gry look, Or thought of bit - ter - ness:
And tri - fles seem to gain a power, Thy in - most soul to vex:
From ev - 'ry earth - ly sha - dow, To the land of per - fect light:

This is the hour for plead - ing, His fin - ished work for thee,—
This is the hour for claim - ing, Thy Lord to fight for thee;
Then is the hour for grasp - ing His hand, who walked the sea;
Then is the hour for feel - ing, "Christ has done all for me;"

This is the time for sing - ing, "His blood was shed for me."
Then is the time for sing - ing, "He doth de - liv - er me."
Then is the hour for sing - ing, "He makes it calm for me."
Then is the time for sing - ing, "He gives the vic - to - ry."

Copyright, 1883, by John J. Hood.

41. By and by.

ANNA H. C. HOWARD. "That where I am, there ye may be also."—John xiv. 3. F. A. BLACKMER.

1. There will be no sin nor pain By and by, by and by,
2. When life's les-sons we shall learn By and by, by and by,
3. We shall see him eye to eye By and by, by and by,

All that's dark will be made plain By and by, by and by;
Je-sus' voice we shall dis-cern By and by, by and by;
We shall meet him in the sky By and by, by and by;

For the Lord will come a-gain— Oh, how glo-ri-ous his reign—
He will ban-ish ev-'ry sigh; Let us lift our heads on high,
We shall hear his tender tone, We shall be no more a-lone,

Like the sunshine aft-er rain . . By and by, by and by.
Our redemption draweth nigh . . By and by, by and by.
He is coming to his own . . By and by, by and by.

Copyright, 1879, by F. A. BLACKMER.

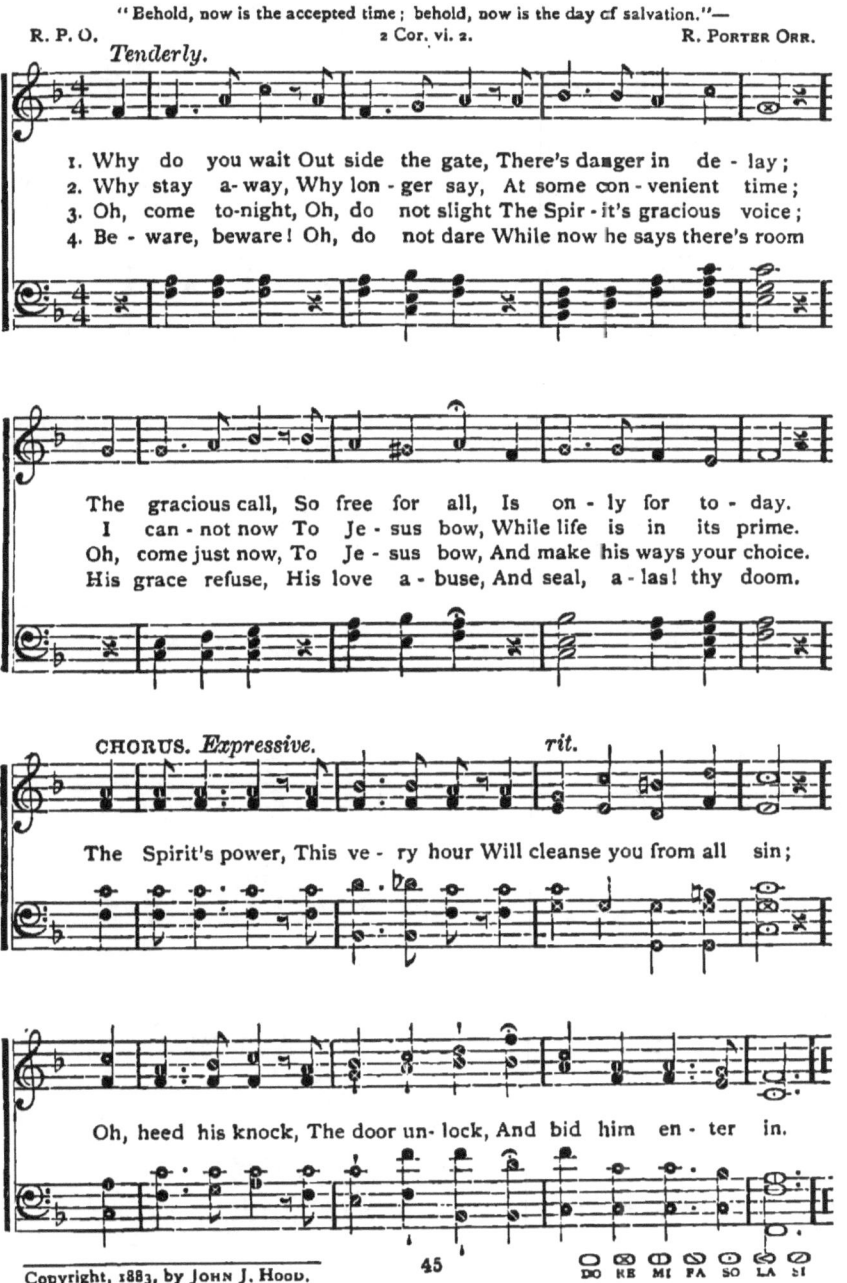

44. "Let the Meeting go on."

"Let me die at my post!"   "Let the meeting go on!"   "All is well!"

WM. HUNTER, D.D.   Lines suggested by the last utterances of Rev. G. D. Kinnear.   T. C. O'KANE.

1. An old sol-dier I stand, With my sword in my hand, Till I catch the glad
2. "Let the meeting go on!" I will short-ly be gone! Let anoth-er the
3. "Let the meeting go on!" When the conquest is won, And the Lord from the
4. When he com-eth to reign, We shall come in his train; To his saints shall the

summons divine! Lo, the sig-nal I see! He is waiting for me! "All is
message repeat, "In the blood that was shed, There is life from the dead; O, ye
opening skies, Shall in glory come down With the long-promised crown, All the
kingdom be given, With our last labor done, And our last battle won, We shall

REFRAIN.

well!"—I am his!—He is mine! "Let the meet-ing go on!" "Let me
ransomed, come, bow at his feet!"
sleep-ers in Christ shall a-rise.
shine as the stars in the heaven.

die at my post!" Let me fall in the van of the conquering host! "Let the

meeting go on!" "Let me die at my post!" "All is well! All is well!"

By permission.

45. "I have Nothing to Do."

"I have fought a good fight."—2 Tim. iv. 7.
Last words of the lamented Rev. Dr. Thos. Guard, of Baltimore.

Mrs. E. C. Ellsworth. W. Warren Bentley.

1. I have fought a good fight, I have nothing to do, My foes he has laid at my feet; I will fear not the grave, he is conquer-or there, My vict'-ry in him is com-plete.
2. I have kept to the faith, and will cling to his word: His promise is dear to my heart: For he nev-er, no nev-er his own will forsake, Tho' heaven and earth should de-part.
3. I am read-y to go,—for a voice I can hear; And yonder my Fath-er I see; He is call-ing me home to the mansions above, Where loved ones are waiting for me.
4. I am read-y to go, I am read-y to go; To earth I have bid-den a-dieu; I shall dwell in a city whose streets are pure gold; Its gates are al-read-y in view.

REFRAIN.

I have nothing to do; I am read-y to go; Sal-va-tion com-plet-ed I see! I'm ac-cept-ed in Christ, and my labors are o'er; In him there is resting for me.

Copyright, 1883, by John J. Hood.

DO RE MI FA SO LA SI

4 Open thou my heart; oh, come,
  Make it now thine earthly home;
  Sup with me, thou welcome guest,
  Give my weary spirit rest.

5 Open thou the door to heaven
  When the last earth-tie is riven;
  When I rise to dwell with thee,
  Open, Lord, the door to me.

From "Fount of Blessing," by per.

51. The Child of a King.

HATTIE E. BUELL. Arr. from Melody by Rev. JOHN B. SUMNER.

1. My Father is rich in houses and lands, He holdeth the wealth of the world in his hands! Of rubies and diamonds, of silver and gold His coffers are full,—he has riches untold.
2. My Father's own Son, the Saviour of men, Once wander'd o'er earth as the poorest of men, But now he is reigning forever on high, And will give me a home in heaven by and by.
3. I once was an outcast stranger on earth, A sinner by choice, an alien by birth! But I've been adopted, my name's written down,—An heir to a mansion, a robe, and a crown.
4. A tent or a cottage, why should I care? They're building a palace for me over there! Tho' exiled from home, yet, still I may sing: All glory to God, I'm the child of a King.

CHORUS.

I'm the child of a King, The child of a King; With Jesus my Saviour I'm the child of a King.

Copyright, 1881, by JOHN J. HOOD.

52 Only Believe.

Rev. J. B. Tuttle. Mark v. 36. E. O. Excell.

1. Sinner, the Saviour is calling for thee, Will you his message of mercy receive?
2. Rest not on works for they never will save, 'Tis in believing that life he will give;
3. Rest not on feeling, but trust in the blood, Jesus will never, no never deceive;
4. Will you not look to him now and be bless'd? Look this moment, he'll freely forgive;

Throw off the burden and come unto me, All that I ask of you, On-ly believe.
No other way but his way can you have, All that he asks of you, On-ly believe.
Trusting in feeling can do you no good, All that he asks of you, On-ly believe.
Burdens will fall and thy soul will find rest, All that he asks of you, Only believe.

CHORUS.

Fall at his feet, his mer-cy entreat; See how he waits to free-ly forgive;

Bid him come in, he'll cleanse you from sin; Joyfully say, Now, Lord, I believe.

From "Sacred Echoes," by per.

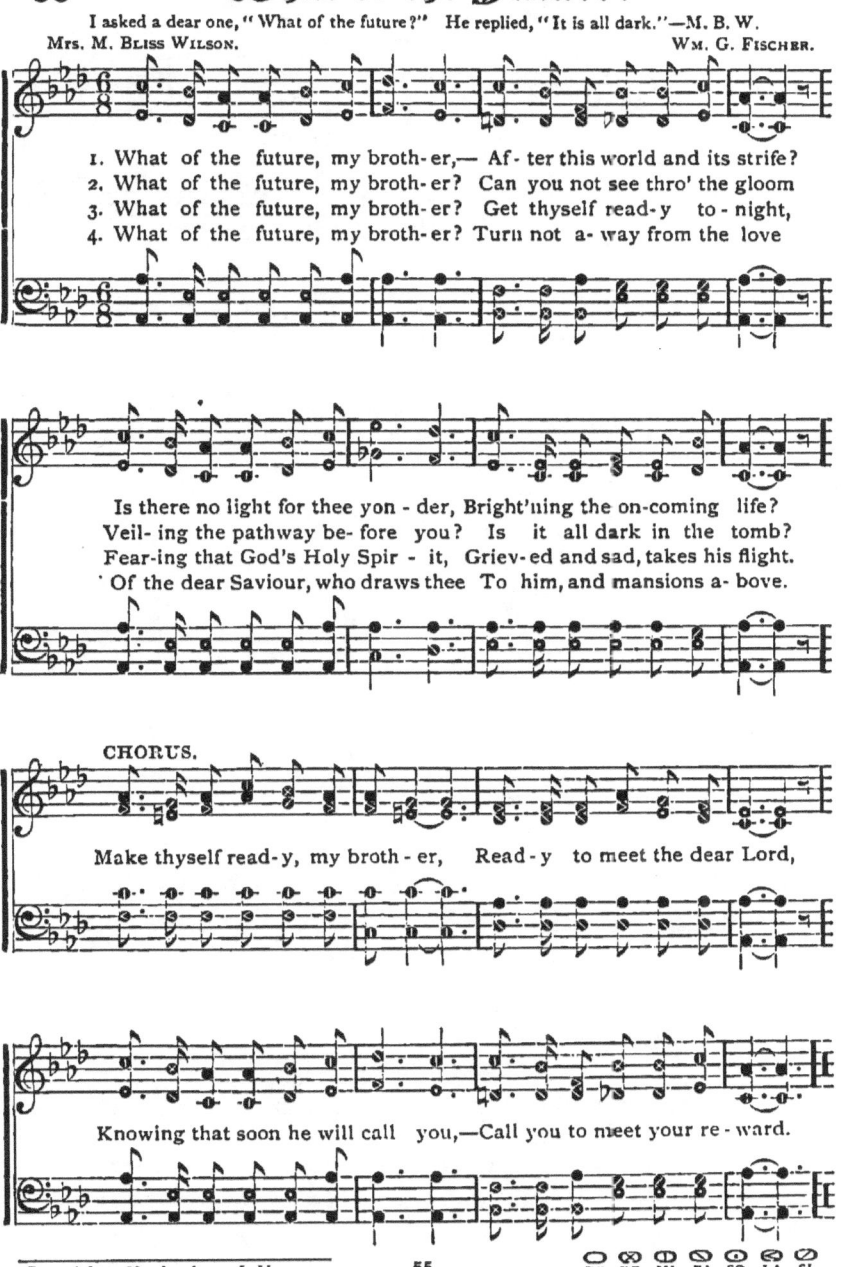

57. Sin No More.

C. C. McCabe.
Wm. J. Kirkpatrick.

1. When did ev-er words so ten-der Fall on mor-tal ears be-fore,
As the bless-ed words of Je-sus,—"Go thy way, and sin no more."
Pardoned! oh, that word of rap-ture! As I knelt at Mercy's door,
Burdened with my sin and sor-row,—"Go thy way, and sin no more."

2. Je-sus spake, and then the pow-er Of his great sal-va-tion came;
All the bonds of sin were broken: Glo-ry! glo-ry! to his name.
"Rise, forgiven, O child of sor-row; Rise, for lo! thy light hath come;
Put thy beauteous garments on thee; Take thy staff, and journey home."

3. "I will know the way thou tak-est Till thou stand on Canaan's shore;
Nev-er, nev-er will I leave thee; Go thy way, and sin no more."
"From the world I will not take thee Till the bat-tle strife is o'er;
From its e-vil I will keep thee; Go thy way, and sin no more."

4 O the fight! I've learned to love it,
For the victory is mine;
In the cross of Christ I glory,
Triumphing in love divine.
O the dawn of heaven's glory!
O the day that has no night!
O the sun that finds no zenith!
O the host in raiment bright!

5 O, the King who dwells among them
In his beauty I shall see;
Heav'n shall ring with loud hosannas
Unto him who died for me.
But, 'mid all the joys of heaven,
I will ne'er forget the hour
When my Saviour said, "Forgiven!
Go thy way, and sin no more."

Copyright, 1882, by John J. Hood.

59. Beneath the Bleeding Side.

Mrs. E. C. Ellsworth. "He was wounded for our transgressions."— Isaiah liii. 5. *A. Barringer.*

1. Come, stand beneath the bleeding side, Beneath the crimson flow;
2. Oh, lift with rev'rent hand the veil That shrouds the Saviour's face,
3. He drinks the dregs, the bitter dregs, Of all this cup of woe,

Come see the wounds thy sins have made,—Their cruel nature know.
That hides the Father's loving smile, And brings such sore disgrace.
That we might taste of heavenly bliss, And thirst might never know.

REFRAIN.

Behold! behold! the Saviour dies, A sacrifice for thee!

Hast thou no heart, no kind return, For love so full, so free?

Copyright, 1883, by John J. Hood.

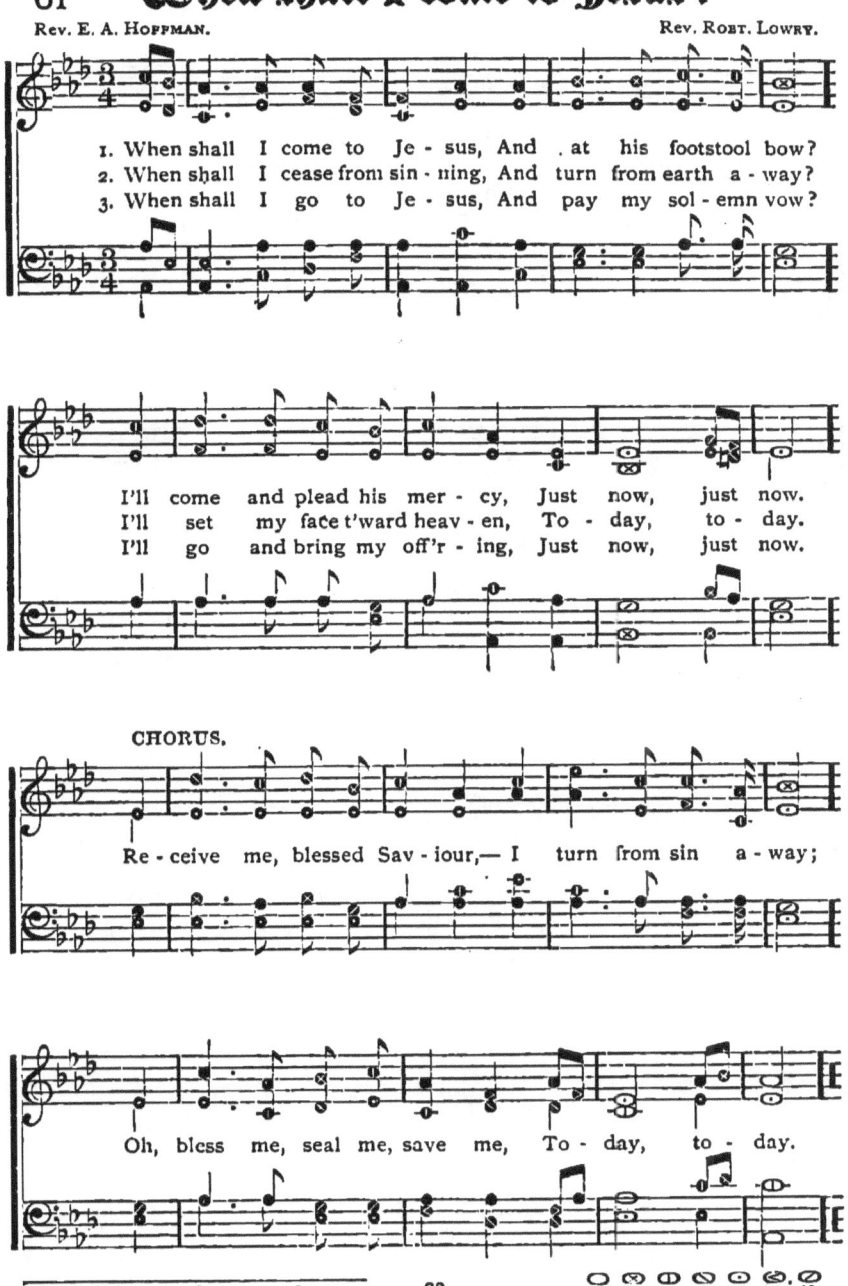

62. I will Follow Thee.

E. A. H.   Rev. E. A. Hoffman.

1. Lead me forth, O blessed Jesus! Out of darkness, out of night,
2. Lead me forth, O blessed Jesus! Leaving all my doubts and fears,
3. Lead me forth, O blessed Jesus! In-to full-er, clearer light,
4. Lead me high-er still and high-er, Draw me near-er, near-er thee;
5. Lead me forth, O blessed Jesus! With a clear eye, fixed a-bove

In-to life and love e-ter-nal, In-to joy and in-to light.
Leaving all my sins and sor-rows, Leaving all my griefs and tears.
Where the sunshine of thy presence Falls up-on my in-ner sight.
Touch my heart with love and fit me, Lord, thy faithful child to be.
On the crown that now is wait-ing In the Par-a-dise of Love.

CHORUS.

I will take my cross and fol-low, I will take my cross and fol-low, I will take my cross and fol-low, I will follow on-ly thee.

By permission.

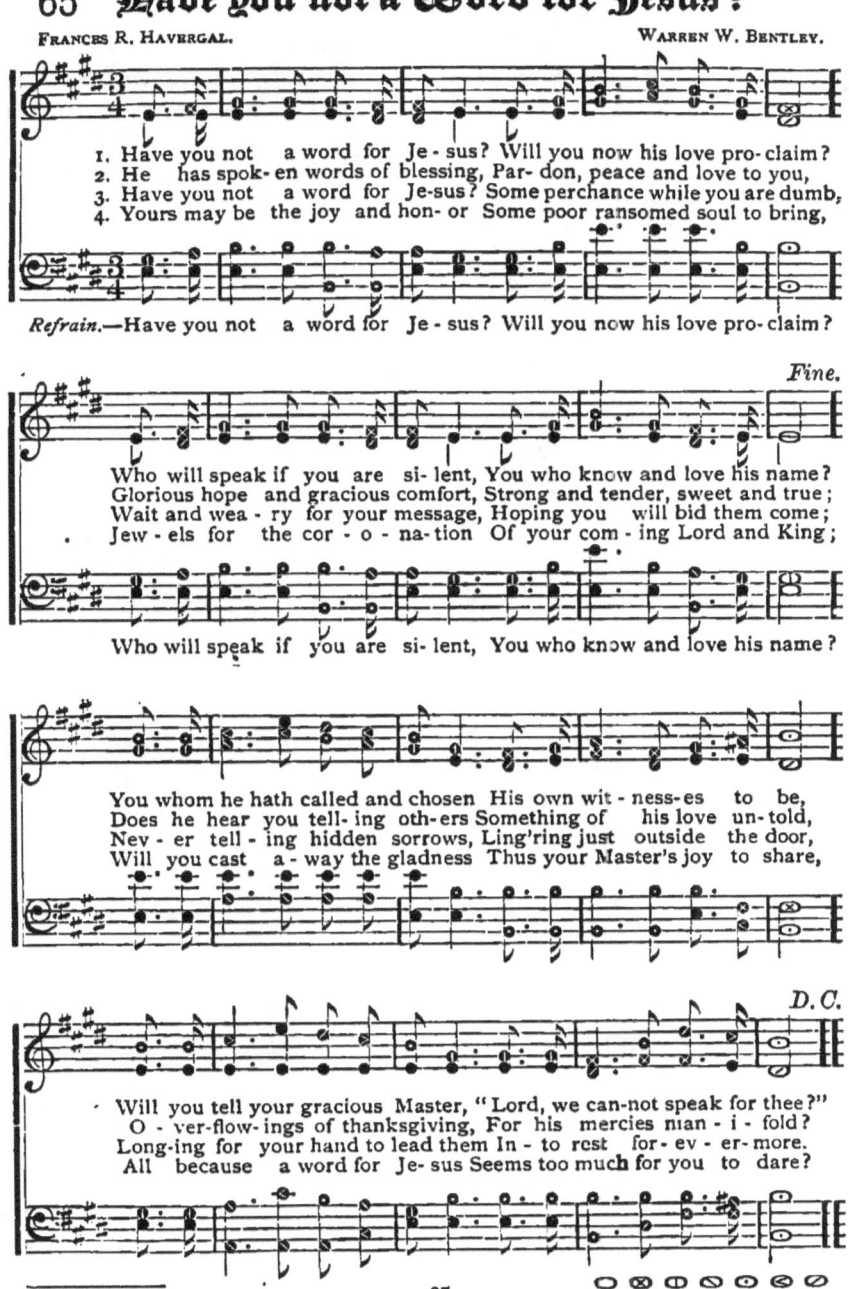

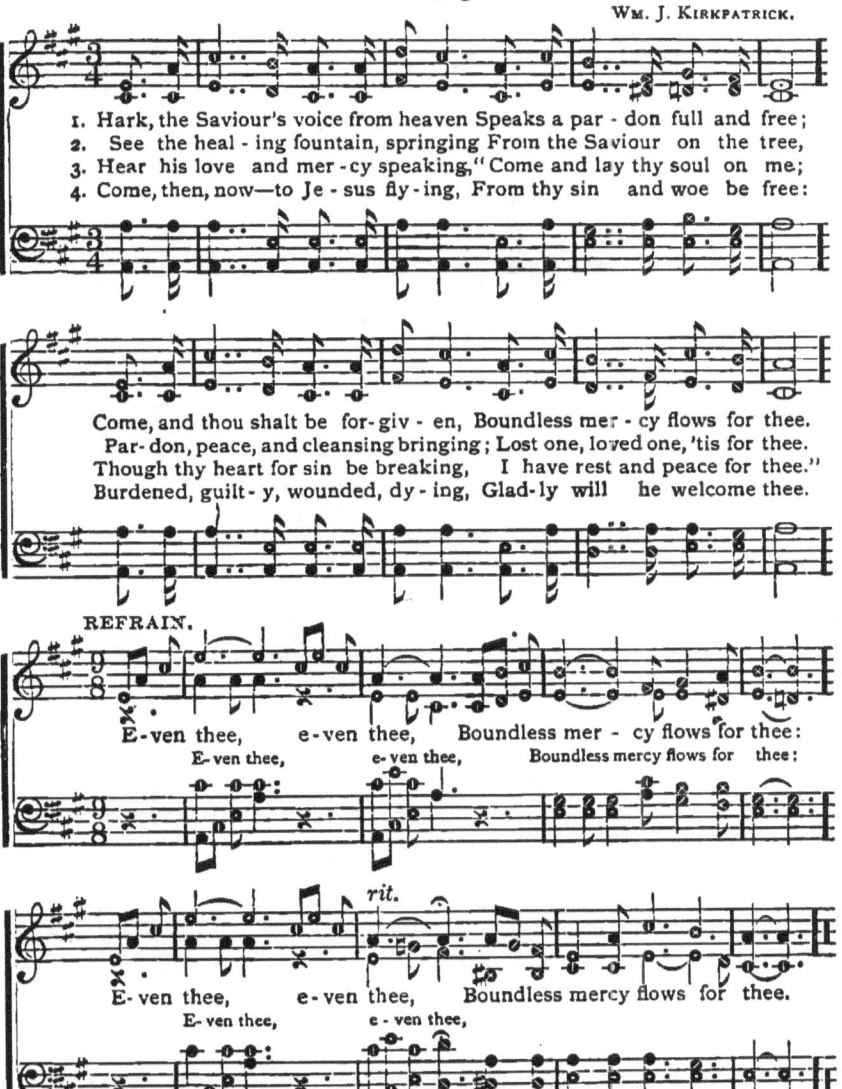

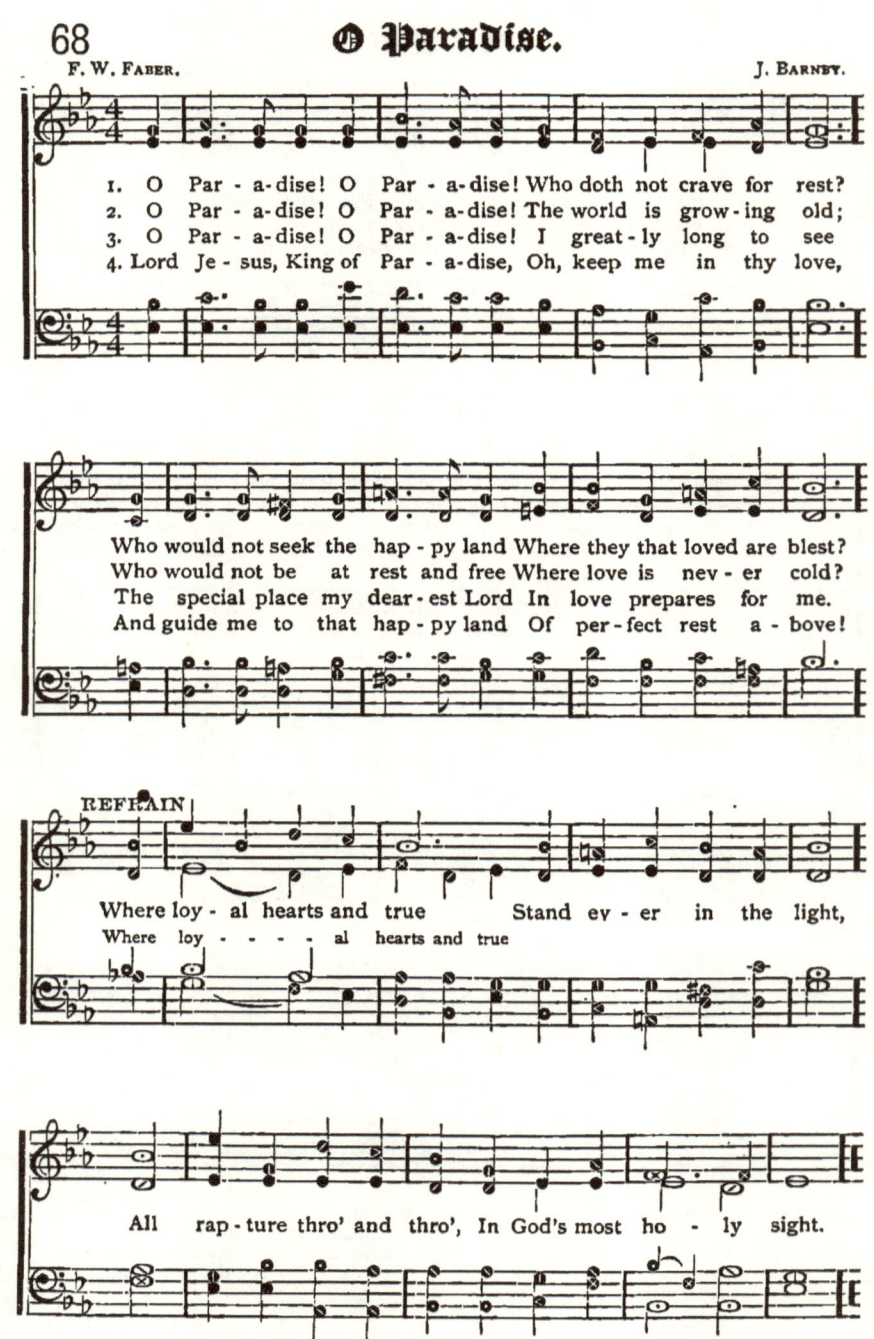

69. Decide To-Night.

"How long halt ye?"—1 Kings. xviii. 21.

W. A. Spencer.

Slow and with expression.

1. Some go a-way from the house to-night, Pu-ri-fied from sin;
2. Some will go out from the house of pray'r, Harden'd by de-lay,
3. Some will go out from the house to-night, Full of trust in God;
4. Wait-ing a mo-ment more for thee, Je-sus still en-treats;

Chorus.—Go-ing a-way from Christ to-night, A-way from his loving care;

Oth-ers re-ject the precious light, And go a-way un-clean:
Yielding to Sa-tan's lur-ing snare, Will hopeless turn a-way;
Hap-py in heart, made pure and white, By Je-sus' precious blood:
Soon will the knocking end-ed be, That now thy closed heart beats:

Go-ing a-way from bless-ed light, To darkness and des-pair.

Lov-ing-ly still the Sav-iour stands, Plead-ing with thy heart;
Nev-er-more shall the Spir-it plead At the bolt-ed door;
Go not a-way, poor wand'rer, stay Till thou too art free!
Stay, sin-ner, stay at Mer-cy's door, Seek the o-pen gate;

Patient-ly knocks with his bleeding hands, Unwill-ing to de-part.
Now is the hour of thy soul's great need, 'Tis now or nev-er-more.
Walking with Christ life's hap-py way, Most bless-ed shalt thou be.
Sinner, de-cide, lest hope be o'er, And thou shouldst be too late.

By permission.

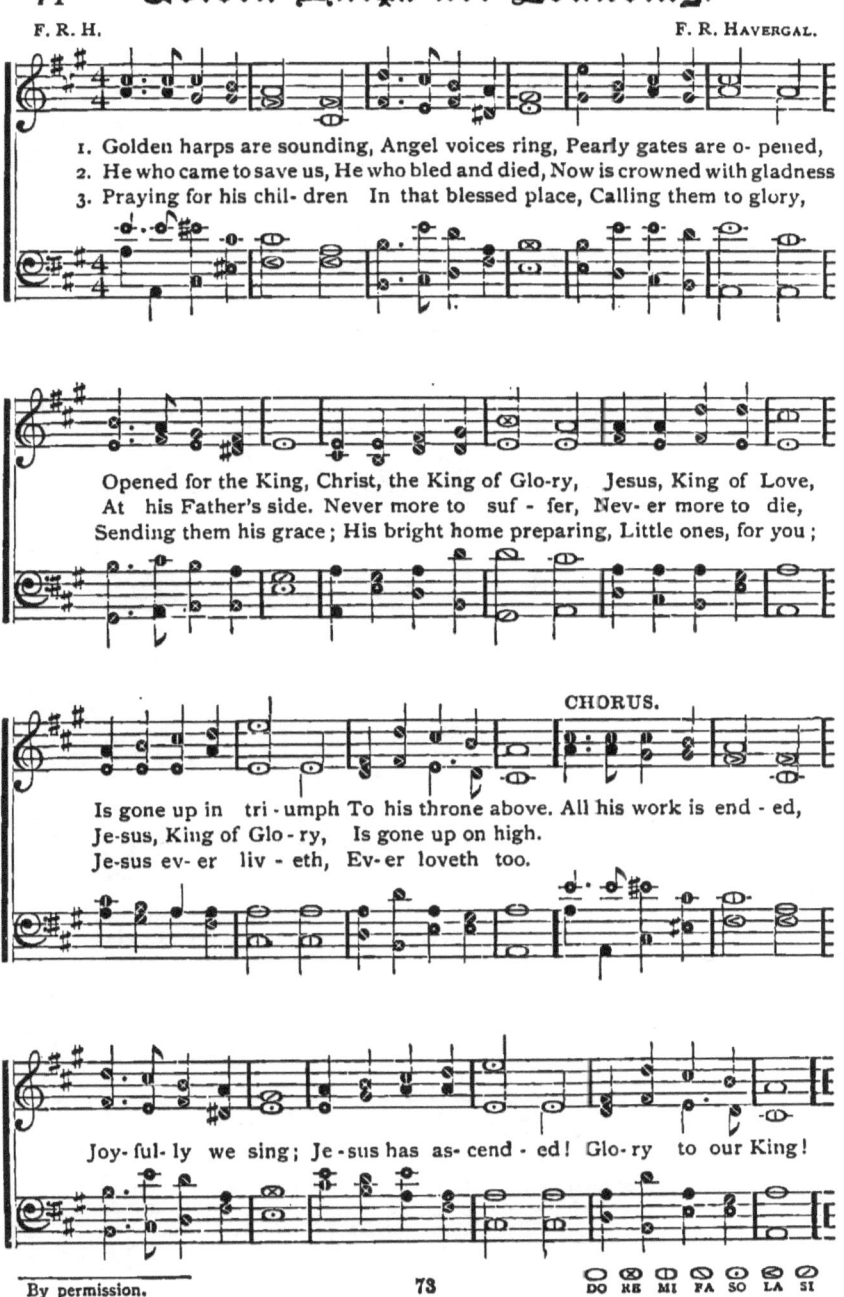

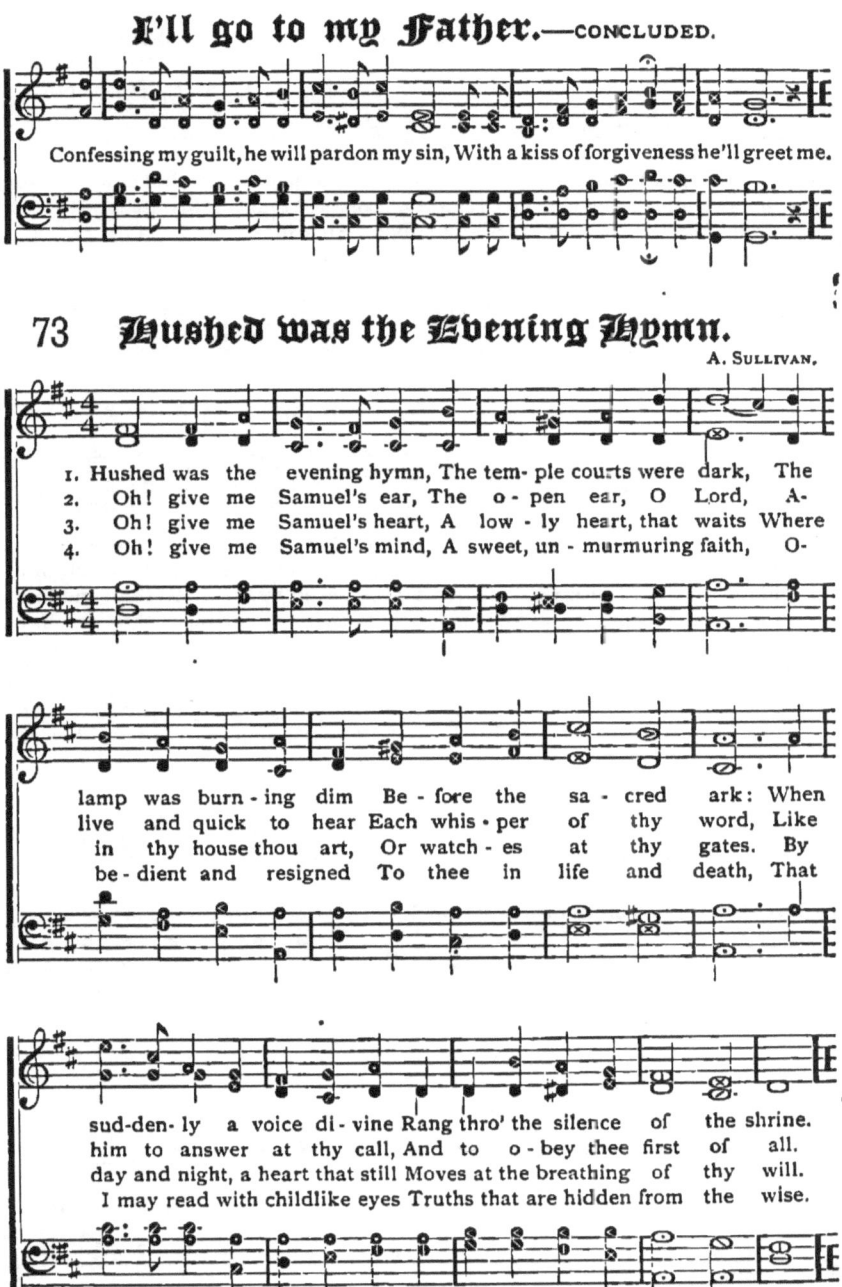

74. Saved Through and Through.

Lizzie Edwards.   Jno. R. Sweney.

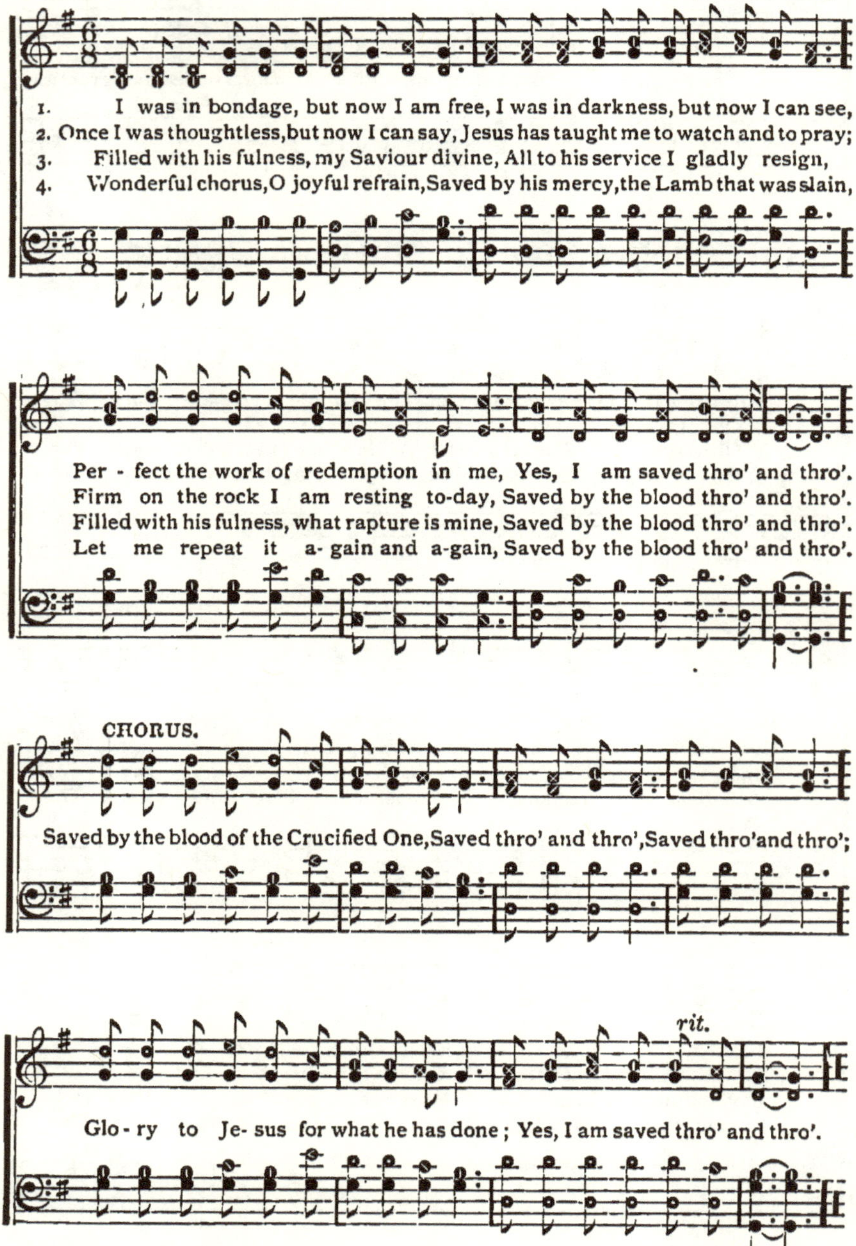

1. I was in bondage, but now I am free, I was in darkness, but now I can see,
2. Once I was thoughtless, but now I can say, Jesus has taught me to watch and to pray;
3. Filled with his fulness, my Saviour divine, All to his service I gladly resign,
4. Wonderful chorus, O joyful refrain, Saved by his mercy, the Lamb that was slain,

Per-fect the work of redemption in me, Yes, I am saved thro' and thro'.
Firm on the rock I am resting to-day, Saved by the blood thro' and thro'.
Filled with his fulness, what rapture is mine, Saved by the blood thro' and thro'.
Let me repeat it a-gain and a-gain, Saved by the blood thro' and thro'.

CHORUS.

Saved by the blood of the Crucified One, Saved thro' and thro', Saved thro' and thro';

Glo-ry to Je-sus for what he has done; Yes, I am saved thro' and thro'.

Copyright, 1882, by John J. Hood.

DO RE MI FA SO LA SI

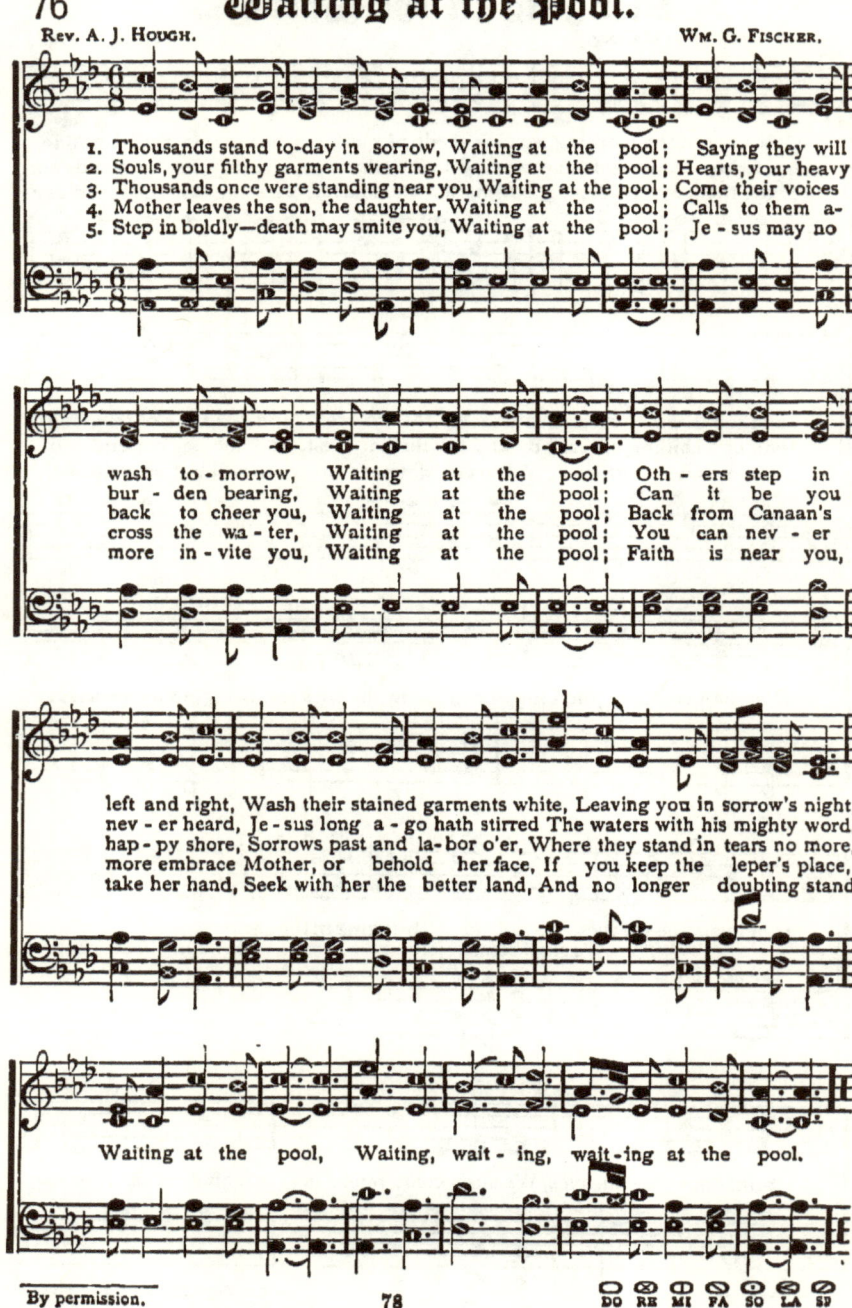

79. It must be Settled to-night.

A miner in England went to church one night and became deeply concerned for the salvation of his soul. When the services were ended he refused to leave the house, although the minister told him it was late, and he must go home and seek the Saviour there, and come again the next night. "No," said the miner, "It must be settled to-night, to-morrow night may be too late." So the minister stayed with him until he found peace. The next day while at work in the mines a mass of rock fell upon him, and he was killed. His last words were, "Thank God, it was settled last night, to-night it would have been too late."

Rev. C. B. KENDALL.   JOHN J. HOOD.

1. "It must be settled to-night, To-morrow may be too late;"
   The an-gel of death may come, And seal for-ev-er my fate.
2. A burden weighs my soul I can no lon-ger bear;
   Un-less removed this night, 'Twill sink me in-to des-pair.
3. I can-not rest till peace En-folds me from a-bove,—
   Till my Re-deemer speaks to me As-surance of his love.
4. Oh, now I know 'tis done! My peace is made with God;
   My par-don's found in Je-sus' name, Thro' faith in Je-sus' blood.

CHORUS.
It must be settled to-night, to-night, I can no lon-ger wait,
Peace with my God I now must have, To-morrow may be too late.

Copyright, 1881, by JOHN J. HOOD.   F 81

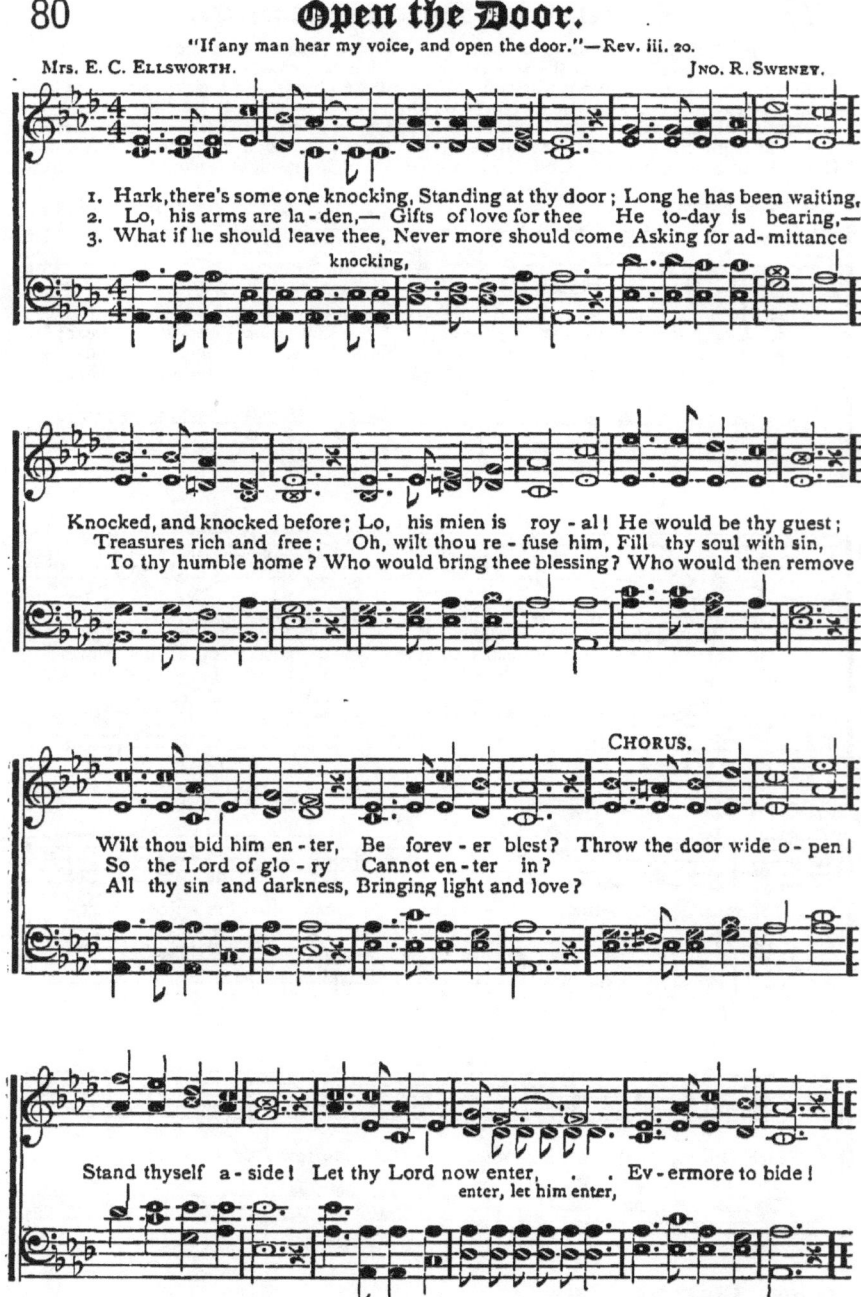

85. Missing.

JULIA H. THAYER.   SOLO OR QUARTETTE.   Dr. H. L. GILMOUR.

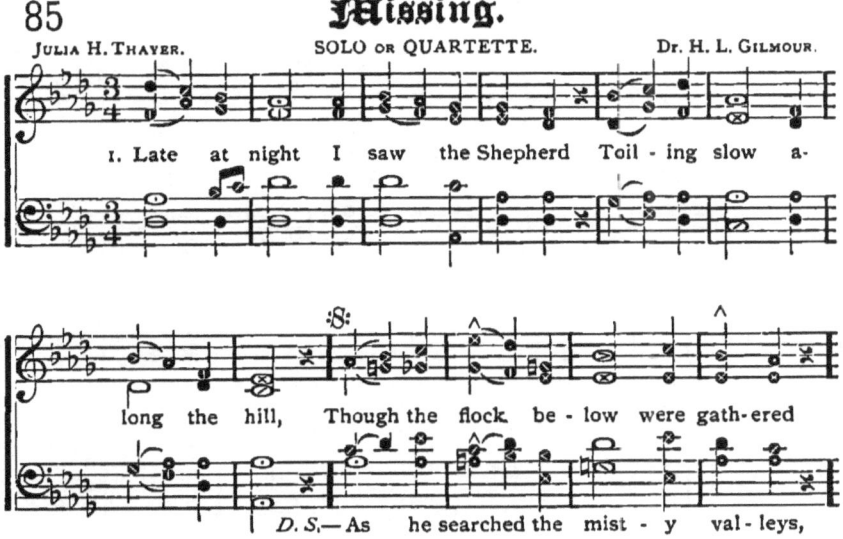

1. Late at night I saw the Shepherd Toil-ing slow a-long the hill, Though the flock be-low were gath-ered
D.S.—As he searched the mist-y val-leys,

In the fold so warm and still; On his face I
As he climbed the frost-y heights.

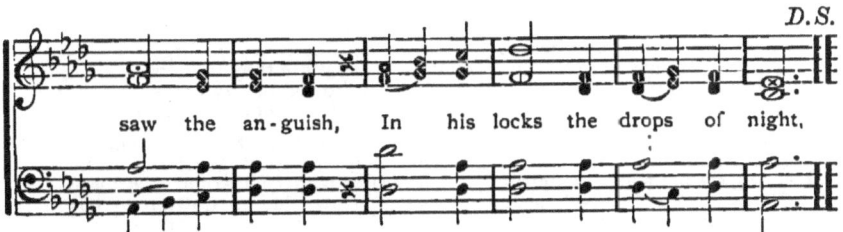

saw the an-guish, In his locks the drops of night.

2 Just one tender lamb was missing,
　When he called them all by name;
While the others heard and followed
　This one, only, never came.
Oft his voice rang thro' the darkness
　Of that long, long night of pain,
Oft he vainly paused to listen
　For an answering tone again.

3 Far away the truant sleeping,
　By the chasm of despair;
Lay unconscious of its danger,
　Shivering in the mountain air.
But at last the Shepherd found it,
　Found it ere in sleep it died,
Took it in his loving bosom,
　And his soul was satisfied.

Copyright, 1882, by H. L. GILMOUR.

86. Abide with me.

Rev. H. F. Lyte.   Wm. H. Monk.

1. Abide with me! Fast falls the eventide, The darkness deepens—Lord, with me abide! When other helpers fail, and comforts flee, Help of the helpless, oh, abide with me!
2. Swift to its close ebbs out life's little day; Earth's joys grow dim, its glories pass a-way; Change and decay in all around I see; O thou who changest not tempter's pow'r? Who, like thyself, my guide and stay can be? Thro' cloud and sunshine, Lord, abide with me!
3. I need thy presence ev'ry passing hour; What but thy grace can foil the

4 I fear no foe, with thee at hand to bless;
Ills have no weight, and tears no bitterness;
Where is death's sting? where, grave, thy victory?
I triumph still, if thou abide with me!

5 Hold thou thy cross before my closing eyes;
Shine through the gloom and point me to the skies;
Heaven's morning breaks, and earth's vain shadows flee;
In life, in death, O Lord, abide with me!

87

Solo.—**The Trundle Bed.**—*Key G.*

1 As I rummaged through the attic,
   List'ning to the falling rain,
As it pattered on the shingles,
   And against the window pane,
Peeping over chests and boxes,
   Which with dust were thickly spread,
Saw I in the farthest corner
   What was once my trundle bed.

2 So I drew it from the recess,
   Where it had remained so long,
Hearing all the while the music
   Of my mother's voice in song,
As she sung in sweetest accents,
   What I since have often read—
"Hush, my dear, lie still and slumber,
   Holy angels guard thy bed."

3 As I listened, recollections
   That I thought had been forgot,
Came with all the gush of mem'ry,
   Rushing, thronging to the spot;
And I wandered back to childhood,
   To those merry days of yore,
When I knelt beside my mother,
   By this bed upon the floor.

4 Then it was, with hands so gently
   Placed upon my infant head,
That she taught my lips to utter
   Carefully the words she said:
Never can they be forgotten,
   Deep are they in mem'ry riven—
"Hallowed be thy name, O Father!
   Father! thou who art in heaven."

5 This she taught me, then she told me
   Of its import, great and deep—
After which I learned to utter
   "Now I lay me down to sleep;"
Then it was, with hands uplifted,
   And in accents sweet and mild,
That my mother asked, "Our Father!
   Father! do thou bless my child."

6 Years have pass'd, and that dear mother
   Long has mouldered 'neath the sod,
And I trust her sainted spirit
   Revels in the home of God:
But that scene at summer twilight
   Never has from mem'ry fled,
And it comes in all its freshness
   When I see my trundle bed.

The Rescue.

"Some on boards, and some on broken pieces of the ship, and so it came to pass they escaped all safe to land."

PHILIP PHILLIPS.

1. A ship was on the might-y deep, With all her sails unfurled,
2. Her deck was throng'd with precious souls, The young and old were there,
3. All drank the cup that pleasure held, But gave no thought to Him,

Tho' scarce a breath, that calm, still morn, The crest-ed bil-low curled.
And some with furrowed brows that woke Full many a trace of care.
Their heavenly Guide, whose bounteous hand Had filled it to the brim.

For many an hour, up-on the wave, That state-ly ves-sel lay,
They glid-ed on,— a week had passed,—The sky was still se-rene;
But see far off, where yon-der sun Is fad-ing to its rest,

Then spread her can-vas to the breeze, And proud-ly sailed a-way.
As if a storm could nev-er change The beau-ty of the scene.
That bank of clouds por-ten-tous rise A-cross the gold-en west!

4. Now peal on peal loud thunders roll, And vi-vid lightnings flash!

And now against the ves-sel's side The an-gry bil-lows dash!

Wild blows the wind! the night is dark! Huge mas-sive rocks are near!

rit.

They stand a-gast, that lone-ly throng, And cheeks are pale with fear.

5. Quick! quick! let ev'ry sail be furled!—But ere the word is given, The helm is

By permission.

91. The Happy Pilgrim.

Words arranged.   Rev. W. M'Donald. By per.

1. I saw a happy pilgrim, In shining garments clad,
   And trav'ling up the mountain, His countenance was glad;
   He had no cares nor burdens, He'd laid them at the cross,
   The blood of Christ, his Saviour, Had wash'd him from all dross.

CHORUS.

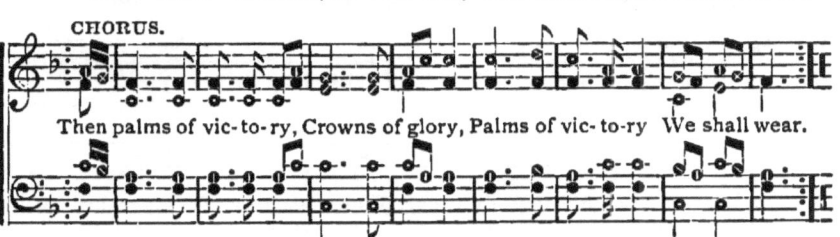

Then palms of victory, Crowns of glory, Palms of victory We shall wear.

2 The summer sun was sinking,
  The sweat was on his brow;
His garments worn and dusty,
  His step seemed very slow;
But he kept pressing onward,
  For he was wending home,
Still shouting as he journeyed,
  Deliverance will come.

3 I saw him in midsummer,
  Still happy on his way,
He'd reached the land of Beulah,
  Where birds sing all the day.
He found a store of honey
  And wine upon the lees,
And fruit in rich abundance
  Upon life's living trees.

4 I saw him in the evening,
  The sun was bending low,
He'd overtopped the mountain
  And reached the vale below;
He saw the golden city,
  His everlasting home,
And shouted loud, Hosanna!
  Deliverance will come.

5 I heard the song of triumph
  They sang upon that shore,
Saying, Jesus has redeemed us,
  To suffer nevermore:
Then casting his eyes backward
  On the race which he had run,
He shouted loud, Hosanna!
  Deliverance has come!

92. Solo.—The Drunkard's Wife. *Key D.*

1 A drunkard reached his cheerless home,
  The storm without was dark and wild;
He forced his weeping wife to roam
  A wanderer, friendless with her child;
As through the falling snow she pressed,
  The babe was sleeping on her breast.

2 And colder still the winds did blow,
  And dark the hours of night came on,
And deeper grew the drifted snow—
  Her limbs were chilled, her strength was gone,
O God! she cried, in accents wild,
  If I must perish, save my child!

3 She stripped the mantle from her breast,
  And bared her bosom to the storm,
As round the child she wrapped the vest,
  She smiled to think that it was warm,
With one cold kiss, a tear of grief,
  The broken-hearted found relief.

4 At morn her cruel husband passed,
  And saw her on her snowy bed;
Her tearful eyes were closed at last;
  Her cheek was pale, her spirit fled;
He raised the mantle from the child;
  The babe looked up and sweetly smiled.

5 Shall this sad warning plead in vain?
  Poor thoughtless one, it speaks to you;
Now break the tempter's cruel chain,
  No more your dreadful way pursue;
Renounce the cup, to Jesus fly—
  Immortal soul, why will you die?

93. Hold up Your Hand for Jesus.

[A LITTLE street boy in London had both legs broken by a dray passing over them. He was laid in one of the beds of the hospital to die, and another little fellow was laid near by, picked up sick with famine and fever. The latter was allowed to lie down by the side of the little crushed boy. He crept up to him and said: "Bubby, did you never hear about Jesus?" "No, I never heard of Him." "Bubby, I went to Mission School once, and they told us that Jesus would take you to Heaven when you die, and you'd never have hunger any more—and no more pain—if you axed Him." "I couldn't ask such a great, big gentleman as He to do anything for me. He wouldn't stop to speak to a little boy like me." "But He'll do all that, if you ax Him." "How can I ax Him if I don't know where He lives: and how can I get there when both my legs is broke?" "Bubby, they told me at Mission School as how Jesus passes by. Teacher says as how He goes around. How do you know but that He might come around to the hospital this very night? You'd know Him if you was to see Him." "But I can't keep my eyes open. My legs feel so awful bad. Doctor says I'll die." "Bubby, hold up your hand, and He'll know what you want when He passes by." They got the hand up. It dropped. Tried again. It slowly fell back. Three times he got up the little hand, only to let it fall. Bursting into tears, he said: "I give it up." "Bubby, lend me yer hand, put yer elbow on my pillar, I can do without it." Soon the hand was propped up. And when they came in the morning the boy lay dead, his hand still held up for Jesus.]

Theo. D. C. Miller, M.D.   W. Warren Bentley.

1. A lit-tle child lay dy-ing, With none to soothe his pain; No
2. "I want to speak of Je-sus Be-fore my eyes grow dim;" The

moth-er's face to cheer him, And give him smiles a-gain; But
poor boy gent-ly whis-pered: "I nev-er heard of him!" "But

one brave lit-tle fel-low Crept slow-ly to his bed, And
he is ev-er near you, And when this life is o'er, He'll

Hold up Your Hand, etc.—CONCLUDED.

3 "I could not ask a stranger
  This dying form to see,
And One so good and noble
  Would never speak to me;
I know not where to find him,
  If he would ease my pain;
But tell me more of Jesus,—
  Oh, speak of him again!"

4 "Just ask for peace and quiet,
  For pleasure when you die;
His love is ever near you,—
  This night he passes by;
In hospital and palace
  His presence doth abide,
And if you wish to see him
  Draw nearer to his side."

5 "The doctor says I'm dying,
  My eyes are growing dim;
In pain I cannot linger,—
  How shall I speak to him?"
"Hold up your hand for Jesus,
  And when he passes by,
He'll take you in his bosom
  And bear you to the sky."

6 The little hand, so feeble,
  Went up, but fell again;
Then twice he sowly raised it,
  But could not bear the pain;
Then propped upon a pillow,
  With sad eyes opened wide,
His hand went up for Jesus,
  And bright with smiles he died.

Published in sheet form by W. J. A. Lieder, 60 Chatham St., N. Y. Used by per.

Nothing Between.—CONCLUDED.

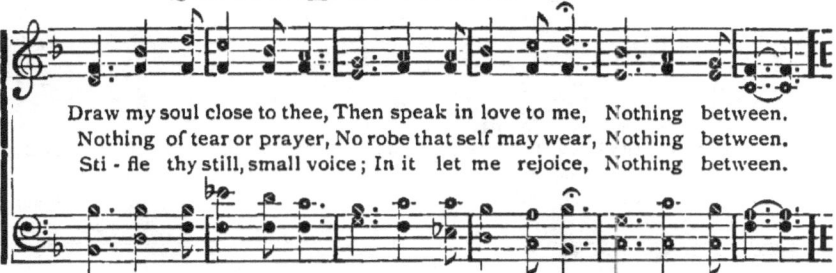

Draw my soul close to thee, Then speak in love to me, Nothing between.
Nothing of tear or prayer, No robe that self may wear, Nothing between.
Sti-fle thy still, small voice; In it let me rejoice, Nothing between.

4 Nothing between, Lord,
  Nothing between;
Shine with unclouded ray,
Chasing each mist away;
O'er my whole heart bear sway,
  Nothing between.

5 Nothing between, Lord,
  Nothing between;
Thus may I walk with thee,
Thee only may I see,
Thine only let me be,
  Nothing between.

6 Nothing between, Lord,
  Nothing between,
Till thine unclouded light,
Rising on earth's dark night,
Bursts on my living sight,
  Nothing between.

7 Nothing between, Lord,
  Nothing between,
Till, the last conflict o'er,
I stand on Canaan's shore
With thee evermore,
  Nothing between.

96 A Sinner like Me.

C. J. B. CHAS. J. BUTLER.

1. I was once far away from the Saviour, And as vile as a sinner could be,
I wondered if Christ the Redeemer, Could save a poor sinner like me.

2 I wandered on in the darkness,
    Not a ray of light could I see,
  And the thought filled my heart with sad-   [ness,
    There's no hope for a sinner like me.

3 I then fully trusted in Jesus,
    And oh, what a joy came to me;
  My heart was filled with his praises,
    For saving a sinner like me.

4 No longer in darkness I'm walking,
    For the light is now shining on me,
  And now unto others I'm telling,
    How he saved a poor sinner like me.

5 And when life's journey is over,
    And I the dear Saviour shall see,
  I'll praise him forever and ever,
    For saving a sinner like me.

Copyright, 1881, by JOHN J. HOOD.

Leave All to Him.—CONCLUDED.

neith - er great nor small, But one vast com - pre - hend - ing
weak - est when they call; For none are might - i - er than
him, he e - ven knows When thou would'st lean too much on
watch - ful, lov - ing eye; And say, "Ful - fill thy will in

plan, Thy-self in - volved ere worlds be-gan; Leave all to him.
those Who on his un - seen arm re - pose; Leave all to him.
these And seek, with them, thy - self to please; Leave all to him.
me, In life, in death, e - ter - nal - ly;" Leave all to him.

99 Only for a Little While.

W. WARREN BENTLEY.

With feeling.

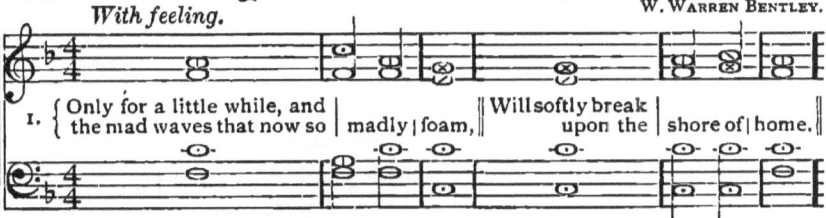

1. { Only for a little while, and | the mad waves that now so | madly | foam, || Will softly break | upon the | shore of | home. ||

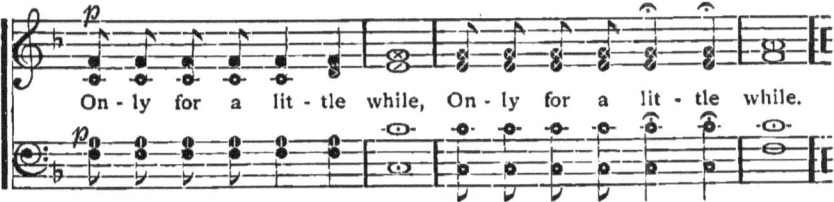

On - ly for a lit - tle while, On - ly for a lit - tle while.

2. Only for a little while to struggle with the | raging | billow, || And then the sleep upon the | quiet | pillow. || Only for a little while.

3. This thought of perfect rest across the water dashing | wild and | high, || Gleams like a star upon a | darkening | sky, || A true image, pure and blest.

By permission.

DO RE MI FA SO LA SI

100 The Wondrous Gift.

1 GRACE! 'tis a charming sound,
　　Harmonious to the ear;
　Heaven with the echo shall resound,
　　And all the earth shall hear.

Ref.—Saved by grace alone,
　　　This is all my plea;
　　Jesus died for all mankind,
　　　And Jesus died for me.

2 Grace first contrived a way
　　To save rebellious man;
　And all the steps that grace display,
　　Which drew the wondrous plan.

3 Grace taught my roving feet
　　To tread the heavenly road;
　And new supplies each hour I meet,
　　While pressing on to God.

4 Grace all the work shall crown,
　　Through everlasting days;
　It lays in heaven the topmost stone,
　　And well deserves our praise.

101 Nothing but Leaves.

1 NOTHING but leaves! The Spirit grieves
　　O'er years of wasted life;
　O'er sins indulged while conscience slept,
　O'er vows and promises unkept,
　　And reap from years of strife
　Nothing but leaves! nothing but leaves!

2 Nothing but leaves! no gathered sheaves
　　Of life's fair ripening grain:
　We sow our seeds; lo! tares and weeds,—
　Words, *idle* words, for earnest deeds,—
　　Then reap, with toil and pain,
　Nothing but leaves! nothing but leaves!

3 Ah, who shall thus the Master meet,
　　And bring but withered leaves?
　Ah, who shall at the Saviour's feet,
　Before the awful judgment seat,
　　Lay down for golden sheaves,
　Nothing but leaves? nothing but leaves?

102 White as Snow.

1 WHAT! "lay my sins on Jesus?"
　　God's well-beloved Son!
　No! 'tis a truth most precious,
　　That God e'en *that* hath done.

Cho.—Hallelujah, Jesus saves me,
　　　He makes me "white as snow."

2 Yes, 'tis a truth most precious,
　　To all who do believe,
　God laid our sins on Jesus,
　　Who did the load receive.

3 What! "bring our guilt to Jesus?"
　　To wash away our stains;
　The act is passed that freed us,
　　And naught to do remains.

103 Knocking, Knocking.

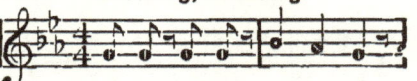

1 KNOCKING, knocking, who is there?
　　Waiting, waiting, oh, how fair!
　'Tis a Pilgrim, strange and kingly,
　　Never such was seen before;
　Ah, my soul, for such a wonder,
　　Wilt thou not undo the door?

2 Knocking, knocking,—still he's there,—
　　Waiting, waiting, wondrous fair;
　But the door is hard to open,
　　For the weeds and ivy-vine,
　With their dark and clinging tendrils,
　　Ever round the hinges twine.

3 Knocking, knocking—what, still there?
　　Waiting, waiting, grand and fair;
　Yes, the pierced hand still knocketh,
　　And beneath the crowned hair
　Beam the patient eyes, so tender,
　　Of thy Saviour, waiting there.

104 How Solemn are the Words.

1 How solemn are the words,
　　And yet to faith how plain,
　Which Jesus uttered while on earth,—
　　"Ye must be born again!"

2 "Ye must be born again!"
　　For so hath God decreed,
　No reformation will suffice—
　　'Tis *life* poor sinners need.

3 "Ye must be born again!"
　　And life *in Christ* must have;
　In vain the soul may elsewhere go—
　　'Tis he *alone* can save.

4 "Ye must be born again!"
　　Or never enter heaven;
　'Tis only blood-washed ones are there—
　　The ransomed are forgiven.

105 The Great Physician.

1 THE great Physician now is here,
　The sympathizing Jesus;
　He speaks the drooping heart to cheer,
　Oh, hear the voice of Jesus.

Cho.—Sweetest note in seraph song,
　　Sweetest name on mortal tongue,
　　Sweetest carol ever sung,
　　Jesus, blessed Jesus.

2 Your many sins are all forgiven,
　Oh, hear the voice of Jesus;
　Go on your way in peace to heaven,
　And wear a crown with Jesus.

3 All glory to the dying Lamb!
　I now believe in Jesus;
　I love the blessed Saviour's name,
　I love the name of Jesus.

4 His name dispels my guilt and fear,
　No other name but Jesus;
　Oh, how my soul delights to hear
　The precious name of Jesus.

5 And when to that bright world above,
　We rise to see our Jesus,
　We'll sing around the throne of love
　His name, the name of Jesus.

106 Come to Jesus.

1 COME to Jesus, come to Jesus,
　Come to Jesus just now;
　Just now come to Jesus,
　Come to Jesus just now.

2 He will save you.　　7 He will cleanse you.
3 He is able.　　　　　8 He'll renew you.
4 He is willing.　　　　9 He'll forgive you.
5 He is waiting.　　　10 If you trust him.
6 He will hear you.　　11 He will save you.

107 Marching to Zion.

1 COME, we that love the Lord,
　And let our joys be known,
　Join in a song with sweet accord,
　And thus surround the throne.

Cho.—We're marching to Zion,
　　Beautiful, beautiful Zion;
　　We're marching upward to Zion,
　　The beautiful city of God.

2 Let those refuse to sing
　Who never knew our God;
　But children of the heavenly King,
　May speak their joys abroad.

3 The hill of Zion yields
　A thousand sacred sweets,
　Before we reach the heavenly fields,
　Or walk the golden streets.

4 Then let our songs abound,
　And every tear be dry;
　We're marching through Immanuel's ground,
　To fairer worlds on high.

108 I Heard the Voice of Jesus.

1 I HEARD the voice of Jesus say,
　"Come unto Me and rest;
　Lay down, thou weary one, lay down
　Thy head upon My breast."

2 I came to Jesus as I was—
　Weary, and worn, and sad;
　I found in him a resting-place,
　And he has made me glad.

3 I heard the voice of Jesus say,
　"Behold, I freely give
　The living water, thirsty one,
　Stoop down, and drink, and live."

4 I came to Jesus, and I drank
　Of that life-giving stream;
　My thirst was quenched, my soul revived,
　And now I live in him.

109 I Love Thy Kingdom.

1 I LOVE thy kingdom, Lord,
　The house of thine abode,
　The Church our blest Redeemer saved
　With his own precious blood.

2 I love thy Church, O God!
　Her walls before thee stand,
　Dear as the apple of thine eye,
　And graven on thy hand.

3 Beyond my highest joy
　I prize her heavenly ways;
　Her sweet communion, solemn vows,
　Her hymns of love and praise.

4 Sure as thy truth shall last,
　To Zion shall be given
　The brightest glories earth can yield,
　And brighter bliss of heaven.

110. Sun of My Soul.

1 SUN of my soul, thou Saviour dear,
  It is not night if thou be near;
  Oh, may no earth-born cloud arise,
  To hide thee from thy servant's eyes.

2 When the soft dews of kindly sleep
  My wearied eye-lids gently steep,
  Be my last thought, how sweet to rest
  Forever on my Saviour's breast.

3 Abide with me from morn till eve,
  For without thee I cannot live;
  Abide with me when night is nigh,
  For without thee I dare not die.

4 Watch by the sick: enrich the poor
  With blessings from thy boundless store;
  Be every mourner's sleep to-night,
  Like infant's slumbers, pure and light.

111. Sing of His Mighty Love.

1 OH, bliss of the purified, bliss of the free,
  I plunge in the crimson tide opened for me;
  O'er sin and uncleanness exulting I stand,
  And point to the print of the nails in his hand.

Cho.—Oh, sing of his mighty love,
    ‖: Sing of his mighty love, :‖
    Mighty to save.

2 Oh, bliss of the purified, Jesus is mine,
  No longer in dread condemnation I pine;
  In conscious salvation I sing of his grace,
  Who lifteth upon me the light of his face.

3 Oh, bliss of the purified, bliss of the pure,
  No wound hath the soul that his blood cannot cure;
  No sorrow-bowed head but may sweetly find rest,
  No tears but may dry them on Jesus' breast.

4 O Jesus the crucified, thee will I sing,
  My blessed Redeemer, my God and my King;
  My soul filled with rapture shall shout o'er the grave,
  And triumph in death in the "Mighty to Save."

112. Revive Thy Work.

1 WE praise thee, O God, for the Son of thy love,
  For Jesus who died, and is now gone above.

Cho.—Hallelujah! thine the glory, hallelujah! amen;
    Hallelujah! thine the glory, revive us again.

2 We praise thee, O God, for thy Spirit of light,
  Who has shown us our Saviour and scattered our night.

3 All glory and praise to the Lamb that was slain,
  Who has borne all our sins, and has cleansed every stain.

4 All glory and praise to the God of all grace,
  Who has bought us, and sought us, and guided our ways.

5 Revive us again, fill each heart with thy love;
  May each soul be rekindled with fire from above.

113. How Sweet the Name.

1 HOW sweet the name of Jesus sounds
  In a believer's ear;
  It soothes his sorrows, heals his wounds,
  And drives away his fear.

2 It makes the wounded spirit whole,
  And calms the troubled breast;
  'Tis manna to the hungry soul,
  And to the weary rest.

3 Jesus, my Shepherd, Saviour, Friend;
  My Prophet, Priest, and King;
  My Lord, my Life, my Way, my End,—
  Accept the praise I bring.

4 I would thy boundless love proclaim
  With every fleeting breath;
  So shall the music of thy name
  Refresh my soul in death.

114. Even Me.

1 LORD, I hear of showers of blessing
  Thou art scattering full and free—
  Showers the thirsty land refreshing;
  Let some droppings fall on me.

Cho.—Even me, even me,
    Let thy blessing fall on me.

2 Pass me not, O gracious Father!
  Sinful though my heart may be;
  Thou might'st leave me, but the rather
  Let thy mercy fall on me.

3 Pass me not, O tender Saviour!
  Let me love and cling to thee;
  I am longing for thy favor;
  Whilst thou'rt calling, oh, call me.

4 Pass me not, O mighty Spirit!
  Thou can'st make the blind to see;
  Witnesser of Jesus' merit,
  Speak the word of power to me.

FAMILIAR HYMNS.

115　Shining Shore.

1 My days are gliding swiftly by,
　And I, a pilgrim stranger,
　Would not detain them as they fly,
　These hours of toil and danger.

Cho.—For oh, we stand on Jordan's strand,
　　Our friends are passing over,
　　And, just before, the shining shore
　　We may almost discover.

2 We'll gird our loins, my brethren dear,
　Our distant home discerning;
　Our absent Lord has left us word,
　Let every lamp be burning.

3 Should coming days be cold and dark,
　We need not cease our singing;
　That perfect rest naught can molest
　Where golden harps are ringing.

4 Let sorrow's rudest tempest blow,
　Each cord on earth to sever;　[home
　Our King says, "Come," and there's our
　For ever, oh, for ever!

116　'Tis Midnight.

1 'Tis midnight; and on Olives' brow,
　The star is dimm'd that lately shone,
　'Tis midnight; in the garden now
　The suff'ring Saviour prays alone.

2 'Tis midnight, and from all removed,
　The Saviour wrestles 'lone with fears;
　E'en that disciple whom he loved
　Heeds not his Master's grief and tears.

3 'Tis midnight; and for others' guilt,
　The Man of Sorrows weeps in blood;
　Yet he who hath in anguish knelt,
　Is not forsaken by his God.

4 'Tis midnight; and from ether-plains
　Is borne a song that angels know;
　Unheard by mortals are the strains
　That sweetly soothe the Saviour's woe.

117　Bread of Heaven.

1 Guide me, O thou great Jehovah,
　Pilgrim through this barren land;
　I am weak, but thou art mighty,
　Hold me with thy powerful hand;
　　Bread of heaven,
　Feed me till I want no more.

2 Open now the crystal fountain,
　Whence the healing waters flow;
　Let the fiery, cloudy pillar
　Lead me all my journey through!
　　Strong deliverer,
　Be thou still my strength and shield.

3 When I tread the verge of Jordan,
　Bid my anxious fears subside;
　Bear me through the swelling current,
　Land me safe on Canaan's side;
　　Songs of praises
　I will ever give to thee.

118　O Holy Spirit, Come.

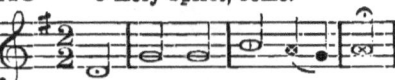

1 O Holy Spirit, come,
　And Jesus' love declare;
　Oh, tell us of our heavenly home,
　And guide us safely there.

2 Our unbelief remove
　By thine almighty breath;
　Oh, work the wondrous work of love,
　The mighty work of faith.

3 Come with resistless power,
　Come with almighty grace,
　Come with the long-expected shower,
　And fall upon this place.

119　Holy Spirit, Faithful Guide.

1 Holy Spirit, faithful guide,
　Ever near the Christian's side;
　Gently lead us by the hand,
　Pilgrims in a desert land;
　Weary souls fore'er rejoice,
　While they hear that sweetest voice
　Whispering softly, wanderer, come!
　Follow me, I'll guide thee home.

2 Ever-present, truest Friend,
　Ever near thine aid to lend,
　Leave us not to doubt and fear,
　Groping on in darkness drear,
　When the storms are raging sore,
　Hearts grow faint, and hopes give o'er,—
　Whispering softly, wanderer, come!
　Follow me, I'll guide thee home!

3 When our days of toil shall cease,
　Waiting still for sweet release,
　Nothing left but heaven and prayer,
　Wond'ring if our names were there;
　Wading deep the dismal flood,
　Pleading nought but Jesus' blood;
　Whispering softly, wanderer, come!
　Follow me, I'll guide thee home!

120 Nearer to Thee.

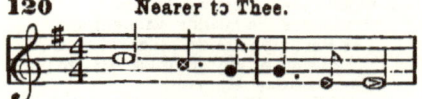

1 NEARER, my God, to thee!
　Nearer to thee,
E'en though it be a cross
　That raiseth me;
Still all my song shall be,
Nearer, my God, to thee,
　Nearer to thee!

2 Though like the wanderer,
　The sun gone down,
Darkness be over me,
　My rest a stone,
Yet in my dreams I'd be,
Nearer, my God, to thee,
　Nearer to thee!

3 There let the way appear,
　Steps unto heaven;
All that thou sendest me,
　In mercy given;
Angels to beckon me
Nearer, my God, to thee,
　Nearer to thee!

121 Antioch.

1 O FOR a thousand tongues, to sing
　My great Redeemer's praise;
The glories of my God and King,
　The triumphs of his grace!

2 My gracious Master and my God,
　Assist me to proclaim,
To spread through all the earth abroad,
　The honors of thy name.

3 Jesus! the name that charms our fears,
　That bids our sorrows cease;
'Tis music in the sinner's ears,
　'Tis life, and health, and peace.

4 He breaks the power of canceled sin,
　He sets the prisoner free;
His blood can make the foulest clean;
　His blood availed for me.

122 Coronation.

1 ALL hail the power of Jesus' name!
　Let angels prostrate fall;
Bring forth the royal diadem,
　And crown him Lord of all.

2 Ye chosen seed of Israel's race,
　Ye ransomed from the fall,
Hail him who saves you by his grace,
　And crown him Lord of all.

3 Sinners, whose love can ne'er forget
　The wormwood and the gall;
Go, spread your trophies at his feet,
　And crown him Lord of all.

4 Let every kindred, every tribe,
　On this terrestrial ball,
To him all majesty ascribe,
　And crown him Lord of all.

5 O that with yonder sacred throng
　We at his feet may fall;
We'll join the everlasting song,
　And crown him Lord of all.

123 Blest be the tie.

1 BLEST be the tie that binds
　Our hearts in Christian love;
The fellowship of kindred minds
　Is like to that above.

2 Before our Father's throne
　We pour our ardent prayers;
Our fears, our hopes, our aims are one,
　Our comforts and our cares.

3 We share our mutual woes,
　Our mutual burdens bear;
And often for each other flows
　The sympathising tear.

4 When we asunder part,
　It gives us inward pain;
But we shall still be joined in heart,
　And hope to meet again.

124 How Gentle. Same tune.

1 How gentle God's commands!
　How kind his precepts are!
Come, cast your burdens on the Lord,
　And trust his constant care.

2 Beneath his watchful eye
　His saints securely dwell;
That hand which bears all nature up
　Shall guard his children well.

3 Why should this anxious load
　Press down your weary mind?
Haste to your heavenly Father's throne,
　And sweet refreshment find.

4 His goodness stands approved,
　Unchanged from day to day:
I'll drop my burden at his feet,
　And bear a song away.

125 What a Friend.

1 WHAT a Friend we have in Jesus,
   All our sins and griefs to bear!
  What a priveledge to carry
   Everything to God in prayer!
  O what peace we often forfeit,
   O what needless pain we bear,
  All because we do not carry
   Everything to God in prayer!

2 Have we trials and temptations?
   Is there trouble anywhere?
  We should never be discouraged,
   Take it to the Lord in prayer.
  Can we find a friend so faithful
   Who will all our sorrows share?
  Jesus knows our every weakness,
   Take it to the Lord in prayer.

126 Rock of Ages.

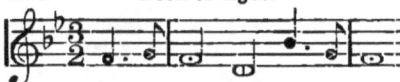

1 ROCK of Ages, cleft for me,
   Let me hide myself in thee;
  Let the water and the blood,
   From thy wounded side which flowed,
  Be of sin the double cure,
   Save from wrath and make me pure.

2 Could my tears forever flow,
   Could my zeal no languor know;
  These for sin could not atone;
   Thou must save, and thou alone;
  In my hand no price I bring,
   Simply to thy cross I cling.

3 While I draw this fleeting breath,
   When my eyes shall close in death,
  When I rise to worlds unknown,
   And behold thee on thy throne,
  Rock of Ages, cleft for me,
   Let me hide myself in thee.

127 Before the Cross.

1 MY faith looks up to thee,
   Thou Lamb of Calvary,
    Saviour divine;
   Now hear me while I pray,
   Take all my guilt away,
   O let me from this day
    Be wholly thine.

2 May thy rich grace impart
   Strength to my fainting heart,
    My zeal inspire;
   As thou hast died for me,
   O may my love to thee
   Pure, warm, and changeless be,—
    A living fire.

3 While life's dark maze I tread,
   And griefs around me spread,
    Be thou my guide;
   Bid darkness turn to day,
   Wipe sorrow's tears away,
   Nor let me ever stray
    From thee aside.

128 Happy Day.

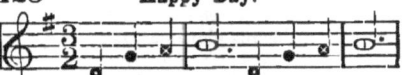

1 O HAPPY day, that fixed my choice
   On thee, my Saviour and my God!
  Well may this glowing heart rejoice,
   And tell its rapture all abroad.

Cho.—Happy day, happy day,
   When Jesus washed my sins away;
  He taught me how to watch and pray,
   And live rejoicing every day;
  Happy day, happy day,
   When Jesus washed my sins away.

2 'Tis done, the great transaction's done—
   I am my Lord's and he is mine;
  He drew me, and I followed on,
   Charmed to confess the voice divine.

3 Now rest, my long divided heart:
   Fixed on this blissful centre, rest
  Nor ever from thy Lord depart,
   With him of every good possessed.

129 Sweet Hour of Prayer.

1 Sweet hour of prayer, sweet hour of prayer,
   That calls me from a world of care,
  And bids me at my Father's throne
   Make all my wants and wishes known!
  In seasons of distress and grief
   My soul has often found relief,
  And oft escaped the tempter's snare
   By thy return, sweet hour of prayer.

2 Sweet hour of prayer, sweet hour of prayer,
   Thy wings shall my petition bear
  To him, whose truth and faithfulness
   Engage the waiting soul to bless:
  And since he bids me seek his face,
   Believe his word, and trust his grace,
  I'll cast on him my every care,
   And wait for thee, sweet hour of prayer.

130. Stand up for Jesus.

1 STAND up, stand up for Jesus,
   Ye soldiers of the cross;
Lift high his royal banner,
   It must not suffer loss:
From victory unto victory
   His army shall he lead,
Till every foe is vanquished
   And Christ is Lord indeed.

2 Stand up, stand up for Jesus,
   The trumpet call obey;
Forth to the mighty conflict,
   In this his glorious day:
"Ye that are men, now serve him,"
   Against unnumbered foes;
Your courage rise with danger,
   And strength to strength oppose.

131. Just as I am.

1 JUST as I am, without one plea,
But that thy blood was shed for me,
And that thou bid'st me come to thee,
   O Lamb of God, I come!

2 Just as I am, and waiting not
To rid my soul of one dark blot,
To thee, whose blood can cleanse each
   O Lamb of God, I come!   [spot,

3 Just as I am—thou wilt receive,
Wilt welcome, pardon, cleanse, relieve;
Because thy promise I believe,
   O Lamb of God, I come!

4 Just as I am—thy love unknown
Hath broken every barrier down;
Now, to be thine, yea, thine alone,
   O Lamb of God, I come!

132. Work, for the night.

1 WORK, for the night is coming,
   Work through the morning hours;
Work, while the dew is sparkling,
   Work 'mid springing flowers;
Work, when the day grows brighter,
   Work in the glowing sun;
Work, for the night is coming,
   When man's work is done.

2 Work, for the night is coming,
   Work through the sunny noon;
Fill brightest hours with labor,
   Rest comes sure and soon.
Give every flying minute
   Something to keep in store;
Work, for the night is coming,
   When man works no more.

133. In the Cross of Christ I glory.

1 IN the cross of Christ I glory,
   Towering o'er the wrecks of time;
All the light of sacred story
   Gathers round its head sublime.

2 When the woes of life o'ertake me,
   Hopes deceive and fears annoy,
Never shall the cross forsake me;
   Lo! it glows with peace and joy.

3 When the sun of bliss is beaming
   Light and love upon my way,
From the cross the radiance streaming
   Adds more lustre to the day.

4 Bane and blessing, pain and pleasure,
   By the cross are sanctified;
Peace is there that knows no measure,
   Joys that through all time abide.

134. The Morning Light.

1 THE morning light is breaking
   The darkness disappears;
The sons of men are waking
   To penitential tears;
Each breeze that sweeps the ocean
   Brings tidings from afar
Of nations in commotion,
   Prepared for Zion's war.

2 See heathen nations bending
   Before the God we love,
And thousand hearts ascending
   In gratitude above;
While sinners, now confessing,
   The gospel call obey,
And seek the Saviour's blessing,
   A nation in a day.

3 Blest river of salvation,
   Pursue thine onward way;
Flow thou to every nation,
   Nor in thy richness stay,
Stay not till all the lowly
   Triumphant reach their home
Stay not till all the holy
   Proclaim, "The Lord is come!"

135 Fountain.

1 THERE is a fountain filled with blood
   Drawn from Immanuel's veins;
   And sinners, plunged beneath that flood,
   Lose all their guilty stains.

2 The dying thief rejoiced to see
   That fountain in his day;
   And there may I, though vile as he,
   Wash all my sins away.

3 Thou dying Lamb! thy precious blood
   Shall never lose its power,
   Till all the ransomed Church of God
   Are saved, to sin no more.

4 E'er since, by faith, I saw the stream
   Thy flowing wounds supply,
   Redeeming love has been my theme,
   And shall be till I die.

136 For Victorious Faith.

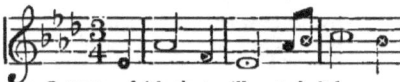

1 O FOR a faith that will not shrink,
   Though pressed by every foe,
   That will not tremble on the brink
   Of any earthly woe!

2 That will not murmur nor complain
   Beneath the chastening rod,
   But, in the hour of grief or pain,
   Will lean upon its God.

3 A faith that keeps the narrow way
   Till life's last hour is fled,
   And with a pure and heavenly ray
   Illumes a dying bed.

4 Lord, give us such a faith as this,
   And then, whate'er may come,
   We'll taste, e'en here, the hallowed bliss
   Of an eternal home.

137 Title Clear.

1 WHEN I can read my title clear
   To mansions in the skies,
   I'll bid farewell to every fear,
   And wipe my weeping eyes.

Cho.—We will stand the storm,
   We will anchor by and by.

2 Should earth against my soul engage,
   And fiery darts be hurled,
   Then I can smile at Satan's rage,
   And face a frowning world.

3 Let cares like a wild deluge come,
   Let storms of sorrow fall,
   So I but safely reach my home,
   My God, my heaven, my all.

4 There I shall bathe my weary soul
   In seas of heavenly rest,
   And not a wave of trouble roll
   Across my peaceful breast.

138 Lord, I am Thine.

1 LORD, I am thine, entirely thine,
   Purchased and saved by blood divine;
   With full consent thine I would be,
   And own thy sovereign right in me.

2 Grant one poor sinner more a place
   Among the children of thy grace;
   A wretched sinner, lost to God,
   But ransomed by Immanuel's blood.

3 Thine would I live—thine would I die;
   Be thine through all eternity;
   The vow is past,—beyond repeal,—
   And now I set the solemn seal.

4 Here, at the cross, where flows the blood
   That bought my guilty soul for God,—
   Thee my new Master now I call,
   And consecrate to thee my all.

139 I am Trusting.

1 I AM coming to the cross;
   I am poor, and weak, and blind;
   I am counting all but dross;
   I shall full salvation find.

Cho.—I am trusting, Lord, in thee,
   Dear Lamb of Calvary;
   Humbly at thy cross I bow;
   Save me, Jesus, save me now.

2 Long my heart has sighed for thee;
   Long has evil reigned within;
   Jesus sweetly speaks to me,
   I will cleanse you from all sin.

3 Here I give my all to thee,—
   Friends, and time, and earthly store;
   Soul and body thine to be—
   Wholly thine—forevermore.

4 Jesus comes! he fills my soul!
   Perfected in love I am;
   I am every whit made whole;
   Glory, glory to the Lamb!

140 Depth of Mercy.

1 DEPTH of mercy! can there be
  Mercy still reserved for me?
  Can my God his wrath forbear?
  Me, the chief of sinners, spare?

Cho.—God is love! I know, I feel;
  Jesus lives, and loves me still;
    Jesus lives,
  He lives and loves me still.

2 I have long withstood his grace,
  Long provoked him to his face:
  Would not hearken to his calls;
  Grieved him by a thousand falls.

3 Now incline me to repent;
  Let me now my sins lament;
  Now my foul revolt deplore,
  Weep, believe, and sin no more.

141 I Hear Thy Welcome Voice.

1 I HEAR thy welcome voice,
    That calls me, Lord, to thee,
  For cleansing in thy precious blood
    That flowed on Calvary.

Cho.—I am coming, Lord,
    Coming now to thee!
  Wash me, cleanse me in the blood
    That flowed on Calvary.

2 Though coming weak and vile,
    Thou dost my strength assure;
  Thou dost my vileness fully cleanse,
    Till spotless all and pure.

3 'Tis Jesus calls me on
    To perfect faith and love,
  To perfect hope, and peace, and trust,
    For earth and heaven above.

4 All hail, atoning blood!
    All hail, redeeming grace!
  All hail, the gift of Christ our Lord,
    Our Strength and Righteousness!

142 The Home Over There.

1 OH, think of the home over there,
    By the side of the river of light,
  Where the saints, all immortal and fair,
    Are robed in their garments of white.
Ref.—Over there, over there,
    Oh, think of the home over there.

2 Oh, think of the friends over there,
    Who before us the journey have trod,
  Of the songs that they breathe on the air,
    In their home in the palace of God.
Ref.—Over there, over there,
    Oh, think of the friends over there.

3 My Saviour is now over there,
    There my kindred and friends are at rest;
  Then away from my sorrow and care,
    Let me fly to the land of the blest.
Ref.—Over there, over there,
    My Saviour is now over there.

4 I'll soon be at home over there,
    For the end of my journey I see;
  Many dear to my heart, over there,
    Are watching and waiting for me.
Ref.—Over there, over there,
    I'll soon be at home over there.

143 He Leadeth Me!

1 HE leadeth me! O blessed thought!
  O words with heavenly comfort fraught!
  Whate'er I do, where'er I be,
  Still 'tis God's hand that leadeth me.

Cho.—He leadeth me, he leadeth me,
  By his own hand he leadeth me;
  His faithful follower I would be,
  For by his hand he leadeth me.

2 Sometimes 'mid scenes of deepest gloom,
  Sometimes where Eden's bowers bloom,
  By waters still, o'er troubled sea,—
  Still 'tis his hand that leadeth me!

3 Lord, I would clasp thy hand in mine,
  Nor ever murmur nor repine,
  Content, whatever lot I see,
  Since 'tis my God that leadeth me!

144 My Country! 'tis of Thee.

1 MY country! 'tis of thee,
  Sweet land of liberty,
    Of thee I sing:
  Land where my fathers died!
  Land of the pilgrims' pride!
    From every mountain side
    Let freedom ring!

2 My native country, thee,
  Land of the noble, free,
    Thy name I love;
  I love thy rocks and rills,
  Thy woods and templed hills:
    My heart with rapture thrills
    Like that above.

3 Our fathers' God! to thee,
  Author of liberty,
    To thee we sing;
  Long may our land be bright
  With freedom's holy light;
    Protect us by thy might,
    Great God, our King!

FAMILIAR HYMNS.

145 Jesus of Nazareth.

1 WHAT means this eager, anxious throng,
  Which moves with busy haste along—
  These wondrous gath'rings day by day?
  What means this strange commotion, pray?
  ||: In accents hushed the throng reply:
  "Jesus of Nazareth passeth by." :||

2 Jesus! 'tis he who once below
  Man's pathway trod, 'mid pain and woe:
  And burdened ones, where'er he came,
  Brought out their sick, and deaf, and lame;
  ||: The blind rejoiced to hear the cry:
  "Jesus of Nazareth passeth by." :||

3 Again he comes! From place to place
  His holy footprints we can trace;
  He pauseth at our threshhold—nay,
  He enters—condescends to stay;
  ||: Shall we not gladly raise the cry—
  "Jesus of Nazareth passeth by." :||

4 Ho! all ye heavy-laden, come:
  Here's pardon, comfort, rest, and home;
  Ye wanderers from a Father's face,
  Return, accept his proffered grace;
  ||: Ye tempted ones, there's refuge nigh:
  "Jesus of Nazareth passeth by." :||

5 But if you still this call refuse,
  And all his wondrous love abuse,
  Soon will he sadly from you turn,
  Your bitter prayer for pardon spurn;
  ||: "Too late! too late!" will be the cry—
  "Jesus of Nazareth *has passed by!*" :||

146 I am Praying for You.

1 I HAVE a Saviour, he's pleading in glory,
  A dear, loving Saviour, tho' earth-friends be few;
  And now he is watching in tenderness o'er me,
  And, oh, that my Saviour, were your Saviour, too!

  Cho.—For you I am praying, :||
    I'm praying for you.

2 I have a Father: to me he has given
  A hope for eternity, blessed and true;
  And soon will he call me to meet him in heaven, [me, too!
  But, oh, that he'd let me bring you with

3 I have a robe: 'tis resplendent in whiteness
  Awaiting in glory my wondering view;
  Oh, when I receive it all shining in brightness,
  Dear friend, could I see you receiving one, too!

147 All to Christ I Owe.

1 I HEAR the Saviour say,
  Thy strength indeed is small;
  Child of weakness, watch and pray,
  Find in Me thine all in all.

  Cho.—Jesus paid it all,
    All to him I owe;
  Sin had left a crimson stain:
    He washed it white as snow.

2 Lord, now indeed I find
  Thy power, and thine alone,
  Can change the leper's spots,
  And melt the heart of stone.

3 For nothing good have I
  Whereby thy grace to claim—
  I'll wash my garment white
  In the blood of Calvary's Lamb.

4 When from my dying bed
  My ransomed soul shall rise,
  Then "Jesus paid it all"
  Shall rend the vaulted skies.

5 And when before the throne
  I stand in him complete,
  I'll lay my trophies down,
  All down at Jesus' feet.

148 What hast thou done for Me?

1 I GAVE my life for thee,
  My precious blood I shed,
  That thou might'st ransomed be,
  And quickened from the dead;
  I gave, I gave My life for thee,
  What hast thou given for Me?

2 My Father's house of light,—
  My glory-circled throne,—
  I left, for earthly night,
  For wand'rings sad and lone;
  I left, I left it all for thee,
  Hast thou left aught for Me?

3 I suffered much for thee,
  More than thy tongue can tell,
  Of bitterest agony,
  To rescue thee from hell;
  I've borne, I've borne it all for thee,
  What hast thou borne for Me?

4 And I have brought to thee,
  Down from My home above,
  Salvation full and free,
  My pardon and My love;
  I bring, I bring rich gifts to thee,
  What hast thou brought to Me?

149 Saviour, like a Shepherd.

1 SAVIOUR, like a shepherd lead us,
  Much we need thy tend'rest care,
In thy pleasant pastures feed us,
  For our use thy folds prepare;
  ||: Blessed Jesus, blessed Jesus,
  Thou hast bought us, thine we are. :||

2 We are thine, do thou befriend us,
  Be the Guardian of our way;
Keep thy flock, from sin defend us,
  Seek us when we go astray;
  ||: Blessed Jesus, blessed Jesus,
  Hear, oh, hear us when we pray. :||

3 Thou hast promised to receive us,
  Poor and sinful though we be;
Thou hast mercy to relieve us,
  Grace to cleanse, and power to free;
  ||: Blessed Jesus, blessed Jesus,
  We will early turn to thee. :||

150 I Love to Tell the Story.

1 I LOVE to tell the Story
  Of unseen things above,
Of Jesus and his glory,
  Of Jesus and his love;
I love to tell the Story,
  Because I know it's true;
It satisfies my longings,
  As nothing else would do.

Cho.—I love to tell the Story!
  'Twill be my theme in glory,
To tell the Old, Old Story
  Of Jesus and his love.

2 I love to tell the Story!
  More wonderful it seems,
Than all the golden fancies
  Of all our golden dreams;
I love to tell the Story!
  It did so much for me;
And that is just the reason
  I tell it now to thee.

3 I love to tell the Story!
  For those who know it best
Seem hungering and thirsting
  To hear it, like the rest;
And when, in scenes of glory,
  I sing the NEW, NEW SONG,
'Twill be the OLD, OLD STORY
  That I have loved so long.

151 Jesus, Lover of My Soul.

1 JESUS, lover of my soul,
  Let me to thy bosom fly,
While the nearer waters roll,
  While the tempest still is high.
Hide me, O my Saviour, hide,
  Till the storm of life is past;
Safe into the haven guide,
  O, receive my soul at last.

2 Other refuge have I none;
  Hangs my helpless soul on thee:
Leave, oh, leave me not alone,
  Still support and comfort me:
All my trust on thee is stayed,
  All my help from thee I bring;
Cover my defenceless head
  With the shadow of thy wing!

3 Thou, O Christ, art all I want;
  More than all in thee I find;
Raise the fallen, cheer the faint,
  Heal the sick, and lead the blind.
Just and holy is thy name,
  I am all unrighteousness;
False and full of sin I am,
  Thou art full of truth and grace.

4 Plenteous grace with thee is found,
  Grace to cover all my sin;
Let the healing streams abound;
  Make and keep me pure within.
Thou of life the fountain art,
  Freely let me take of thee:
Spring thou up within my heart,
  Rise to all eternity.

152 There is a Land.

1 THERE is a land of pure delight,
  Where saints immortal reign;
Eternal day excludes the night,
  And pleasures banish pain;
There everlasting Spring abides,
  And never-whith'ring flowers;
Death, like a narrow sea, divides
  This heavenly land from ours.

2 Sweet fields beyond the swelling flood
  Stand dressed in living green;
So to the Jews old Canaan stood,
  While Jordan rolled between;
Could we but climb where Moses stood,
  And view the landscape o'er, [flood
Not Jordan's stream, nor death's cold
  Should fright us from the shore.

INDEX.

A
Abide with me! fast falls. 86
A little child lay dying, . 93
All hail the power of Je-. 122
ANGELS' SONG, . . 30
An old soldier I stand, . 44
Are you ready for the . 55
ARE YOU READY TO GO? 2
Are you willing, my sister 48
A ship was on the mighty. 89
A SINNER LIKE ME, . 96
Away from friends, from. 72

B
BEHOLD THE BRIDE- . 55
BENEATH THE BLOOD- . 59
BE NOT THOU AFRAID, . 40
Blest be the tie that binds 123
BRINGING IN THE SHEA. 75
BY AND BY, . . . 41

C
Called to the feast by the. 11
CLINGING, . . . 6
Close to thee, O Lamb of 7
COME AND REST, . . 5
COME, PRODIGAL, COME, 28
Come, stand beneath the . 59
Come to Jesus, come to . 106
COME TO ME, . . 83
Come, we that love the . 107
COMING TO JESUS, . 47

D
DECIDE TO-NIGHT, . 69
Depth of mercy! can . 140
DIVINE UNION, . . 25
Down at the cross where . 94
Do you know the won- . 7
Drifting away, drifting a- 63

E
Each day a little nearer, . 21
EVEN THEE, . . . 67

F
FREELY SPEAK FOR JE- 50
From Calvary's mountain 84

G
GLORY TO HIS NAME, . 94
Golden harps are sound- 71
GOOD BYE TILL WE . 81
Grace! 'tis a charming . 100
Guide me, O thou great. 117

H
Hark, hark my soul, . 30
Hark, the Saviour's voice 67
Have mercy, Lord, on me, 9
Have you not a word for. 65
He has come! He has . 70
He leadeth me! O blessed 143
HOLD UP YOUR HAND . 93
Holy, holy, holy, . . 58
Holy Spirit, faithful guide 119
How gentle God's com-. 124
How sad it would be, if . 6
How solemn are the . 104
How sweet the name of . 113
Humbly the penitent . 39
Hushed was the evening. 73

I
I am coming to the cross, 139
I AM SAVED BY HIS . 2
I AM THE DOOR, . . 23
I gave my life for thee, . 148
I have a Saviour, he's . 146
I have fought the good . 45
I HAVE NOTHING TO DO 45
I heard the voice of Je- . 108
I hear the Saviour say, . 147
I hear thy welcome voice, 141
I'LL GO TO MY FATHER. 72
I love to tell the Story, . 150
I love thy kingdom, . 109
In life's twilight hours I . 40
I now am so happy in Je- 4
IN SIGHT OF THE CRYS- 90
In the cross of Christ I . 133
I sat alone with life's . 90
I saw a happy pilgrim, . 91
IT IS GOOD TO BE HERE. 78
It must be settled to-night 79
I've a message of great . 77
I want thy heart, I wait-. 60

I was in bondage, but . 74
I was once far away from 96
I weep no more with sad- 8
I WILL FOLLOW THEE, . 62

J
Jerusalem the golden, . 26
Jesus is pleading with my 64
Jesus, lover of my soul, . 151
JESUS, SAVE ME NOW, . 22
"Jesus wept!"—those . 33
Just as I am, without one 131

K
KEEP ME EVER, . . 8
KNEELING, PLEADING, . 9
Knocking, knocking, . 103

L
Late at night I saw . 85
Lead me forth, O blessed 62
Leave all to him who . 98
LET THE MEETING GO . 44
Lord, I am thine, entirely 138
Lord, I hear of showers . 114
Lord, I know I am not . 9
Lord, my heart is bruised 22
Look to Jesus, burdened 49

M
MISSING, . . . 85
More love to thee, O . 3
My country! 'tis of thee, 144
My days are gliding swift- 115
My faith looks up to thee 127
My Father is rich in . 51

N
Nearer, my God, to thee, 120
NO ROOM IN HEAVEN, . 6
Nothing between, Lord, . 95
Nothing but leaves! The 101
NOT WORTHY, . . 19

O
O for a faith that will not 136
O for a thousand tongues, 121
O happy day, that fixed . 128

111

Oh, bliss of the purified,.	111	
Oh, freely speak for Jesus,	50	
OH, LET ME IN, . .	60	
O Holy Spirit, come, .	118	
Oh, the wondrous love of	29	
Oh, think of the home .	142	
Oh, trust thyself to Jesus,	35	
Oh, while the moments .	38	
O Jesus, at thy cross I fall,	10	
ONE BY ONE WE'RE .	34	
ONLY BELIEVE, . .	52	
Only for a little while, .	99	
O Paradise! O Paradise!	68	
Open thou mine eyes, O.	46	
O soul oppressed with .	23	

P

Pray thou for me, . . 24

R

Rejoice with me, the lost.	3
REMEMBERED, . .	27
Rock of Ages, cleft for .	126

S

Sad and weary, lone and.	8
SAVED THROUGH AND .	74
SAVE ME, GRACIOUS GOD	10
Saviour, blessed Saviour,	88
Saviour, like a Shepherd .	149
SAY, ARE YOU READY?.	54
SHALL I BE SAVED TO-.	64
Should the death angel .	54
Simply a doorkeeper, .	20
Sinner, the Saviour is .	52
SIN NO MORE, . .	57

Some go away from the .	69
SOUL OF MINE, . .	77
Sowing in the morning,.	75
Speak to me, Jesus, .	66
Stand up, stand up for .	130
Step by step we're on the	34
Sun of my soul, thou .	110
Sweet hour of prayer, .	129

T

The blood that flowed on	14
THE CHILD OF A KING,	51
THE CLEANSING BLOOD,	14
THE DRUNKARD'S WIFE	92
The fountain of salvation	28
The great Physician now	105
THE HAPPY PILGRIM, .	91
The love of Christ is .	36
The Master has come .	3
The morning light is .	134
THE PENITENT, . .	39
THE PRECIOUS BLOOD .	18
There is a fountain filled.	135
There is a heavenly land.	5
There is a land of pure .	152
There's a land far away,.	81
THE RESCUE, . .	89
There will be no sin nor.	41
The Saviour called so lov-	12
THE SPIRIT AND THE .	5
THE TRUNDLE BED, .	87
THE WONDROUS STORY,	7
They are coming to the .	56
Thousands stand to-day.	76
'Tis midnight; and on .	116
Trust on! trust on! be-.	31

TRUST THYSELF TO JE-	35

U

Up and away like the dews 27

W

WAITING AT THE POOL,	76
WEIGHED IN THE BAL-.	97
We march, we march to.	82
We praise thee, O God,.	112
We will pray for one an-	37
What a Friend we have .	125
What! "lay my sins on .	102
What means this eager,.	145
What of the future my .	53
WHAT WILT THOU .	48
When did ever words so.	57
When I can read my .	137
When shall I come to Je-	61
WHEN THE KING COMES	11
WHEN THE SHEAVES .	32
When the woes of life .	16
WHILE THE MOMENTS .	38
Who can unfold the bliss	25
Who is on the Lord's .	42
WHOSOEVER BELIEV- .	84
Why do you wait?. .	43
WHY NOT COME TO HIM	4
With my sin-wounded .	47
With tearful eyes I look.	83
With thee, precious Lord.	78
WONDROUS LOVE OF JE-	29
Work, for the night is .	132

Y

Ye who are burdened . 15

SONGS

OF

REDEEMING LOVE

*"Redeeming Love has been my theme,
And shall be till I die."*

EDITED BY

JNO. R. SWENEY,   C. C. McCABE,
    T. C. O'KANE,   W. J. KIRKPATRICK.

PHILADELPHIA: | CINCINNATI:
JOHN J. HOOD, | WALDEN & STOWE,
1018 Arch Street. | St. Louis and Chicago.

Copyright, 1882, by WALDEN & STOWE and JOHN J. HOOD.

PREFACE.

"FEAR not, for I have redeemed thee, I have called thee by thy name; thou art mine."

"Therefore the redeemed of the LORD shall return, and come with singing unto Zion; and everlasting joy shall be upon their head; they shall obtain gladness and joy, and sorrow and mourning shall flee away."

"Break forth into joy, sing together, ye waste places of Jerusalem: for the LORD hath comforted his people, he hath redeemed Jerusalem."

"Who gave himself for us, that he might redeem us from all iniquity."

"Ye were not redeemed with corruptible things, as silver and gold; but with the precious blood of Christ, as of a lamb without blemish and without spot."

"Unto him that loved us,
and washed us from our sins in his own blood,
and hath made us kings and priests unto God and his Father,
to him be glory and dominion for ever and ever.

AMEN.

Copyright, 1882, by Walden & Stowe and John J. Hood.   Hood's Notation Copyright 1880.

4 Oh! shout aloud, ye sons of men,
Tell the glad tidings o'er again,—
Redeeming love! Redeeming love!
From east to west, from south to north,
Still let the sound go reaching forth,—
Redeeming love! Redeeming love!

5 Let distant lands take up the strain,
Till love on earth entire shall reign,
Redeeming love! Redeeming love!
O earth, be glad! O heaven, above,
Sing ye the song,—Redeeming love!
Redeeming love! Redeeming love!

The Song of the Soul.

Rev. Henry A. von Dulsem. T. C. O'Kane.

1. Oh, the song of the soul shall not die nor grow old, Nor languish nor pine, in the home of our King! But as a-ges fly onward new chords shall un-fold, New mel-o-dies meeting, in-spire us to sing.
2. In the beau-ti-ful land far a-way o'er the tide, The jasper-walled home of the An-cient of Days, Where the ransomed ones shine as the sun in his pride, Our long hal-le-lu-jahs of glo-ry we'll raise.
3. And the fair, golden harps in the hands of the blest, Shall thrill to a touch that no an-gel can give, As we sing in that land where the wea-ry shall rest, Of One who hath died that a sin-ner might live.
4. And as a-ges fly onward, tho' worlds cease to be, And per-ish the stars that in heav-en do throng, Still the joy of the soul shall be deathless and free, And deathless and free the sweet notes of her song.

REFRAIN.

Oh, the song of the soul! Oh, the song of the soul!
For-ev-er in glo-ry the song of the soul!

From "Reedeemer's Praise," by per.

DO RE MI FA SO LA SI

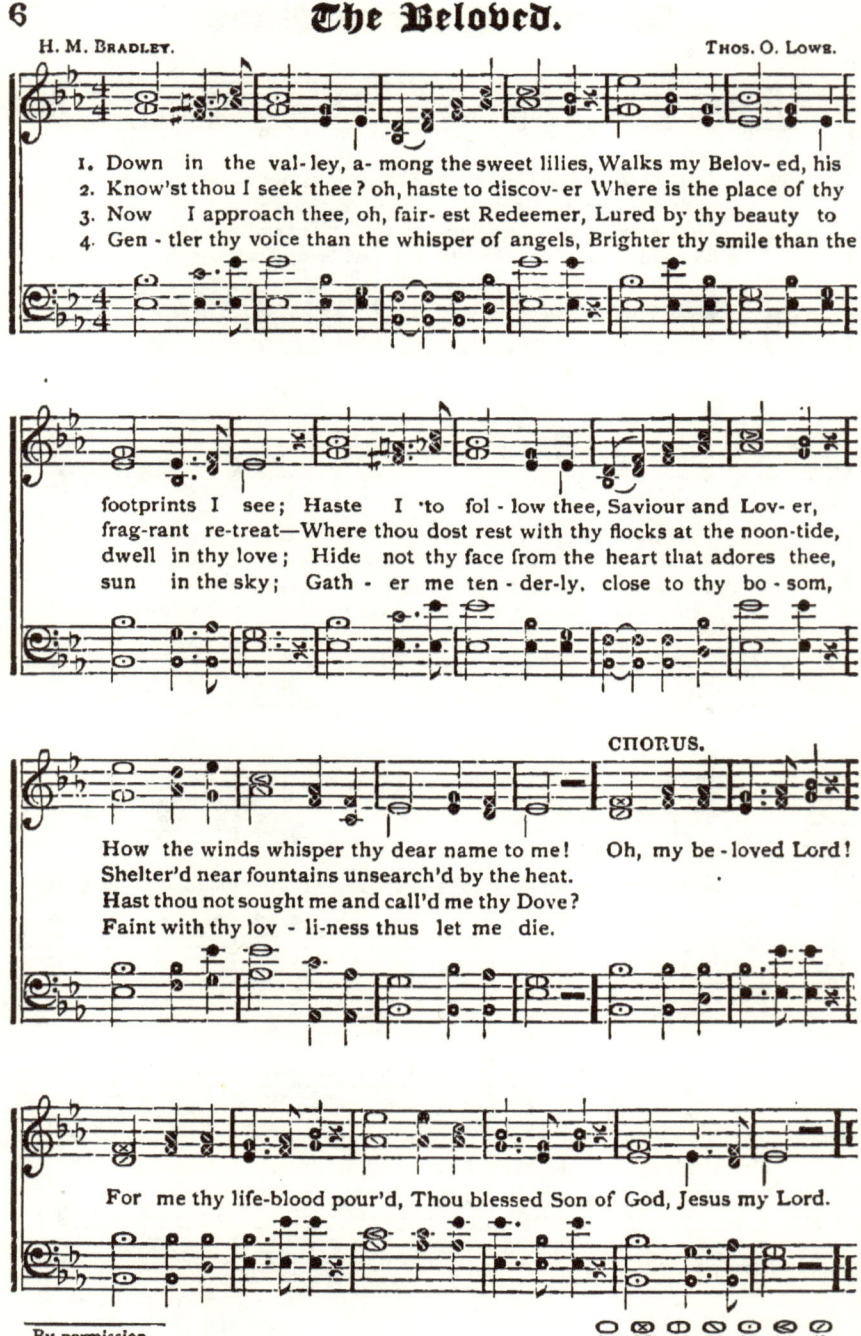

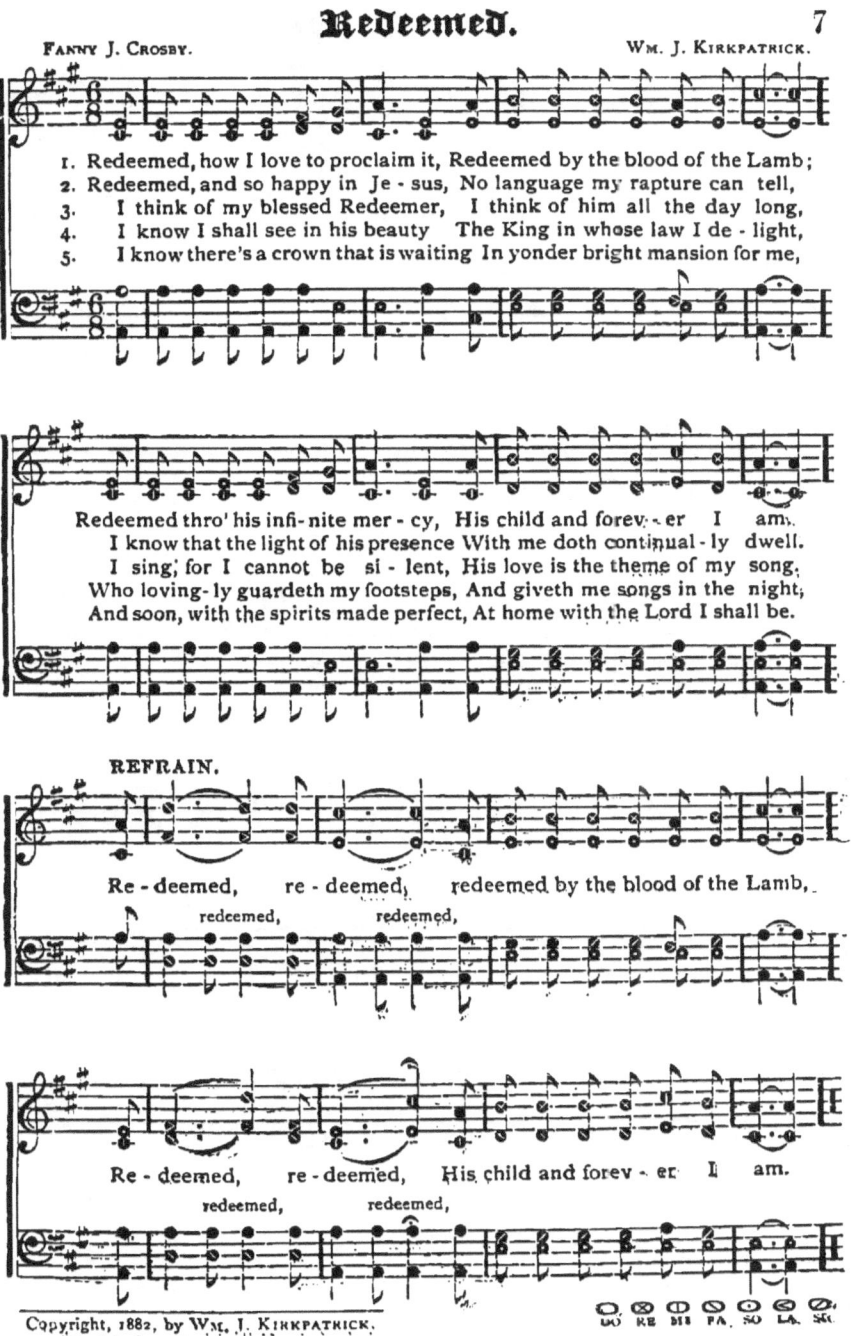

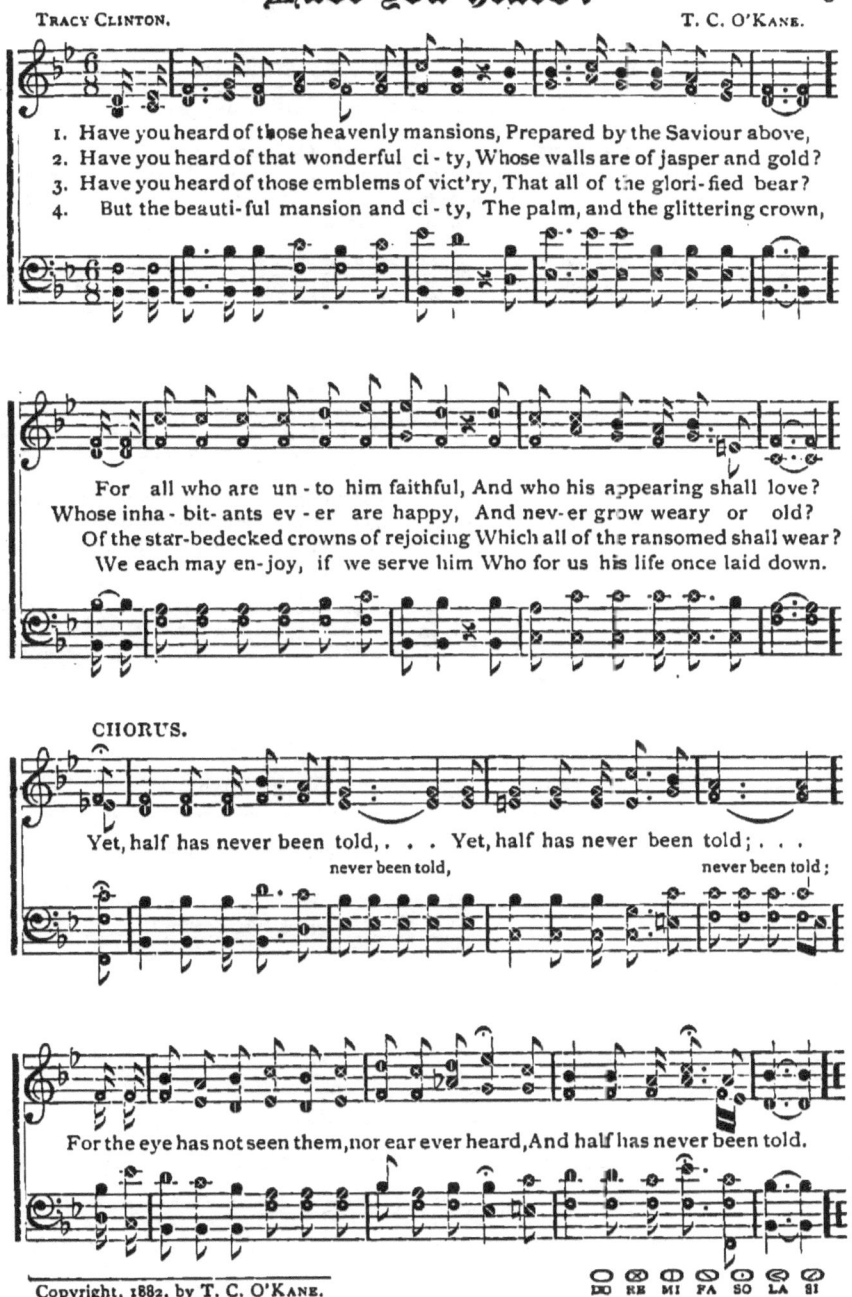

Once for All the Saviour Died. 11

Rev. J. H. MARTIN. T. C. O'KANE.

1. Once for all the Saviour died, Christ the Lord was cru-ci-fied;
2. Once for all our sins he bore, Bought our peace forev-er-more;
3. Once for all the Saviour rose, Vic-tor o'er his mighty foes;
4. Once for all as-cending high, Throned and crowned above the sky,

Once for all he shed his blood, Bearing forth a pur-ple flood.
Once for all our debt he paid, Full, complete a-tonement made.
With their glorious King and Head, Saints shall waken from the dead.
There he in-tercedes and reigns,—Praise him in tri-umphant strains.

From "Redeemer's Praise."

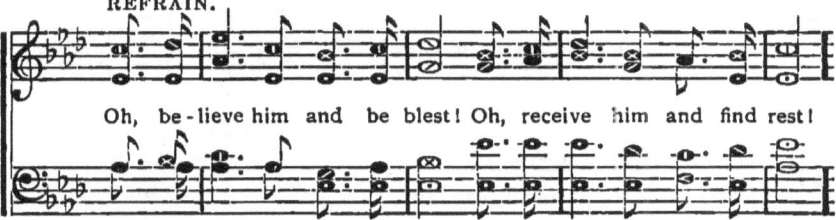

REFRAIN.

Oh, be-lieve him and be blest! Oh, receive him and find rest!

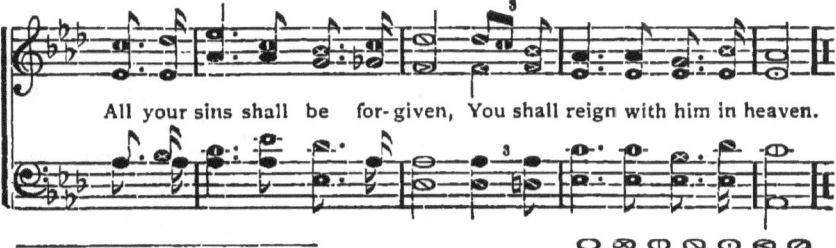

All your sins shall be for-given, You shall reign with him in heaven.

Copyright, 1881, by T. C. O'KANE.

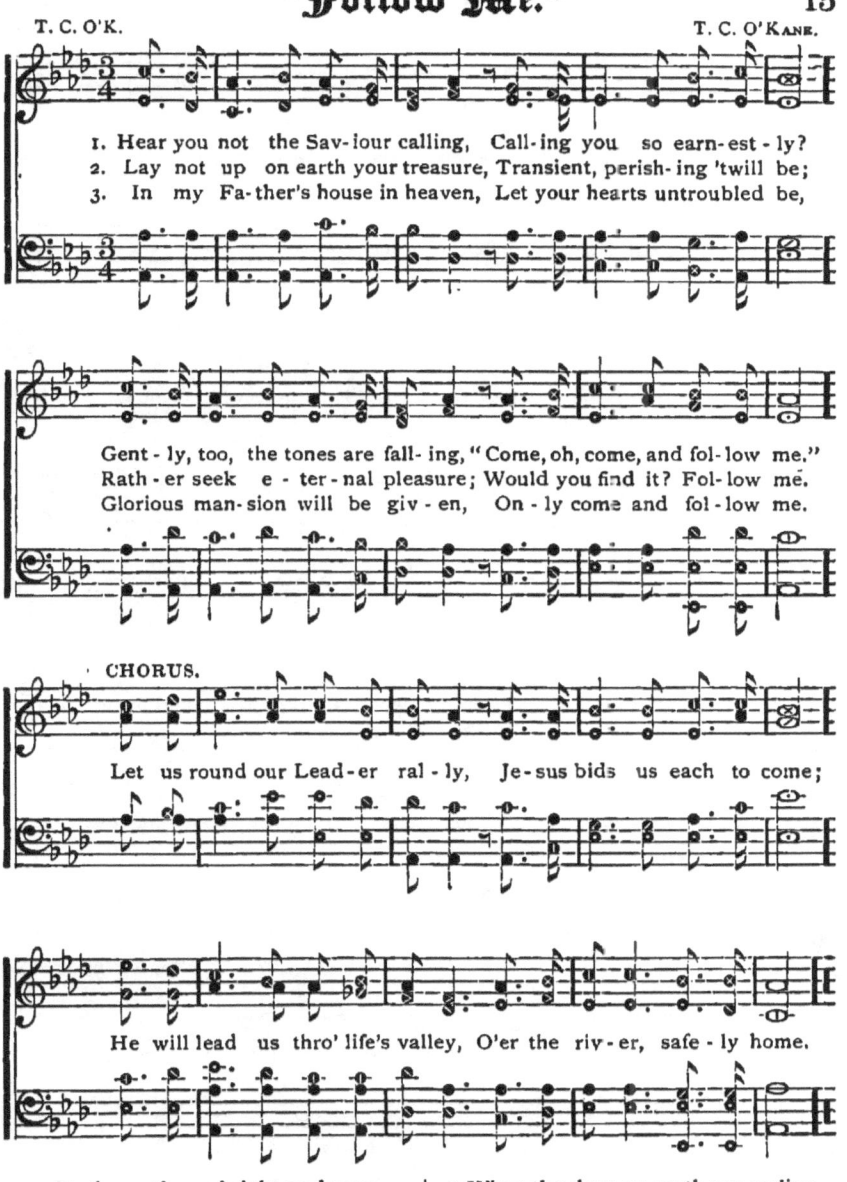

18. Beautiful Day.

W. J. K.   Wm. J. Kirkpatrick.

1. Beau-ti-ful day, love-ly thy light; Ho-ly each ray, ban-ishing night;
2. Beau-ti-ful day, calm was thy dawn; Joyous the lay, blessed the morn,
3. Beau-ti-ful day, perfect-ly bright; Je-sus al-way, boundless delight,
4. Beau-ti-ful day, ha-ven of rest; Ev'ry one may come and be bless'd;

Cloudless thy sky; peaceful my stay Here in the sunlight of beautiful day.
When in my heart, over my way, First shone the noontide of beautiful day.
Bliss all around, heaven by the way, Shining in fulness, oh, beautiful day.
Glory to God! naught can dismay; Christ is the light of this beautiful day.

REFRAIN.

Beau-ti-ful, beauti-ful day, Evermore shine on my way;
Beau-ti-ful, beau-ti-ful day, Ev-ermore shine on my way;

Saviour, I pray, keep me al-way Safe in this beauti-ful day.

beauti-ful day.

By permission.

DO RE MI FA SO LA SI

Coming to Jesus.

Rev. W. H. Burrell.   Jno. R. Sweney.

1. With my sin-wounded soul, To be made ful-ly whole, And thy perfect sal-
2. O, how long have I tried To re-sist nature's tide, All in vain have I
3. I thy promise believe, That in thee I shall live, Thro' thy blood shed so
4. To be thine, wholly thine, Precious Saviour divine; With my all conse-

va-tion to see; With my heart stained by sin, To be washed and made clean,
sighed to be free; In myself all undone, 'Neath the waves sinking down,
free-ly for me To ob-tain a pure heart, To secure this "good part,"
crat-ed to thee; To be kept ev'ry hour, By thy love's wondrous power,

REFRAIN.

I am coming, dear Saviour, to thee, I am coming, dear Saviour, to thee, I am coming, dear Saviour, to thee; With my heart stained by sin, To be washed and made clean, I am coming, dear Saviour, to thee.

By permission.

Marching Onward.

Mrs. R. N. Turner. Wm. J. Kirkpatrick.

1. We are marching, marching onward, Strong to dare, and strong to do!
2. As he leads us, so we'll fol-low, For his light illumes our way;
3. We are marching, marching onward With a courage true and strong;

With our ban-ner float-ing o'er us, And our Leader, Christ in view!
Ev - er on-ward, ev - er on-ward, Step by step, and day by day!
For the vic-t'ry shall not fail us, Tho' the war-fare may be long!

Sin, with all its tempting pleasures, Beckons us with lur - ing hand;
'Tis a grand and glorious ar - my; And the King whose name we bear,
No! the heart that trusts in Je - sus Shall not fall in weakness down;

But with true and earnest purpose, For our Mas-ter we will stand.
Watches o'er us, and sustains us, With a strong and ten - der care!
Strength he gives, the cross to car - ry, Strength to win the victor's crown!

CHORUS.

March-ing on - ward, marching on - ward, Bearing forth the
Marching on - ward, marching on - ward,

Copyright, 1882, by John J. Hood.

DO RE MI FA SO LA SI

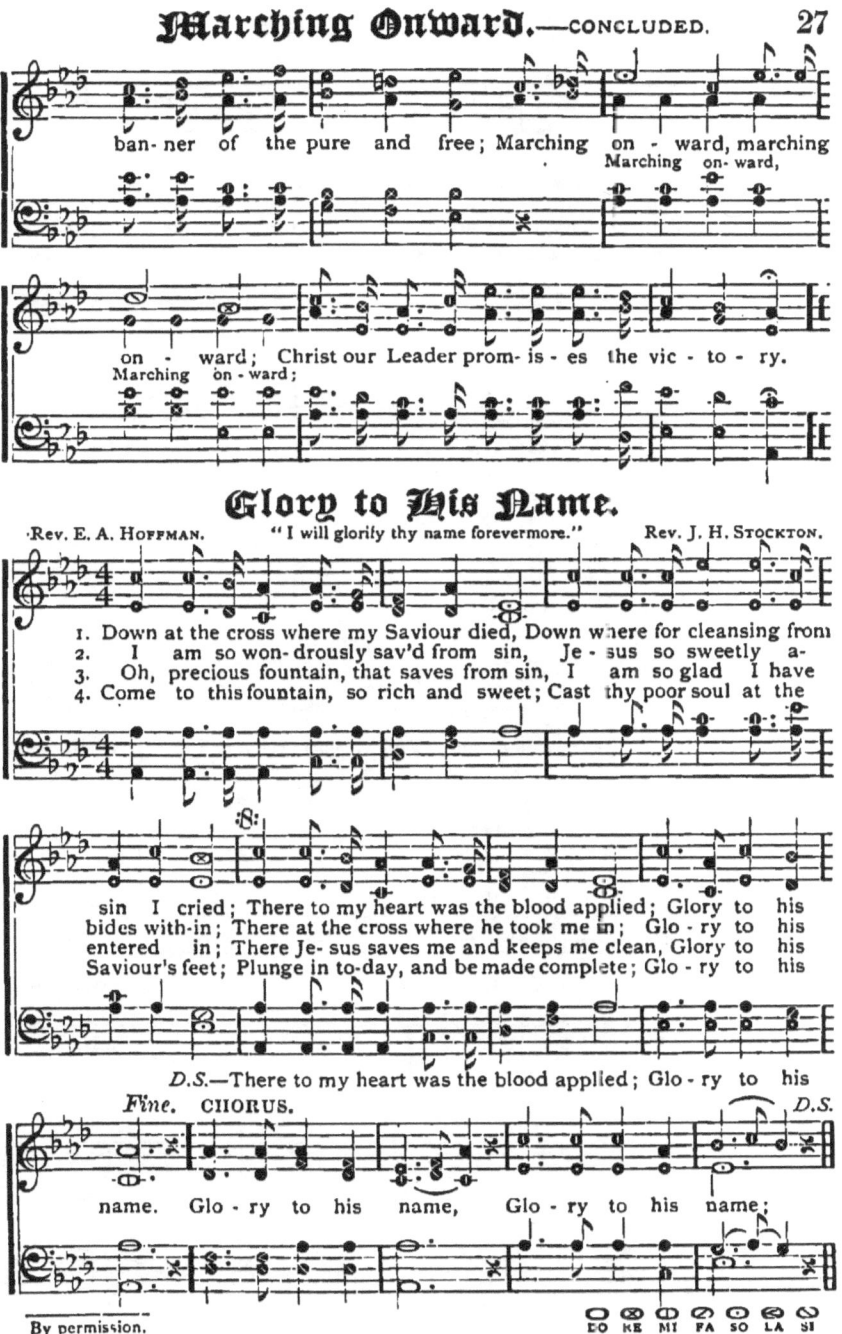

28. Tell it to Jesus.

J. E. Rankin, D.D. — Matt. xiv. 12. — E. S. Lorenz.

1. Are you wea-ry, are you heavy-heart-ed? Tell it to Je-sus,
2. Do the tears flow down your cheeks unbidden? Tell it to Je-sus,
3. Do you fear the gath'ring clouds of sor-row? Tell it to Je-sus,
4. Are you trou-bled at the thought of dy-ing? Tell it to Je-sus,

Tell it to Je-sus; Are you griev-ing o-ver joys de-part-ed?
Tell it to Je-sus; Have you sins that to man's eye are hid-den?
Tell it to Je-sus; Are you anx-ious what shall be to-mor-row?
Tell it to Je-sus; For Christ's coming Kingdom are you sigh-ing?

CHORUS.

Tell it to Je-sus a-lone. Tell it to Je-sus, Tell it to Je-sus, He is a friend that's well known; You have no oth-er such a friend or broth-er, Tell it to Je-sus a-lone.

By permission.

DO RE MI FA SO LA SI

Rejoicing Evermore.

JOHN NEWTON. R. E. HUDSON.

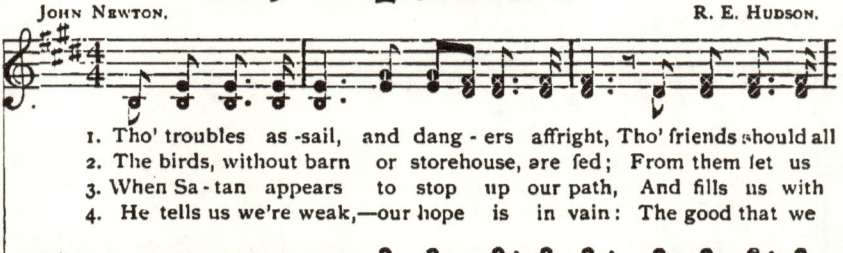

1. Tho' troubles as-sail, and dang-ers affright, Tho' friends should all
2. The birds, without barn or storehouse, are fed; From them let us
3. When Sa-tan appears to stop up our path, And fills us with
4. He tells us we're weak,—our hope is in vain: The good that we

CHORUS.—Yes, I will re-joice, re-joice in the Lord, Yes, I will re-

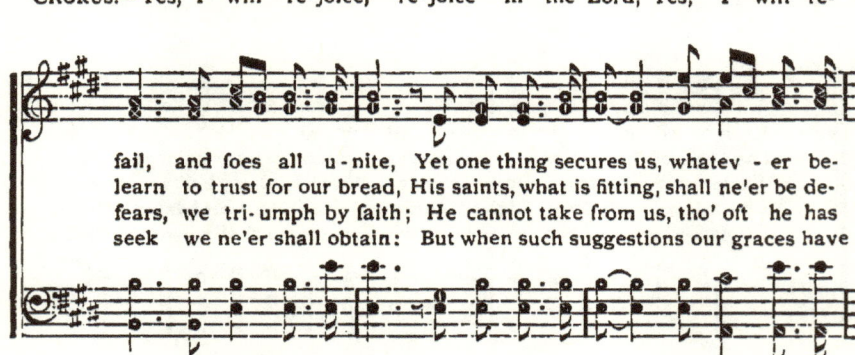

fail, and foes all u-nite, Yet one thing secures us, whatev-er be-
learn to trust for our bread, His saints, what is fitting, shall ne'er be de-
fears, we tri-umph by faith; He cannot take from us, tho' oft he has
seek we ne'er shall obtain: But when such suggestions our graces have

joice, re-joice in the Lord, Yes, I will re-joice, re-joice in the

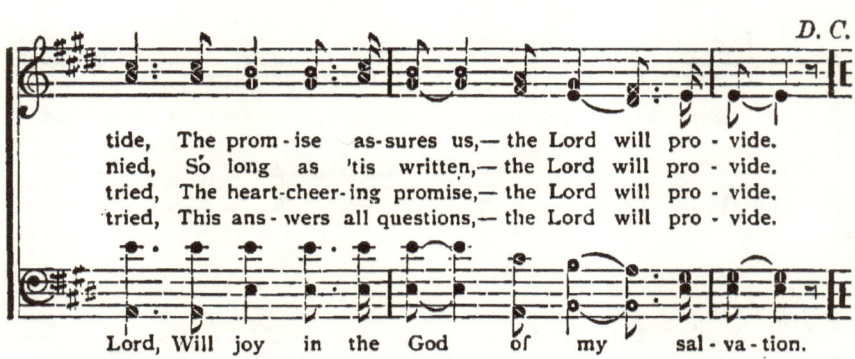

tide, The prom-ise as-sures us,—the Lord will pro-vide.
nied, So long as 'tis written,—the Lord will pro-vide.
tried, The heart-cheer-ing promise,—the Lord will pro-vide.
tried, This ans-wers all questions,—the Lord will pro-vide.

Lord, Will joy in the God of my sal-va-tion.

5 No strength of our own, nor goodness we claim;
Our trust is all thrown on Jesus' great [name:
In this our strong tower for safety we hide;
The Lord is our power,—the Lord will provide,

6 When life sinks apace, and death is in view,
The word of his grace shall comfort us through:
Not fearing or doubting, with Christ on [our side,
We hope to die shouting,—the Lord will provide,

From "Salvation Echoes," by per.

DO RE MI FA SO LA SI

Is not this the Land of Beulah.

1. I am dwelling on the mountain, Where the golden sunlight gleams
   O'er a land whose wondrous beauty Far exceeds my fondest dreams;
   Where the air is pure, ethereal, Laden with the breath of flowers,
   They are blooming by the fountain, 'Neath the amaranthine bowers.

2. I can see far down the mountain, Where I wandered weary years,
   Often hindered in my journey By the ghosts of doubts and fears,
   Broken vows and disappointments Thickly sprinkled all the way,
   But the Spirit led, unerring, To the land I hold to-day.

3. I am drinking at the fountain, Where I ever would abide;
   For I've tasted life's pure river, And my soul is satisfied;
   There's no thirsting for life's pleasures, Nor adorning, rich and gay,
   For I've found a richer treasure, One that fadeth not away.

Cho.—Is not this the land of Beulah, Blessed, blessed land of light,
Where the flowers bloom forever, And the sun is always bright.

4 Tell me not of heavy crosses,
   Nor the burdens hard to bear,
For I've found this great salvation
   Makes each burden light appear;
And I love to follow Jesus,
   Gladly counting all but dross,
Worldly honors all forsaking
   For the glory of the Cross.

5 Oh, the Cross has wondrous glory!
   Oft I've proved this to be true;
When I'm in the way so narrow
   I can see a pathway through;
And how sweetly Jesus whispers:
   Take the Cross, thou need'st not fear,
For I've tried this way before thee,
   And the glory lingers near.

32. Is my Name written There?

M. A. K.
Frank M. Davis.

1. Lord, I care not for riches, Neither silver nor gold; I would make sure of heaven, I would enter the fold; In the book of thy kingdom, With its pages so fair, Tell me, Jesus, my Saviour, Is my name written there?
2. Lord, my sins they are many, Like the sands of the sea, But thy blood, O my Saviour! is sufficient for me; For thy promise is written, In bright letters that glow, "Tho' your sins be as scarlet, I will make them like snow."
3. Oh! that beautiful city, With its mansions of light, With its glorified beings, In pure garments of white; Where no evil thing cometh, To spoil what is fair; Where the angels are watching,—Is my name written there?

REFRAIN.

Is my name written there, On the page white and fair? In the book of thy kingdom, Is my name written there?

By permission.

DO RE MI FA SO LA SI

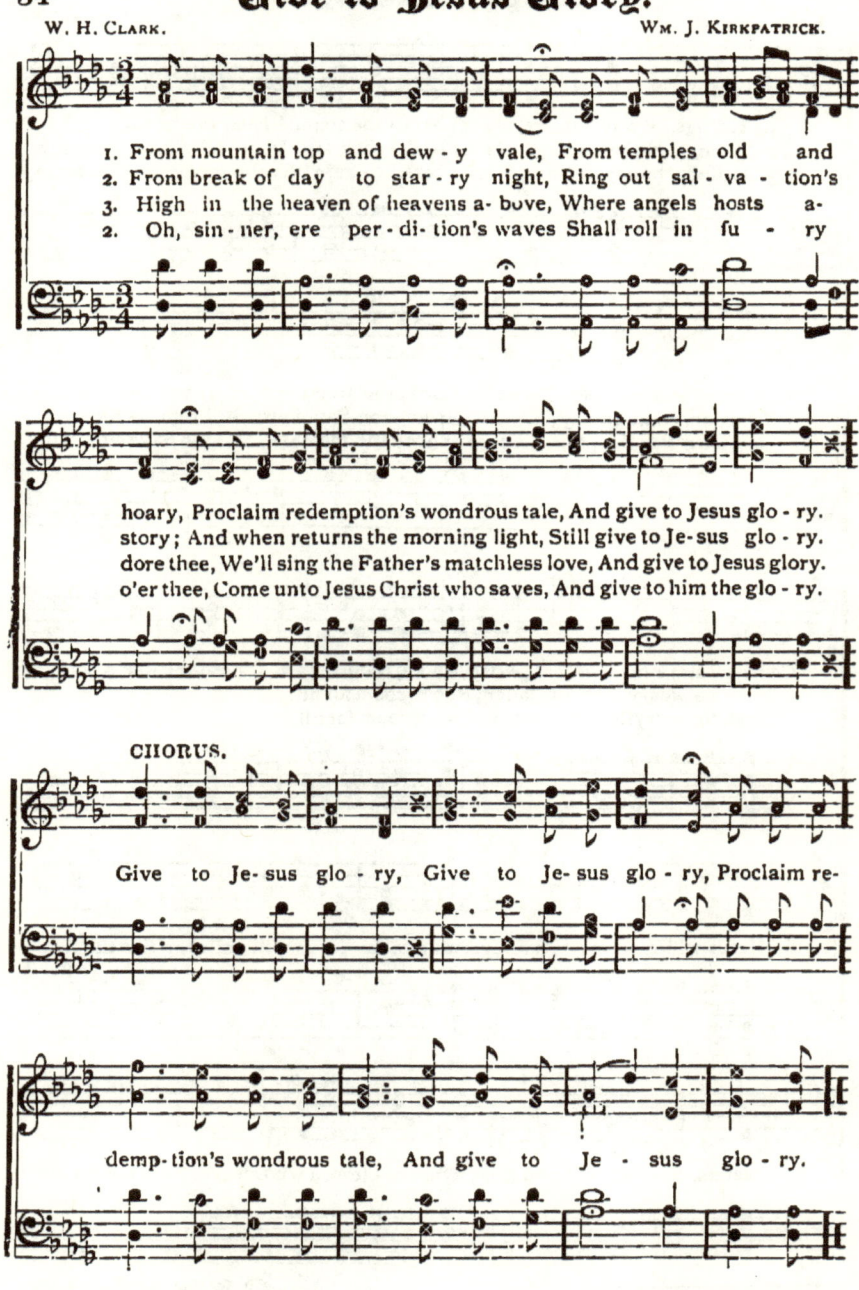

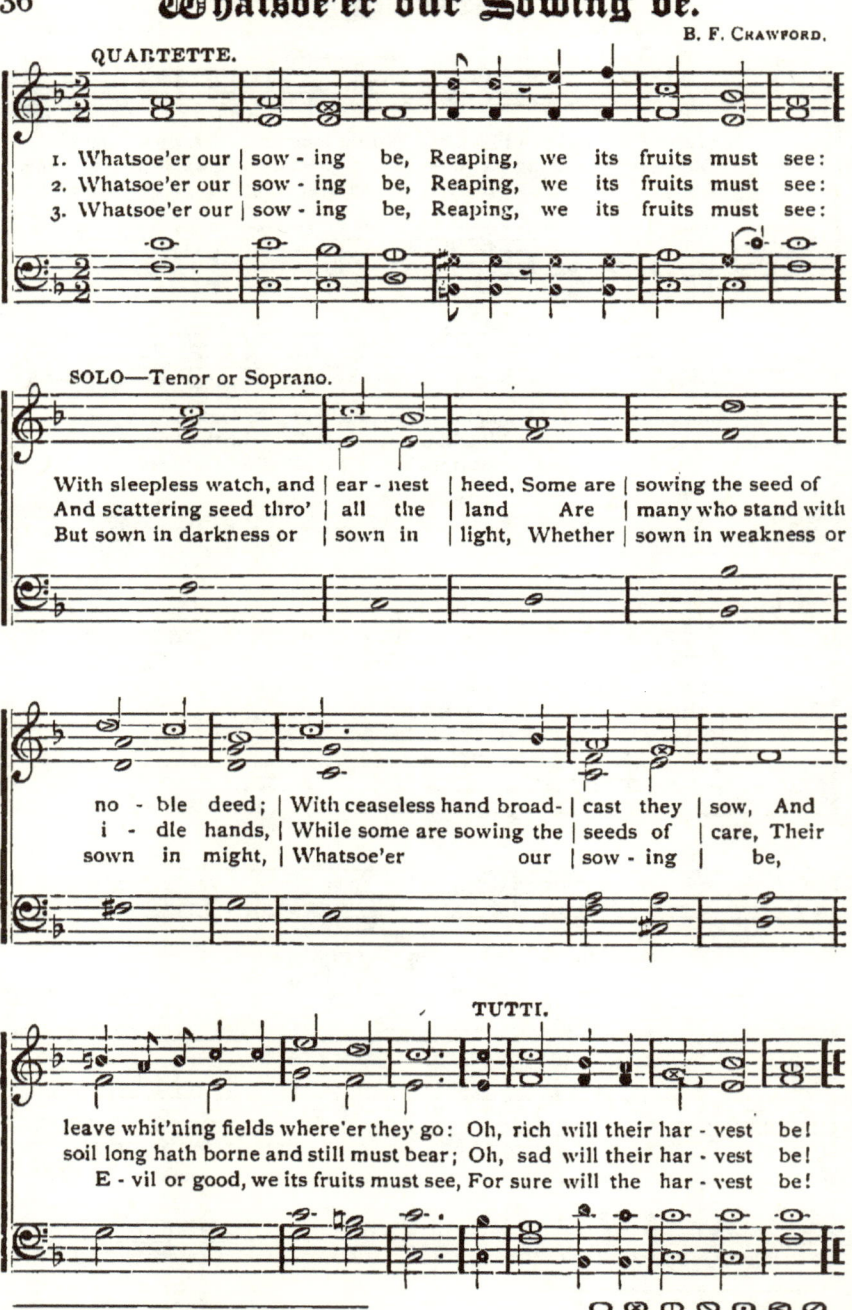

Say, are You Ready?

A. S. Kieffer. "Therefore be ye also ready."—Matt. xxiv. 44 T. C. O'Kane.

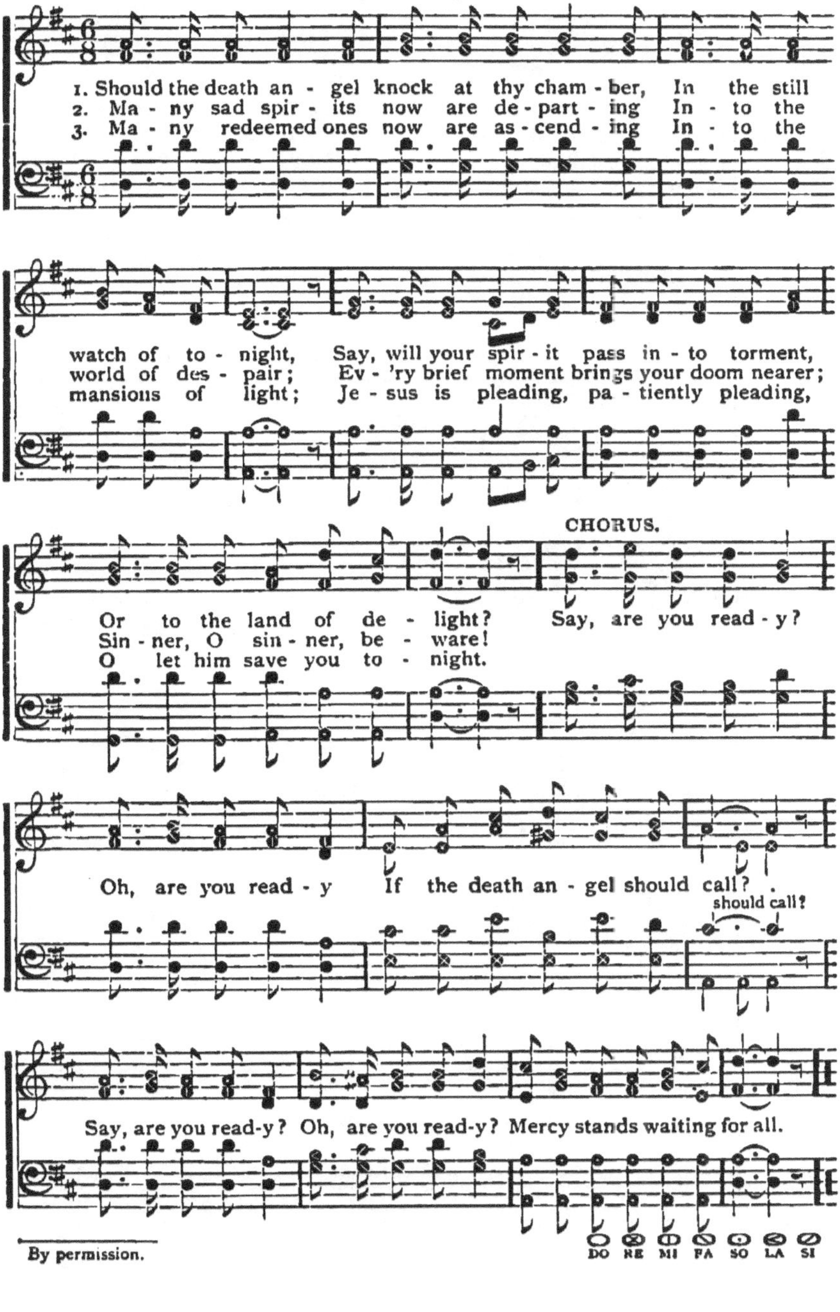
1. Should the death an - gel knock at thy cham - ber, In the still watch of to - night, Say, will your spir - it pass in - to torment, Or to the land of de - light?
2. Ma - ny sad spir - its now are de - part - ing In - to the world of des - pair; Ev - 'ry brief moment brings your doom nearer; Sin - ner, O sin - ner, be - ware!
3. Ma - ny redeemed ones now are as - cend - ing In - to the mansions of light; Je - sus is pleading, pa - tiently pleading, O let him save you to - night.
CHORUS.
Say, are you read - y? Oh, are you read - y If the death an - gel should call?
should call?
Say, are you read-y? Oh, are you read-y? Mercy stands waiting for all.
DO RE MI FA SO LA SI

By permission.

38. Freely to all.

Tracy Clinton. T. C. O'Kane.

1. Jesus now of-fers forgiveness of sin Free-ly to all, free-ly to all;
2. Jesus the water of life will give Free-ly to all, free-ly to all;
3. Jesus has promised the bread of heav'n Freely to all, free-ly to all;
4. Haste to accept of his proffered love,—Free-ly to all, free-ly to all;

Pardon and pur-i-ty,—peace within,—Free-ly, yes, free-ly to all.
Life un-to all who on him will believe, Free-ly, yes, free-ly to all.
Ne'er shall they hunger to whom it is giv'n,—Free-ly, yes, free-ly to all.
So you may win a crown promised above, Free-ly, yes, free-ly to all.

REFRAIN.

Come to Je-sus, his blessing receive; Come to Je-sus, in him you may live;

He is waiting sal-va-tion to give, Free-ly, yes, free-ly to all.

Copyright, 1883, by T. C. O'Kane.

DO RE MI FA SO LA SI

42. Going Home Rejoicing.

FANNY J. CROSBY.   JNO. R. SWENEY.

1. We are going home rejoicing, Where our Father's dwelling stands, We are going home rejoicing, To a house not made with hands; We are going home to Jesus, Who redeemed us with his blood, Hallelujah! hallelujah! Soon we'll cross the swelling flood.

2. We are going in a vessel That we know is firm and strong: 'Tis the good old ship of Zion That has stood the storm so long; Countless millions it has anchored, And will anchor millions more, In the port of life eternal, On the bright, celestial shore.

3. We are going home rejoicing; Praise the Lord, we're going home! Where forever and forever, With the Saviour we shall roam; Clad in robes that he has brought us,—Precious garments of his grace,—We shall see him in his glory, And behold him face to face.

CHORUS.

Soon we'll cross the swelling flood of the Jordan, And the happy, happy

Copyright, 1882, by JOHN J. HOOD.

5 Behold the Lamb of God!
  From earth's foundation slain,
That we, if faithful unto death,
  With him might live and reign.

6 Behold the Lamb of God,
  Whom now by faith we see;
Oh, tell the wonders of his grace.
  And shout redemption free.

Copyright, 1882, by JOHN J. HOOD.

Dayspring.

ENGLISH.   T. C. O'KANE.

1. Come, thou "Bright and Morning Star," Light of lights, without be-ginning,
2. As the soft re-freshing dew Falls on drooping herb and flower,
3. Let thy love's pure fire de-stroy All our earth-ly taint and leaven,
4. Ah! thou dayspring from on high, Grant that at thy next ap-pearing,
5. Light us to those heavenly spheres, Sun of grace in glo-ry shrouded;

Shine up-on us from a-far, That we may be kept from sin-ning;
Let thy Spir-it shed a-new Life on ev'-ry wearied pow-er;
Kindling love and ho-ly joy With the dawning east-ern heav-en;
We who in the grave do lie May a-rise, thy summons hearing,
Lead us thro' this vale of tears To the land where days un-clouded,

Drive a-way by thy clear light Our dark night, our dark night;
Bless thy flock from thy rich store, Ev-er-more, ev-er-more;
Let us tru-ly rise ere yet Life has set, life has set;
And re-joice in our new life, Far from strife, far from strife;
Pur-est joy and per-fect peace Nev-er cease, nev-er cease;

Drive a-way by thy clear light Our dark night.
Bless thy flock from thy rich store, Ev-er-more.
Let us tru-ly rise ere yet Life has set.
And re-joice in our new life, Far from strife.
Pur-est joy and per-fect peace Nev-er cease.

Copyright, 1883, by T. C. O'KANE.

DO RE MI FA SO LA SI

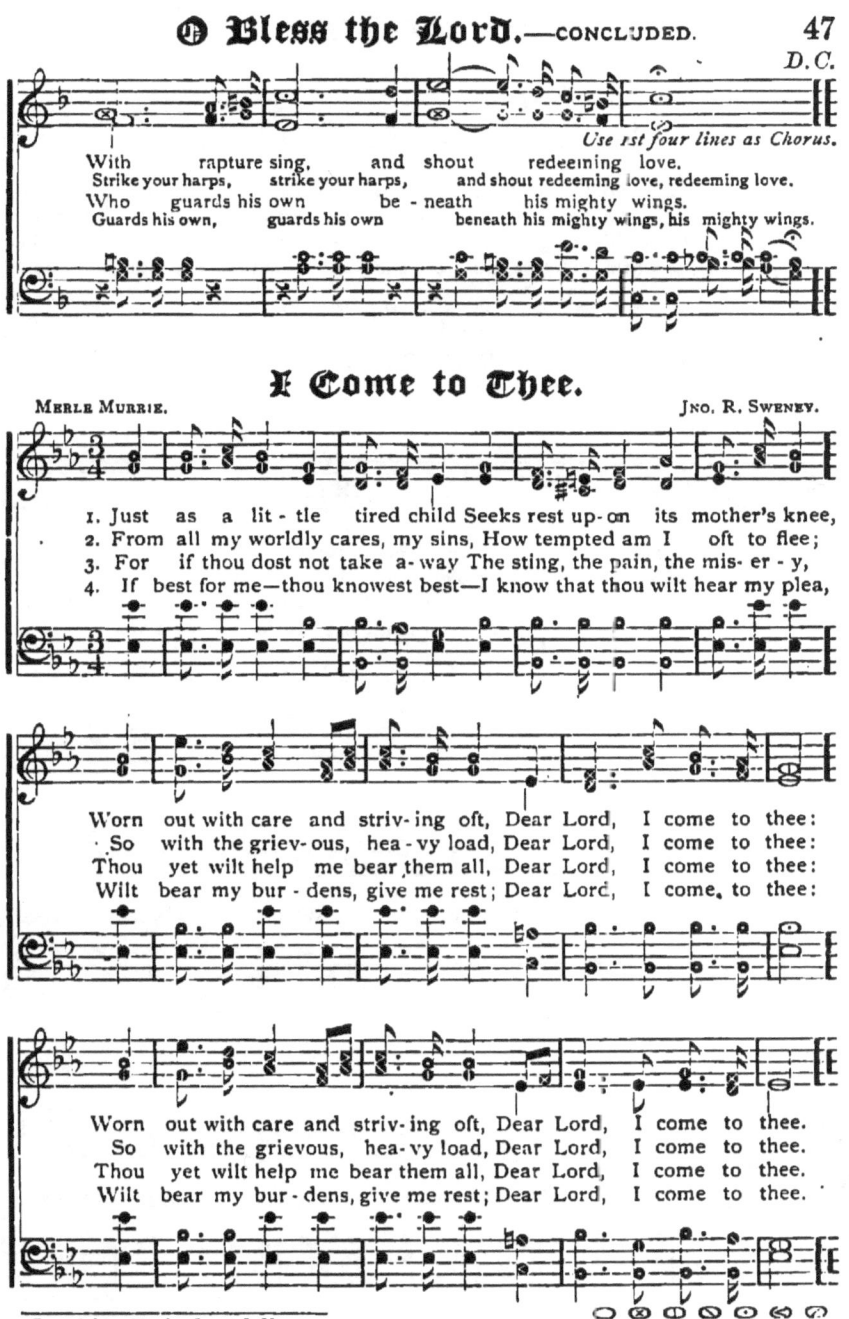

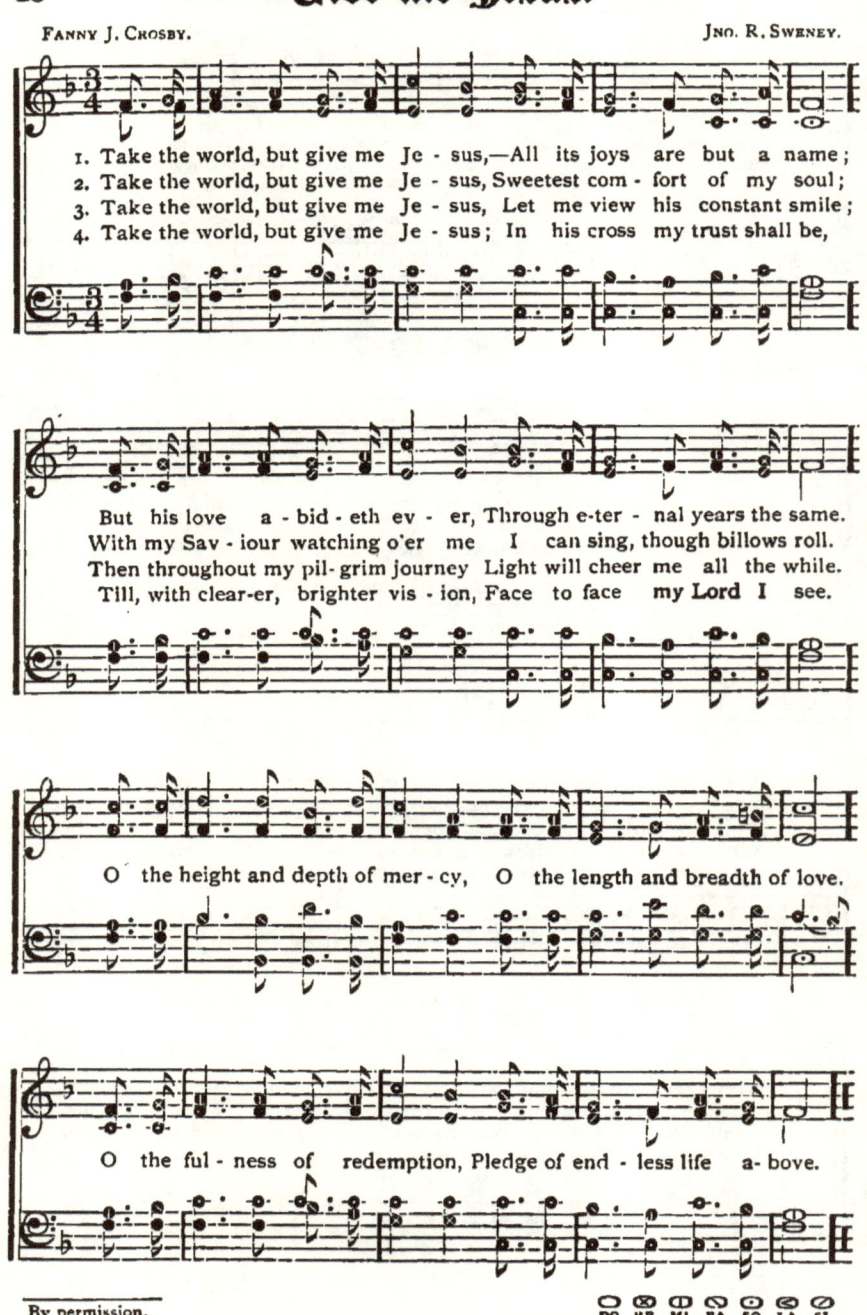

What of the Future?

I asked a dear one, "What of the future?" He replied, "It is all dark."—M. B. W.

Mrs. M. Bliss Wilson.   Wm. G. Fischer.

1. What of the future, my broth-er,— Af-ter this world and its strife?
2. What of the future, my broth-er? Can you not see thro' the gloom
3. What of the future, my broth-er? Get thyself read-y to-night,
4. What of the future, my broth-er? Turn not a-way from the love

Is there no light for thee yon-der, Bright'ning the on-coming life?
Veil-ing the pathway be-fore you? Is it all dark in the tomb?
Fear-ing that God's Holy Spir-it, Griev-ed and sad, takes his flight.
Of the dear Saviour, who draws thee To him, and mansions a-bove.

CHORUS.

Make thyself read-y, my broth-er, Read-y to meet the dear Lord,

Knowing that soon he will call you,—Call you to meet your re-ward.

Copyright, 1883, by John J. Hood.

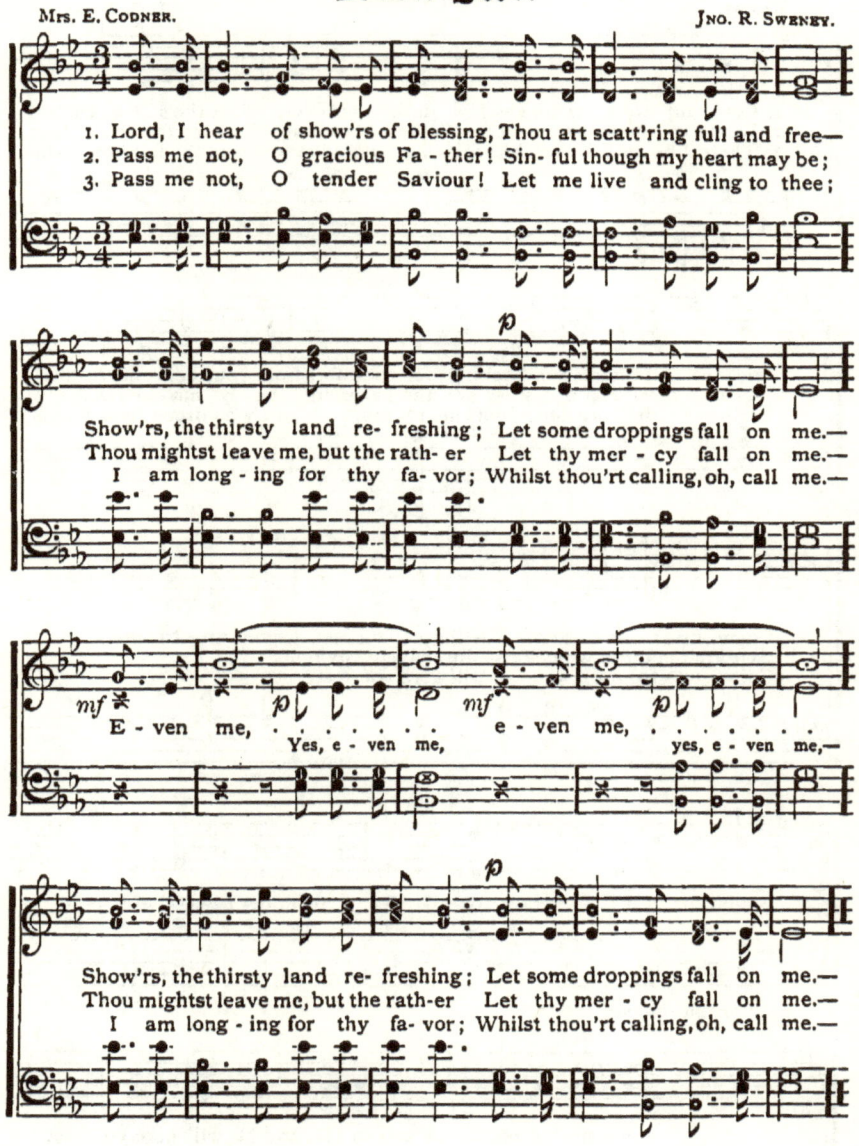

4 Pass me not, O mighty Spirit!
  Thou can'st make the blind to see;
  Witnesser of Jesus' merit,
    Speak the word of power to me,—
      Even me, even me, etc.

5 Love of God, so pure and changeless;
  Blood of Christ, so rich and free;
  Grace of God, so strong and boundless,
    Magnify them all in me,—
      Even me, even me, etc.

From "The Garner," by per.

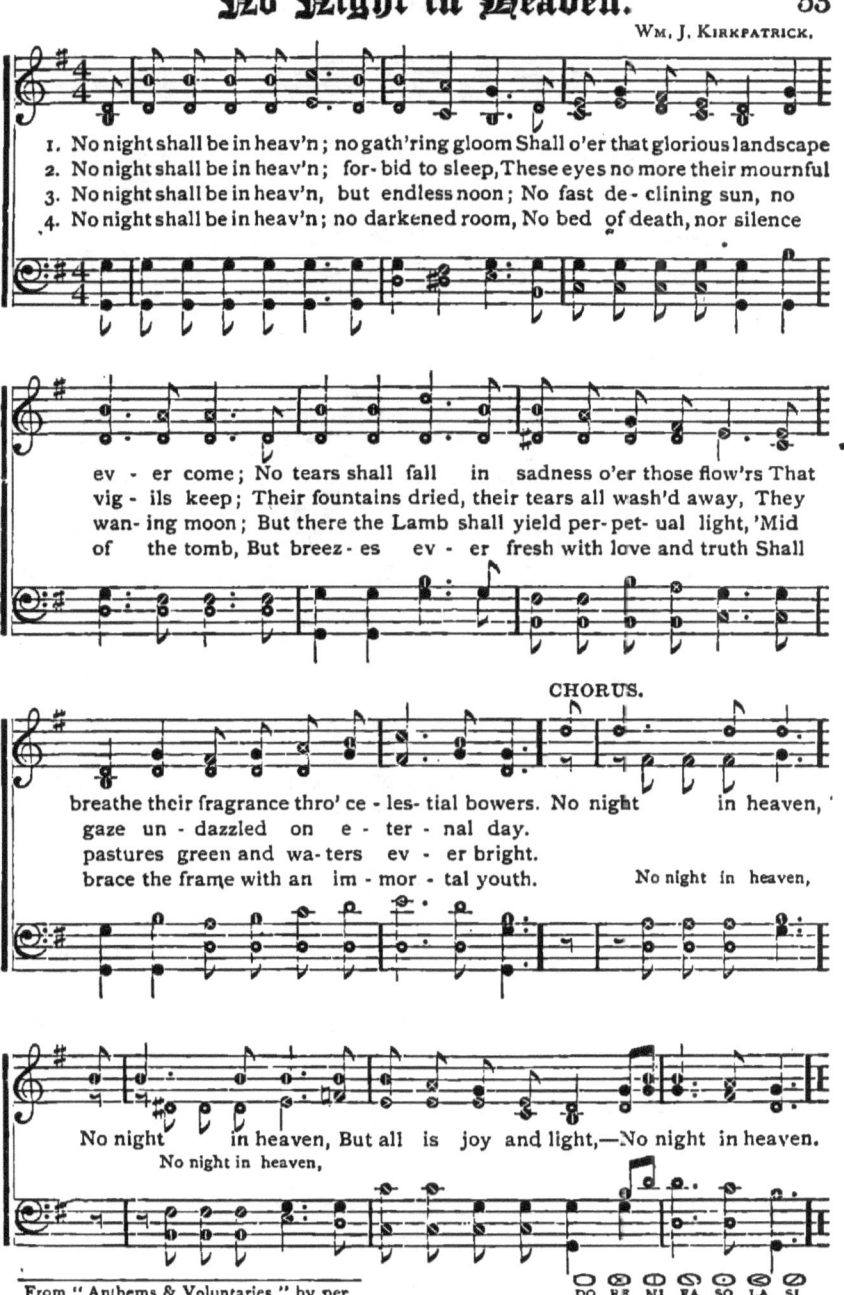

Sin No More.

C. C. McCabe.   Wm. J. Kirkpatrick.

1. When did ev-er words so ten-der Fall on mor-tal ears be-fore,
As the bless-ed words of Je-sus,—"Go thy way, and sin no more."
Pardoned! oh, that word of rap-ture! As I knelt at Mercy's door,
Burdened with my sin and sor-row,—"Go thy way, and sin no more."

2. Je-sus spake, and then the pow-er Of his great sal-va-tion came;
All the bonds of sin were broken: Glo-ry! glo-ry! to his name.
"Rise, forgiven, O child of sor-row; Rise, for lo! thy light hath come;
Put thy beauteous garments on thee; Take thy staff and journey home."

3. "I will know the way thou tak-est Till thou stand on Canaan's shore;
Nev-er, nev-er will I leave thee; Go thy way, and sin no more."
"From the world I will not take thee Till the bat-tle strife is o'er;
From its e-vil I will keep thee; Go thy way, and sin no more."

4 O the fight! I've learned to love it,
For the victory is mine;
In the cross of Christ I glory,
Triumphing in love divine.
O the dawn of heaven's glory!
O the day that has no night!
O the sun that finds no zenith!
O the host in raiment bright!

5 O, the King who dwells among them
In his beauty I shall see;
Heav'n shall ring with loud hosannas
Unto him who died for me.
But, 'mid all the joys of heaven,
I will ne'er forget the hour
When my Saviour said, "Forgiven!
Go thy way, and sin no more."

Copyright, 1882, by John J. Hood.

DO RE MI FA SO LA SI

The Child of a King. 57

HATTIE E. BUELL.   Arr. from Melody by Rev. JOHN B. SUMNER.

1. My Fa-ther is rich in houses and lands, He holdeth the wealth of the
2. My Father's own Son, the Saviour of men, Once wander'd o'er earth as the
3. I once was an out-cast stranger on earth, A sin-ner by choice, an
4. A tent or a cot-tage, why should I care? They're building a palace for

world in his hands! Of ru-bies and diamonds, of silver and gold His
poorest of men, But now he is reigning for-ev-er on high, And will
al-ien by birth! But I've been a-dopt-ed, my name's written down,—An
me o-ver there! Tho' exiled from home, yet, still I may sing: All

CHORUS.

cof-fers are full,—he has riches un-told. I'm the child of a King, The
give me a home in heaven by and by.
heir to a man-sion, a robe, and a crown.
glo-ry to God, I'm the child of a King.

ad lib.

child of a King; With Je-sus my Saviour I'm the child of a King.

Copyright, 1881, by JOHN J. HOOD.   DO RE MI FA SO LA SI

Now the Sowing and the Weeping. 59

F. R. HAVERGAL.   WM. J. KIRKPATRICK.

1. Now the sow-ing and the weep-ing, Working hard and wait-ing long;
2. Now the pruning, sharp, unspar-ing; Scattered blossom, bleeding shoot!
3. Now, the long and toilsome du - ty, Stone by stone to carve and bring:

Af - terward, the gold- en reap- ing, Har-vest home and grate-ful song.
Af - terward, the plenteous bearing Of the Master's pleasant fruit.
Af - terward, the per- fect beau- ty Of the pal- ace of the King!

CHORUS.
Then work, work for Je - sus; Toil through the cloud or sun; Till the
Mas - ter bids thee rest From la - bor—when thy work is done.

4. Now, the spirit conflict-riven,
   Wounded heart, unequal strife;
   Afterward, the triumph given,
   And the victor-crown of life!

5. Now, the training, strange and lowly,
   Unexplained and tedious now;
   Afterward, the service holy,
   And the Master's "Enter thou!"

By permission.

Softly fades the twilight ray.

Wm. Church, Jr.

1. Softly fades the twilight ray
   Of the holy Sabbath day;
   Gently as life's setting sun,
   When the Christian's course is run.
   Night her solemn mantle spreads
   O'er the earth as daylight fades;
   All things tell of calm repose,
   At the holy Sabbath's close.

2. Peace is on the world abroad;
   'Tis the holy peace of God,
   Symbol of the peace within
   When the spirit rests from sin.
   Saviour, may our Sabbaths be
   Days of joy and peace in thee,
   Till in heaven our souls repose,
   Where the Sabbath ne'er shall close.

From "Anthems & Voluntaries," by per.

DO RE MI FA SO LA SI

Ho, ev'ry one that thirsteth. 63

T. C. O'KANE.

1. Ho! ev-'ry one that thirst-eth, Ho! ev-'ry one that thirst-eth, Ho! ev-'ry one that thirst-eth, Come to the wa-ter of life.
2. "Come," saith the Ho-ly Spir-it, "Come," saith the Holy Spir-it, "Come," saith the Ho-ly Spir-it, Come to the wa-ter of life.
3. Come, ev-'ry one that hear-eth, Come, ev-'ry one that hear-eth, Come, ev-'ry one that hear-eth, Come to the wa-ter of life.
4. Come, whoso-ev-er list-eth, Come, whoso-ev-er list-eth, Come, who-so-ev-er list-eth, Come to the wa-ter of life.

CHORUS.

Come, for ev-'rything is read-y,— Je-sus is waiting; hear him call, "Come and buy with-out mon-ey,"—"Je-sus paid it all."

By permission.

One by One. 67

Rev. E. H. Stokes, D. D.
Jno. R. Sweney.

1. One by one, our loved ones slowly Pass beyond the bounds of time;
2. One by one, soon we shall gather, Not as we have gathered here—
3. One by one, our ranks are thinning, Thinning here but swelling there;
4. Good bye! hail! the fondly cherished, Tears and joy are ours to-day;

One by one, a-mong the ho-ly, Sing the vic-tor's song sublime.
Bowed and broken, but the rather, In e-ter-nal youth ap-pear.
One by one, bright crowns are winning, Crowns they shall forever wear.
Some have gone, and lo! the others Hast-en on the shortening way.

CHORUS.

One by one, one by one; We shall soon, yes, soon be there;

One by one, yes, one by one, We shall end-less glo-ry share.

Copyright, 1882, by John J. Hood.

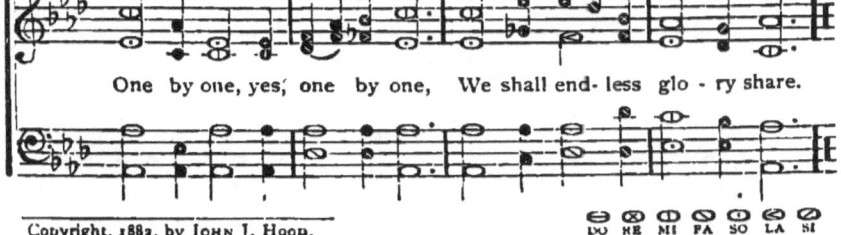

What a Gath'ring that will be.

J. H. K.
"Gather my saints together unto me."—Ps. l. 5.
J. H. KURZENKNABE.

1. At the sounding of the trumpet, when the saints are gather'd home, We will
2. When the angel of the Lord proclaims that time shall be no more, We shall
3. At the great and final judgement, when the hidden comes to light, When the
4. When the golden harps are sounding, and the angel bands proclaim, In tri-

greet each other by the crystal sea, With the friends and all the lov'd ones there a-
gather, and the saved and ransom'd see, Then to meet again to-gether, on the
Lord in all his glo-ry we shall see; At the bidding of our Saviour, "Come, ye
umphant strains the glorious jubilee; Then to meet and join to sing the song of

wait-ing us to come, What a gath'ring of the faith-ful that will be!
bright ce-lestial shore, What a gath'ring of the faith-ful that will be!
bless-ed, to my right, What a gath'ring of the faith-ful that will be!
Mos-es and the Lamb, What a gath'ring of the faith-ful that will be!

CHORUS.

What a gath - - 'ring, gath - - 'ring, At the
What a gath'ring of the loved ones when we'll meet with one an-oth-er,

sounding of the glorious ju-bi - lee! What a gath - - 'ring,
ju-bi-lee! What a gath'ring when the friends and all the

From "Song Treasury," by per.

DO RE MI FA SO LA SI

70. Come, Sinner, Come.

"Come unto me, all ye that labor and are heavy-laden."—Matt. xi. 28

Will. E. Witter.   H. R. Palmer. By per.

1. While Jesus whispers to you, Come, sinner, come!
2. Are you too heavy laden? Come, sinner, come!
3. Oh, hear his tender pleading, Come, sinner, come!

While we are praying for you, Come, sinner, come!
Jesus will bear your burden, Come, sinner, come!
Come and receive the blessing, Come, sinner, come!

Now is the time to own him, Come, sinner, come!
Jesus will not deceive you, Come, sinner, come!
While Jesus whispers to you, Come, sinner, come!

Now is the time to know him, Come, sinner, come!
Jesus can now redeem you, Come, sinner, come!
While we are praying for you, Come, sinner, come!

Copyright, 1879, by H. R. Palmer.

DO RE MI FA SO LA SI

72. Wilt thou be made whole?

W. J. K.
Wm J. Kirkpatrick.

1. Hear the foot-steps of Jesus, He is now passing by, Bearing balm for the wounded, Healing all who apply; As he spake to the suff'rer Who lay at the pool, He is saying this moment, "Wilt thou be made whole?"

2. 'Tis the voice of that Saviour, Whose merciful call Freely offers salvation To one and to all; He is now beck'ning to him Each sin tainted soul, And lovingly asking, "Wilt thou be made whole?"

3. Are you halting and struggling, O'erpowered by your sin, While the waters are troubled Can you not enter in? Lo, the Saviour stands waiting To strengthen your soul, He is earnestly pleading, "Wilt thou be made whole?"

4. Blessed Saviour, assist us To rest on thy word; Let the soul-healing power On us now be out-poured: Wash away ev'ry sin-spot, Take perfect control, Say to each trusting spirit, "Thy faith makes thee whole."

REFRAIN.

Wilt thou be made whole? Wilt thou be made whole? O come, weary suff'rer, O come, sin-sick soul; See, the life-stream is flowing, See, the

By permission.

Memories of Galilee.

ROBERT MORRIS, LL. D. "Jesus walked in Galilee."—John vii. 1. H. R. PALMER.

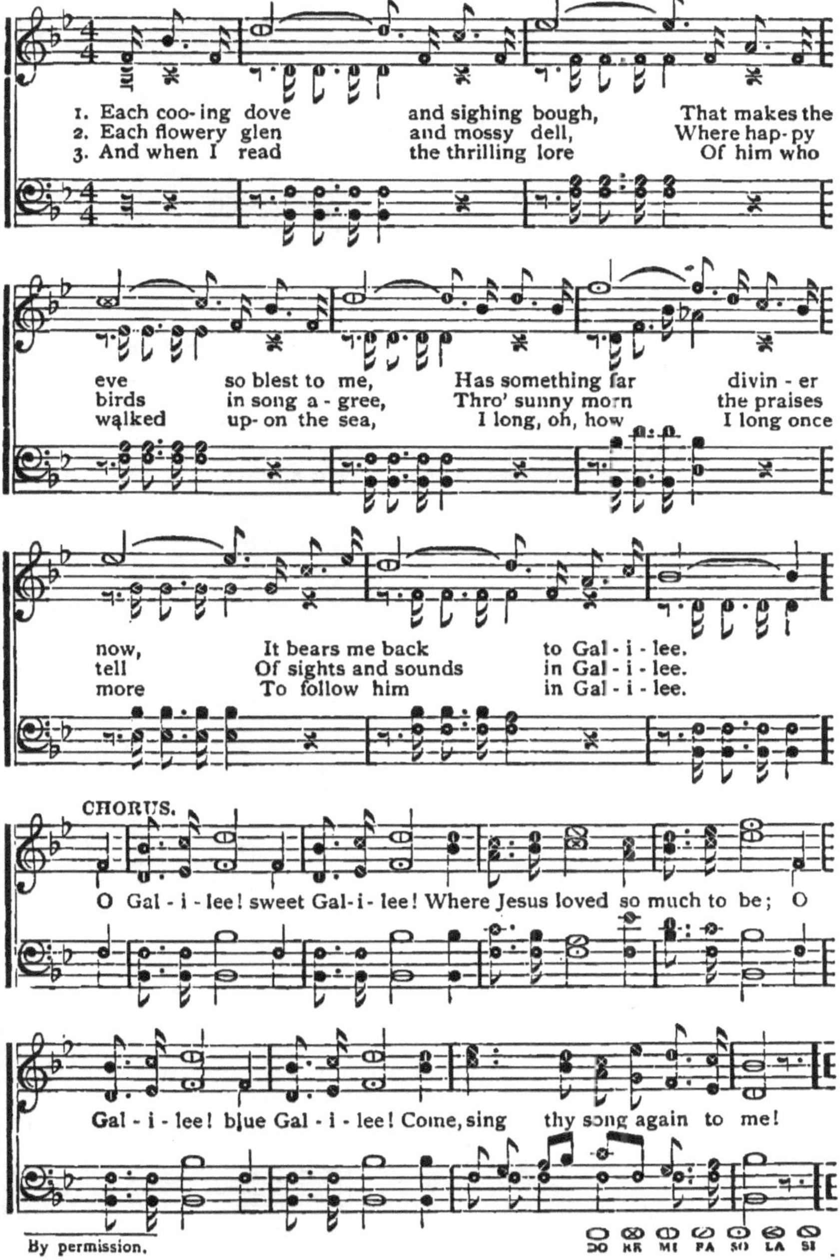
1. Each coo-ing dove and sighing bough, That makes the eve so blest to me, Has something far divin - er now, It bears me back to Gal - i - lee.
2. Each flowery glen and mossy dell, Where hap-py birds in song a - gree, Thro' sunny morn the praises tell Of sights and sounds in Gal - i - lee.
3. And when I read the thrilling lore Of him who walked up-on the sea, I long, oh, how I long once more To follow him in Gal - i - lee.
CHORUS.
O Gal - i - lee! sweet Gal-i - lee! Where Jesus loved so much to be; O Gal - i - lee! blue Gal - i - lee! Come, sing thy song again to me!
DO RE MI FA SO LA SI

By permission.

We Shall Know.—CONCLUDED.

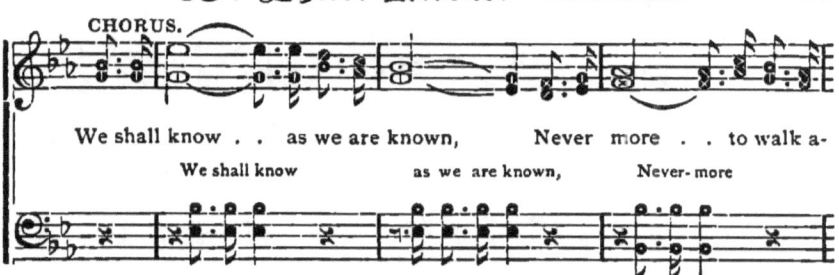

Bringing in the Sheaves.

Words from "Songs of Glory."
Geo. A. Minor.

1. Sowing in the morning, sowing seeds of kindness, Sowing in the noon-tide,
2. Sowing in the sunshine, sowing in the shadows, Fearing neither clouds nor
3. Go, then, ev-er weeping, sowing for the Master, Tho' the loss sustained our

and the dew-y eves; Waiting for the har-vest, and the time of reap-ing,
winter's chilling breeze; By and by the har-vest, and the la-bor end-ed,
spir-it oft-en grieves; When our weeping's over, he will bid us welcome,

CHORUS.

We shall come re-joic-ing, bringing in the sheaves. Bringing in the sheaves,

bringing in the sheaves, bringing in the sheaves,
We shall come rejoicing, Bringing in the sheaves,

bringing in the sheaves, We shall come rejoic-ing, bringing in the sheaves,

By permission.

DO RE MI FA SO LA SI

Take me as I am.

ANON. Rev. J. H. STOCKTON.

1. Je-sus, my Lord, to thee I cry, Unless thou help me I must die;
2. Helpless I am, and full of guilt, But yet for me thy blood was spilt,
3. I thirst, I long to know thy love, Thy full sal-vation I would prove;
4. If thou hast work for me to do, Inspire my will, my heart renew,
5. And when at last the work is done, The bat-tle o'er, the vic-t'ry won,

Oh, bring thy free sal-va-tion nigh, And take me as I am!
And thou can'st make me what thou wilt, But take me as I am!
But since to thee I can-not move, Oh, take me as I am!
And work both in and by me, too, But take me as I am!
Still, still my cry shall be a-lone, Oh, take me as I am!

D. S.— bring thy free sal-va-tion nigh, And take me as I am!

REFRAIN.

Take me as I am, Take me as I am; Oh,
Take me, take me as I am, Take me, take me as I am;

Copyright, 1878, by JOHN J. HOOD

CHARLOTTE ELLIOTT.   **JUST AS I AM.**   Tune and Chorus above.

1 JUST as I am, without one plea,
But that thy blood was shed for me,
And that thou bid'st me come to thee,
O Lamb of God, I come!

2 Just as I am, and waiting not
To rid my soul of one dark blot,
To thee whose blood can cleanse each
O Lamb of God, I come! [spot,

3 Just as I am, though tossed about
With many a conflict, many a doubt,
Fightings within, and fears without,
O Lamb of God, I come!

4 Just as I am—poor, wretched, blind;
Sight, riches, healing of the mind,
Yea, all I need, in thee to find,
O Lamb of God, I come!

5 Just as I am—thou wilt receive,
Wilt welcome, pardon, cleanse, relieve;
Because thy promise I believe,
O Lamb of God, I come!

6 Just as I am—thy love unknown
Hath broken every barrier down,
Now, to be thine, yea, thine alone,
O Lamb of God, I come!

Church of God, Awake.—CONCLUDED. 81

Send the Gos - pel's joy-ful sound Un-to earth's remot-est bound.
Oh, send the Gos - pel's joy-ful sound

The happy Pilgrim.

Words arranged. By per.

1. I saw a hap-py pil-grim, In shin-ing garments clad,
   He had no cares nor bur-dens, He'd laid them at the cross,
   And trav-'ling up the mountain, His coun-tenance was glad;
   The blood of Christ, his Sav-iour, Had wash'd him from all dross.

CHORUS.
Then palms of vic-to-ry, Crowns of glory, Palms of vic-to-ry We shall wear.

2 The summer sun was sinking,
     The sweat was on his brow;
   His garments worn and dusty,
     His step seemed very slow;
   But he kept pressing onward,
     For he was wending home,
   Still shouting as he journeyed,
     Deliverance will come.

3 I saw him in midsummer,
     Still happy on his way,
   He'd reached the land of Beulah,
     Where birds sing all the day.
   He found a store of honey
     And wine upon the lees,
   And fruit in rich abundance
     Upon life's living trees.

4 I saw him in the evening,
     The sun was bending low,
   He'd overtopped the mountain
     And reached the vale below;
   He saw the golden city,
     His everlasting home,
   And shouted loud, Hosanna!
     Deliverance will come.

5 I heard the song of triumph
     They sang upon that shore,
   Saying, Jesus has redeemed us,
     To suffer nevermore:
   Then casting his eyes backward
     On the race which he had run,
   He shouted loud, Hosanna!
     Deliverance has come!

My Shepherd.—CONCLUDED.

3 When called to surrender my faltering breath,
And pass through the vale of the shadow of death,
The presence of Jesus will brighten the tomb,
With hope and with gladness dispelling its gloom.
   With gladness dispelling its gloom.

4 For me his free bounty a table has spread;
And blessings unmeasured he pours on my head;
My cup with abundance and joy overflows;
He dries all my tears, and he heals all my woes.
   He heals all my woes, all my woes.

5 His goodness and mercy shall crown all my days,
My mouth shall be filled with thanksgiving and praise;
I'll dwell in his temple of glory above,
And sing evermore of his grace and his love.
   And sing of his grace and his love.

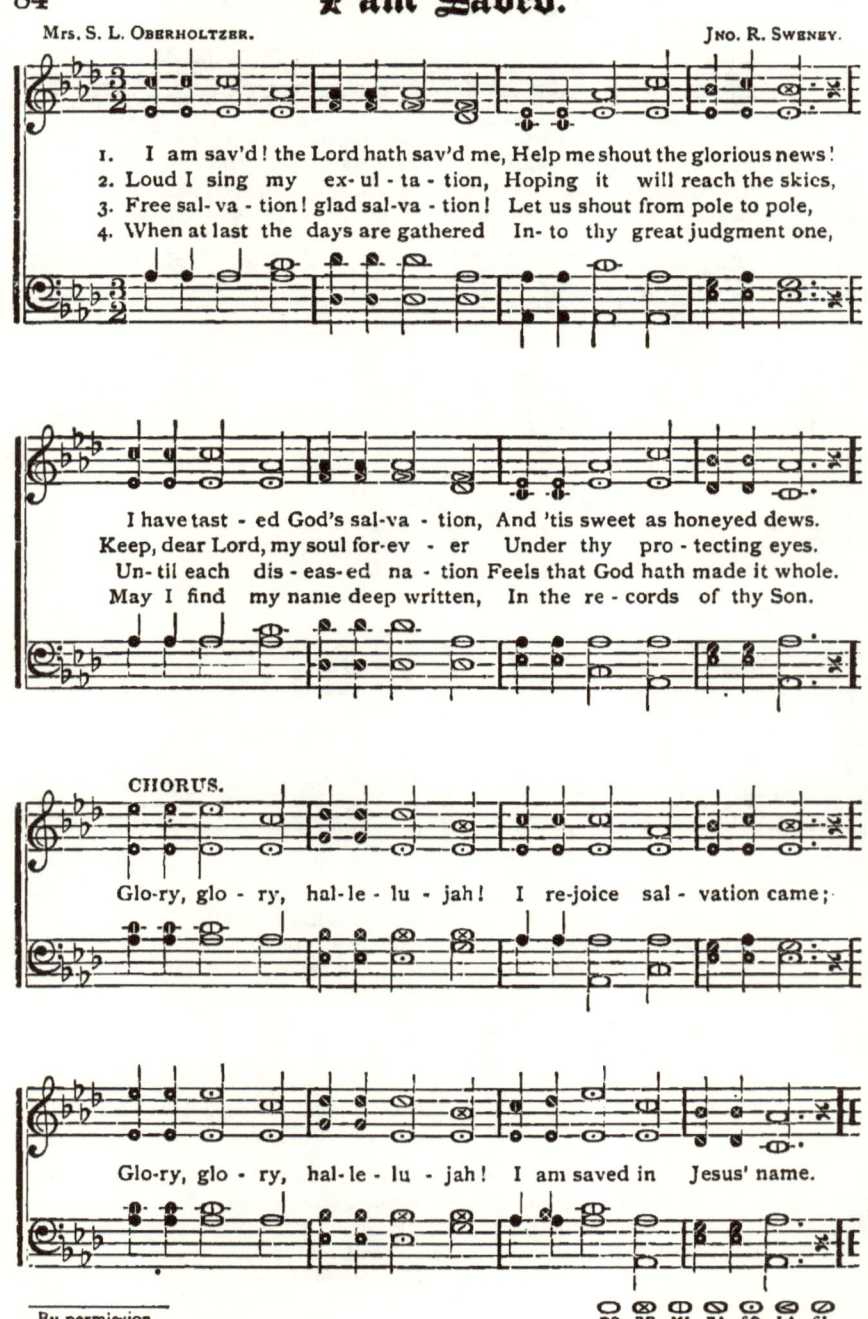

86. The Rock that is Higher than I.

E. Johnson.   Wm. G Fischer.

1. Oh, sometimes the shadows are deep, And rough seems the path to the goal,
2. Oh, sometimes how long seems the day, And sometimes how weary my feet;
3. Oh, near to the Rock let me keep, Or blessings, or sorrows prevail;

And sorrows, sometimes how they sweep Like tempests down over the soul.
But toil-ing in life's dusty way, The Rock's blessed shadow, how sweet!
Or climbing the mountain-way steep, Or walking the shadow-y vale.

CHORUS.

Oh, then, to the Rock let me fly, let me fly, To the Rock that is high-er than I: is high-er than I, Oh, then, to the Rock let me fly, let me fly, To the Rock that is high-er than I.

By permission.

DO RE MI FA SO LA SI

Nearer Home. 87

Wm. Church, Jr.

1. One sweetly solemn thought [Comes to me o'er and o'er,— I'm nearer home to-day Than [I ever have been be-fore. | Nearer my Father's house, Where the many | mansions be; Nearer the great white throne; [Nearer the crystal sea; Home, home, sweet, sweet home,—Pre-pare me, dear Sav-iour, for glo-ry, my home.

2. Nearer the bound of life, [Where we lay our burdens down; Nearer leaving the cross; . [Nearer gaining-the crown. | But lying darkly between, Winding down | thro' the night, Is the deep and unknown [stream That leads at last to-the light.

3. Father, perfect my trust! [Strengthen the might of-my faith; Let me feel as I would when I [stand On the rock of the shore of death: | Feel as I would when my feet Are slipping | o- ver-the brink. For it may be, I'm nearer [home—Nearer now than-I think!

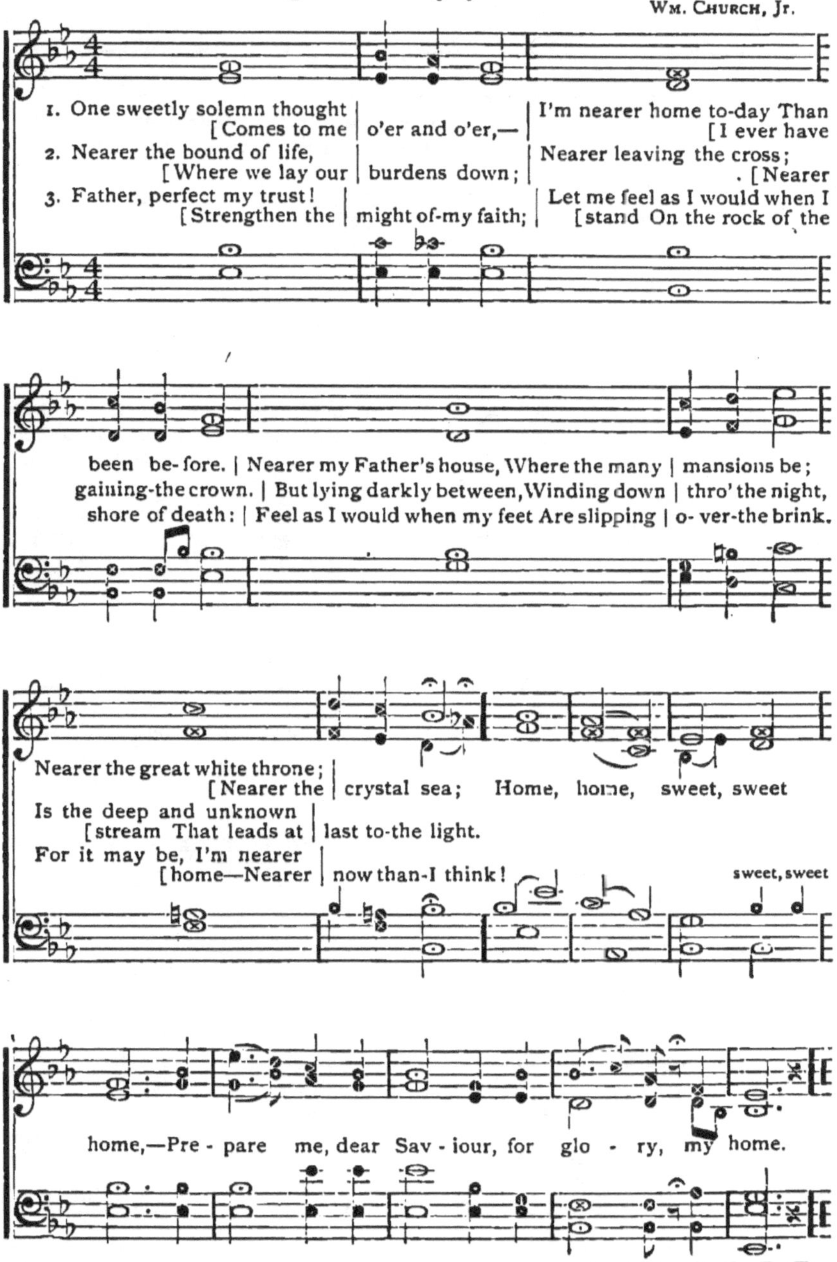

From "Anthems & Voluntaries," by per.

DO RE MI FA SO LA SI

Come unto Me.

J. P. Mills. T. C. O'Kane.

1. "Come un-to me,"—in measured tones and slow, "Come unto me," how sweet the accents flow, "Come un-to me," oh, gen-tle voice di-vine!
2. "Come un-to me,"—the lips with mercy stream, "Come unto me,"—the eyes with love-light beam; "Come unto me," the out-held hands implore,
3. "Come un-to me," dear toiling ones, o-bey, "Come unto me," oh, sinners, hear to-day! "Come un-to me,"—the welcome is to all.

CHORUS.

"Come un-to me," de-sire and love combine. Weary-lad-en souls, what-
"Come un-to me," such words none spake before.
"Come un-to me,"—'tis Jesus makes the call.

e'er your bur-den be, Seeking af-ter rest, Come un-to me, Come un-to me, come unto me, I will give you rest, whate'er your burdens be.

By permission.

DO RE MI FA SO LA SI

Jesus Comes.

Mrs. Phœbe Palmer.   Wm. J. Kirkpatrick.

1. Watch, ye saints, with eyelids waking, Lo, the pow'rs of heav'n are shaking,
2. Lo! the promise of your Saviour, Pardoned sin and purchased favor,
3. Kingdoms at their base are crumbling, Hark, his chariot wheels are rumbling,
4. Nations wane, tho' proud and stately, Christ his kingdom hasteneth greatly,

Keep your lamps all trimm'd and burning, Ready for your Lord's return-ing.
Blood-wash'd robes and crowns of glory; Haste to tell redemption's sto - ry.
Tell, O, tell of grace abound- ing, Whilst the seventh trump is sounding.
Earth her latest pangs is summing, Shout, ye saints, your Lord is coming.

REFRAIN.

Lo! he comes, lo! Jesus comes; Lo! he comes, he comes all glorious!

Je-sus comes to reign victo-rious, Lo! he comes, yes, Je-sus comes.

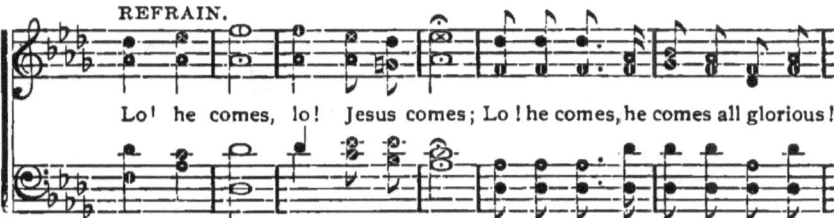

5. Lamb of God!—thou meek and lowly,
Judah's Lion!—high and holy,
Lo! thy Bride comes forth to meet thee,
All in blood-washed robes to greet thee,

6. Sinners, come, while Christ is pleading,
Now for you he's interceding;
Haste, ere grace and time diminished
Shall proclaim the mystery finished.

Copyright, 1882, by Wm. J. Kirkpatrick.

DO RE MI FA SO LA SI

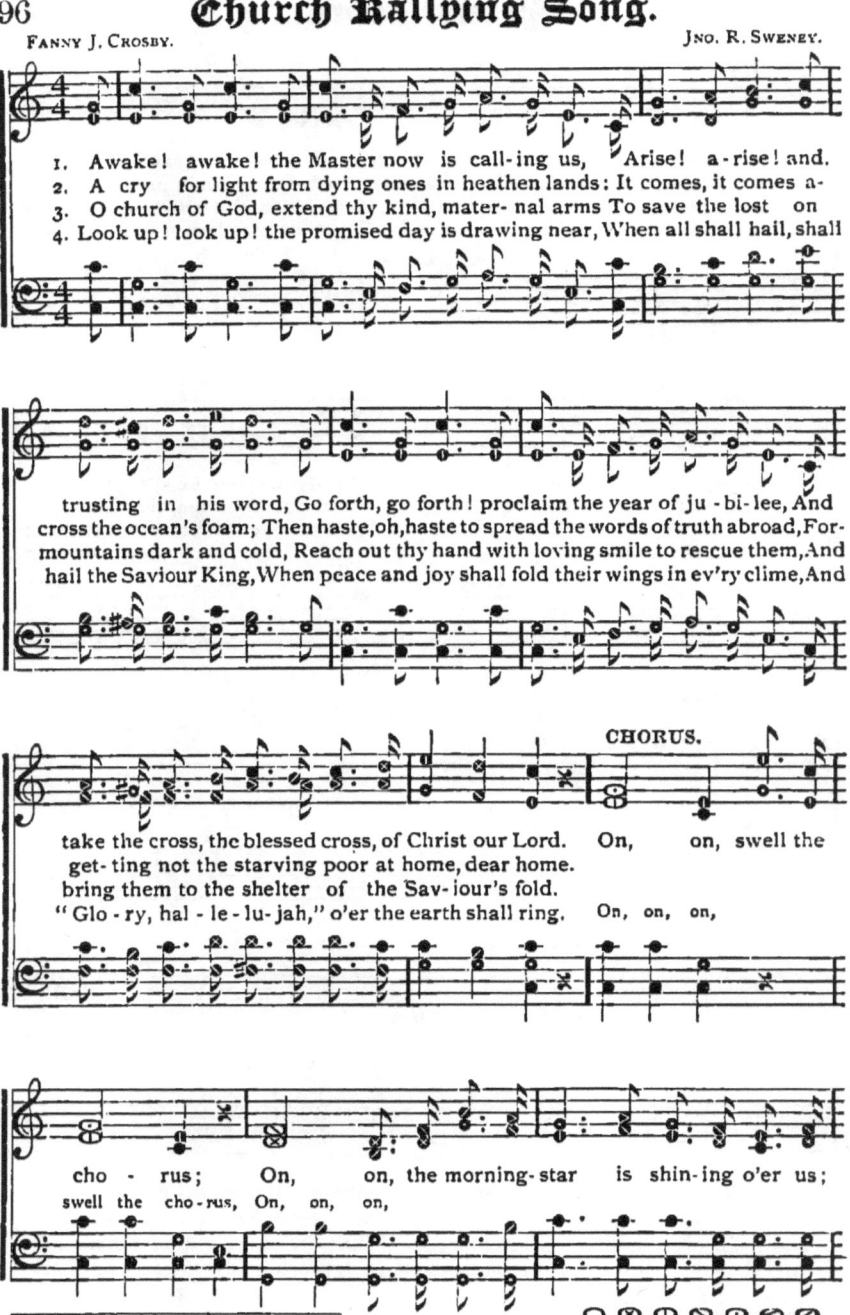

Church Rallying Song.—CONCLUDED. 97

On, on, while before us Our mighty, mighty Saviour leads the way:

{ Glo-ry, glo-ry, hear the ev-erlasting throng }
{ Shout ho-sanna, while we boldly march along; } Faithful soldiers here below,

On-ly Jesus will we know, Shouting "free salvation" o'er the world we go.

F. J. C.   Christmas Carol.—Awake! awake!   Tune above.

1 Awake! awake! our festive day is dawning now,
Awake! awake! and hail its golden light;
Rejoice! rejoice! behold the Sun of Righteousness
Arising in its beauty o'er a long, long night.

Cho.—Come, come, join the chorus,
Come, come, the angel hosts are bending o'er us;
Come, come, join the chorus,—
All glory be to God, to God above.
Oh, the rapture of the bright angelic form,
Oh, the rapture while the anthem rolls along.
Hark! the merry, merry bells,
Everywhere their music swells;
Hark! the merry chiming of the grand old bells.

3 Good news, good news resounding o'er the earth again,
Good news, good news: behold a Saviour born;
Make room, make room in every heart to welcome him,
And shout aloud, hosanna! on his birthday morn.

4 He comes, he comes, the captive's cruel chain to break,
He comes, he comes to give his people rest;
Break forth, break forth, his mighty, mighty love proclaim;
In him shall every nation, every clime, be blessed.

From "Hood's Carols," by per.

Thy precious, precious Fold.

SALLIE SMITH. JNO. R. SWENEY.

1. Sav-iour, though long I have slighted thee, Still thou hast kind-ly in-
2. No more the night com-eth drear-i-ly, No more my feet wan-der
3. Sav-iour, how gent-ly thou guidest me, How in thy mer-cy thou
4. Saved by thy grace, and so ten-der-ly, Glo-ry and praise I will

vit-ed me, Praise for the love that united me To thy precious, precious fold.
weari-ly, Sweet is thy voice and how cheerily It has led me to thy fold.
hidest me, All that I need thou providest me, In thy precious, precious fold.
render thee, Thou in thy mercy remembered me, Thou hast brought me to thy fold.

REFRAIN.

I am hap-py now, I am hap-py now, How my heart is swell-ing, all his mer-cy tell-ing; I am hap-py how, I am hap-py now, In thy precious, precious fold.

By permission.

Joy cometh in the morning.

"Weeping may endure for a night, but joy cometh in the morning."—Psalm xxx. 5.

Mrs. M. M. Weinland. E. S. Lorenz.

1. Oh, wea-ry pilgrim, lift your head, For joy cometh in the morn-ing!
2. Ye feeble saints, dismiss your fears, For joy cometh in the morn-ing!
3. Let ev-'ry tear-ful eye be dry, For joy cometh in the morn-ing!
4. Our God will wipe our tears away, For joy cometh in the morn-ing!

For God in his own word has said That joy cometh in the morn-ing!
And weeping mourners, dry your tears, For joy cometh in the morn-ing!
And ev-'ry trembling sinner hope, For joy cometh in the morn-ing!
Sor-row and sighing flee a-way, For joy cometh in the morn-ing!

CHORUS.

Joy cometh in the morning! Joy cometh in the morning! Weeping may en-dure, may en-dure for a night, But joy cometh in the morn-ing.

From "Holy Voices," by per.

DO RE MI FA SO LA SI

Soldiers of th' Eternal King.

101

J. H.
Mrs. Jos. F. Knapp.

1. Soldiers of th' eternal King, Speed the watchword, give it wing, Let it thro' the churches ring, Up! for Jesus stand. Write it on the temple's spire, Ut-ter it with tongues of fire, Sire to son and son to sire, Up! for Jesus stand ; Sire to son and son to sire, Up! for Jesus, Je-sus stand. Up! for Jesus stand, Up! for Jesus stand; Speed the watchword, give it wing, And up! for Jesus stand.

2. La-bel it on ev-'ry door, Place it high the pulpit o'er, Let it stand for-ev-er-more! Up! for Je-sus stand. Blazon it in mansion-halls, Pencil it on prison walls ; Do and dare, as duty calls, Up! for Jesus stand. Do and dare, as duty calls, Up! for Jesus, Je-sus stand.

3. Place it on the chisel'd stone, Where the mourners weep alone; Grave it on the monarch's throne! Up! for Je-sus stand. Let the press, whose wheels of might Roll for reason and for right, Flash it on the nation's sight ; Up! for Jesus stand. Flash it on the nation's sight; Up! for Jesus, Je-sus stand.

CHORUS.

By permission.

DO RE MI FA SO LA SI

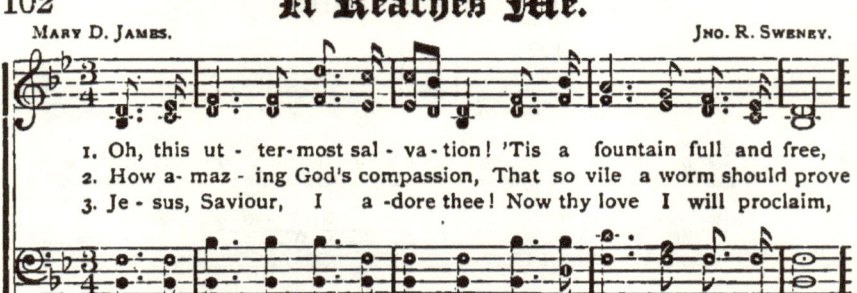

It Reaches Me.

Mary D. James.   Jno. R. Sweney.

1. Oh, this ut-ter-most sal-va-tion! 'Tis a fountain full and free,
2. How a-maz-ing God's compassion, That so vile a worm should prove
3. Je-sus, Saviour, I a-dore thee! Now thy love I will proclaim,

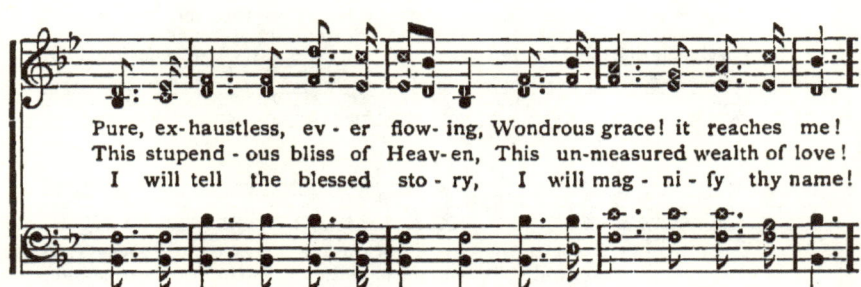

Pure, ex-haustless, ev-er flow-ing, Wondrous grace! it reaches me!
This stupend-ous bliss of Heav-en, This un-measured wealth of love!
I will tell the blessed sto-ry, I will mag-ni-fy thy name!

CHORUS.

It reaches me! it reaches me! Wondrous grace! it reaches me!

Pure, ex-haustless, ev-er flowing, Wondrous grace! it reaches me!

From "The Garner," by per.

Joy in Heaven.

103

PRISCILLA J. OWENS.
WM. J. KIRKPATRICK.

Moderato.

There is joy, there is joy, There is joy in heaven:

Andante.

1. A ransomed soul re-turns, The paths of sin for-sak-ing,
2. A weep-ing sin-ner kneels, The chains of death are bro-ken,
3. No news of pain or care, The jas-per sea o'er-reach-ing,
4. O then to God re-turn,—Come back and be for-giv-en,

And while his sad heart mourns, The harps of God are wak-ing.
And soon his glad heart feels The Sav-iour's welcome spok-en.
But sweet is echoed there The con-trite heart's beseech-ing.
And soon thy heart shall learn To know the joy of heav-en.

CHORUS. *Allegro.*

{ All the gold-en bells are ring-ing, }
{ All the an-gel choirs are sing-ing, } All the lov-ing an-gels say,

"There is joy in heav'n to-day, There is joy, there is joy, joy, joy to-day."

Copyright, 1882, by JOHN J. HOOD.

DO RE MI FA SO LA SI

104. Washed in the Blood.

Rev. E. A. Hoffman.   T. C. O'Kane.

1. I am bowed at the cross, Washed from sin and its dross, In the all-cleansing blood of the Lamb; Joy and rapture are mine, Peace and comfort divine. Fully saved thro' his mercy I am.
2. I have come to the blood; And the Spir-it of God Pours the sin-cleansing tide thro' my soul, Till it burns with pure love To the Saviour above, By whose grace I am saved and made whole.
3. Oh, the wonderful fount Ope'd on Calvary's mount! There believing and wait-ing I am. Lo! the all-cleansing tide To my heart is applied; I am washed in the blood of the Lamb.

REFRAIN.

I am washed in the blood, In the blood of the Lamb; Lo! the all-cleansing tide To my heart is applied, I am washed in the blood of the Lamb.

From "Reedeemer's Praise," by per.

DO RE MI FA SO LA SI

Rest Yonder. 105

H. BONAR.
J M. BLACK.

1. This is not my place of resting,—Mine's a ci-ty yet to come; Onward to it I am hast-ing, On to my e-ter-nal home; In it all is light and glo-ry, O'er it shines a nightless day; Ev-'ry trace of sin's sad story, All the curse has pass'd away. Blessed home bright and fair, Sin can nev - - - er en-ter there; All the

2. There the Lamb, our Shepherd, leads us By the stream of life along, On the fresh-est pastures feeds us, Turns our sigh-ing in-to song; Soon we'll pass this des-ert drea-ry,—Soon we'll bid farewell to pain,—Nev-er more be sad or weary, Never, never sin again.

Fine. CHORUS.

blessed home bright and fair, Sin can nev-er, sin can nev-er en-ter there, en-ter there;

D. S.—saved of earth shall gather In that ci-ty of de-light, There to praise their dear Redeemer, Clad in garments white.

D. S.

Copyright, 1882, by JOHN J. HOOD.

DO RE MI FA SO LA SI

110. When the King comes in.

J. E. Landor.
Rev. E. S. Lorenz.

1. Call'd to the feast by the King are we, Sitting, perhaps, where his people be: How will it fare, then, with thee and me,
2. Crowns on the head where the thorns have been, Glorified he who once died for men; Splendid the vision before us then,
3. Like lightning's flash will that instant show Things hidden long from both friend and foe, Just what we are ev-'ry one will know,
4. Joyful his eye shall on each one rest Who is in white wedding garments dressed—Ah! well for us if we stand the test,

REFRAIN.

When the King comes in? When the King comes in, brother, When the King comes in! How will it fare with thee and me When the King comes in?

From "Songs of Grace," by per.

DO RE MI FA SO LA SI

Sacred Rest.

111

"For we who have believed do enter into rest."

Mrs. Mary D. James.   Heb. iv. 3.   Wm. J. Kirkpatrick.

1. How sweet the sacred rest it brings To nestle 'neath his shelt'ring wings,—The Lover of my soul! "A covert" from the pelting storms, "A refuge" from life's dread alarms, When raging billows roll.
2. 'Tis rest no angel's tongue can tell; 'Tis joy untold, unspeak-a-ble, My Saviour's love to know; To see him smile, and hear him say, "I'll guide thro' all the dang'rous way Each step that thou shalt go."
3. Oh, full salvation, hallowed bliss! No creature joys compare with this Di-vine, unbroken rest:—The sacred calm the soul receives, The peace of God which Jesus gives, While leaning on his breast.
4. Oh, wondrous, condescending grace! That we may bask in his bright rays, His wealth of blessing prove! And lifted to the glorious height Of fellowship with saints in light, What magnitude of love!

REFRAIN.

Oh, glo-ry be to Je-sus! How sweetly I am blest!—In trusting my Redeemer I am finding perfect rest.

Copyright, 1883, by John J. Hood.

DO RE MI FA SO LA SI

Our Way of Duty. 113

WM. H. RUDDIMAN.   WM. J. KIRKPATRICK.

1. We have each our work to do, Let us strive, let us strive, For eternal things are pressing near; While the glowing hours still shine, Oh, improve the gift divine, Lest too soon the night ap-pear.
2. We have sins to o-vercome, Let us strive, let us strive, That the Spir-it in our hearts may dwell, Planting sacred longings there, Ripening fruits of faith and pray'r, While our lives their fragrance tell.
3. We have upward paths to tread, Let us strive, let us strive, In the Master's loving will to grow; May his ev-er-gu-ding hand Lead us to the farther strand, And his radiant honors show.

CHORUS.

We'll serve, serve on, serve on, Dear Saviour, for thee toil on, toil on, Till the promised rest we gain, On the high resplendent plain, And with thee in bliss sit down.

From "Precious Songs," by per.   4H   DO RE MI FA SOL LA SI

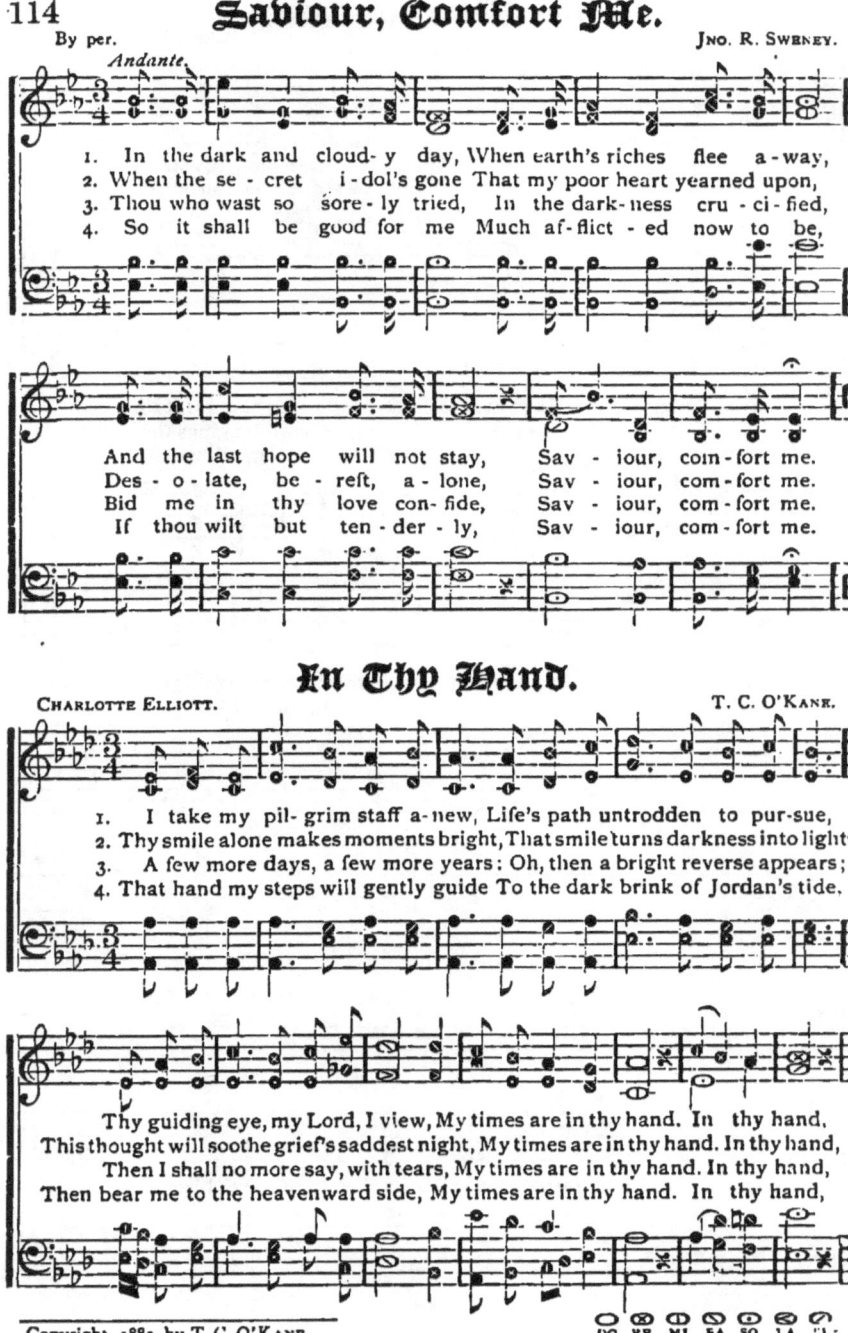

In Thy Hand.—CONCLUDED. 115

in thy hand, Thy guiding eye, my Lord, I view, My times are in thy hand.
in thy hand, This thought will soothe grief's saddest night, My times are in thy hand.
in thy hand, When I shall no more say, with tears, My times are in thy hand.
in thy hand, Then bear me to the heavenward side, My times are in thy hand.

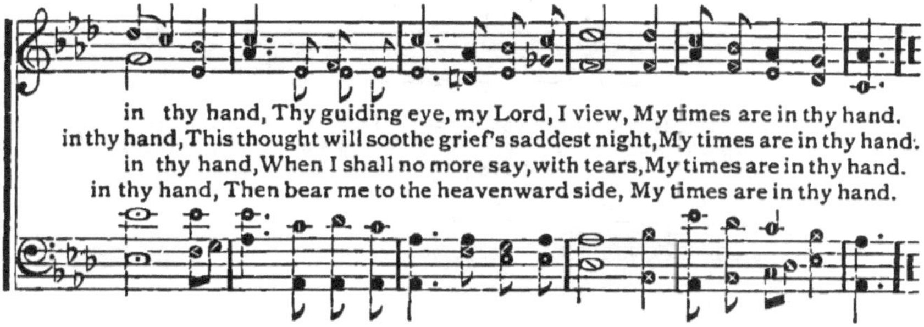

Jesus Loves the Little Ones.

H. W. M.   WM. J. KIRKPATRICK.

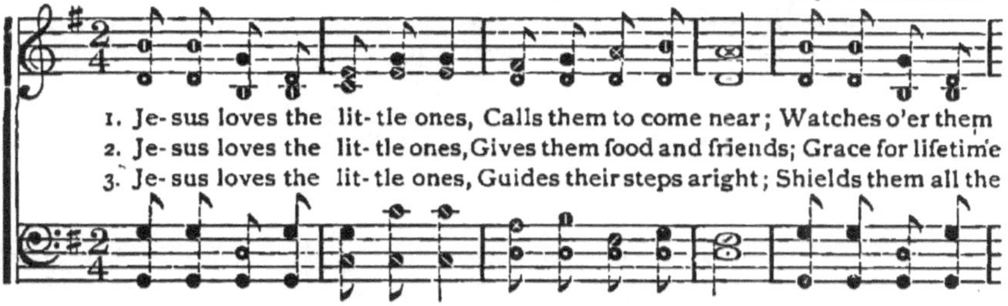

1. Je-sus loves the lit-tle ones, Calls them to come near; Watches o'er them
2. Je-sus loves the lit-tle ones, Gives them food and friends; Grace for lifetime
3. Je-sus loves the lit-tle ones, Guides their steps aright; Shields them all the

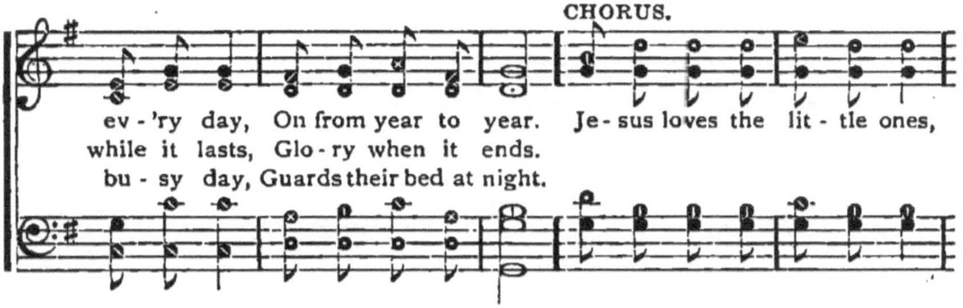

ev-'ry day, On from year to year. Je-sus loves the lit-tle ones,
while it lasts, Glo-ry when it ends.
bu-sy day, Guards their bed at night.

CHORUS.

Yes, yes, yes; All who come to him by prayer He loves to bless.

4 Jesus loves the little ones,
Bears their sin and care;
Loves to hear them lisp his name
In his praise or prayer.

5 Jesus loves the little ones,
Wheresoe'er they roam;
Then he takes them when they die
To his heavenly home.

Copyright, 1882, by JOHN J. HOOD.

DO RE MI FA SO LA SI

119. The Lord will Provide.

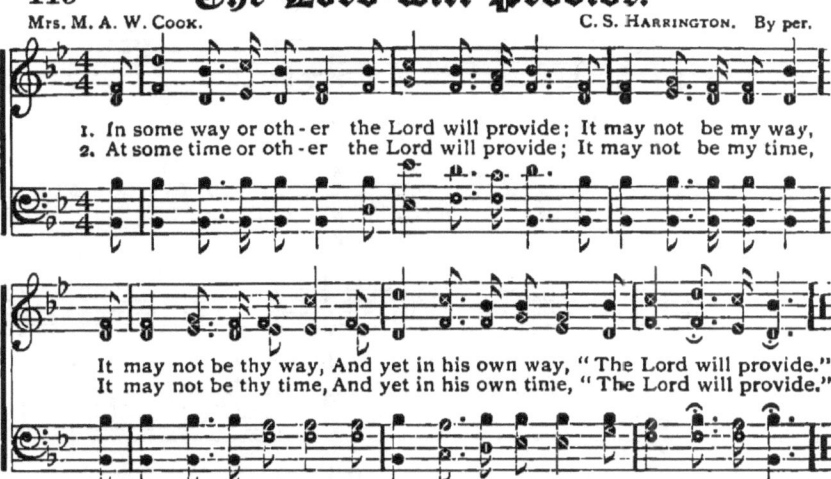

Mrs. M. A. W. Cook. — C. S. Harrington. By per.

1. In some way or oth-er the Lord will provide; It may not be my way,
2. At some time or oth-er the Lord will provide; It may not be my time,

It may not be thy way, And yet in his own way, "The Lord will provide."
It may not be thy time, And yet in his own time, "The Lord will provide."

3 Despond then no longer,
   The Lord will provide;
   And this be the token—
   No word he hath spoken
   Was ever yet broken,—
   "The Lord will provide."

4 March on, then, right boldly;
   The sea shall divide;
   The pathway made glorious,
   With shoutings victorious,
   We'll join in the chorus,
   "The Lord will provide."

120. The Altered Motto.

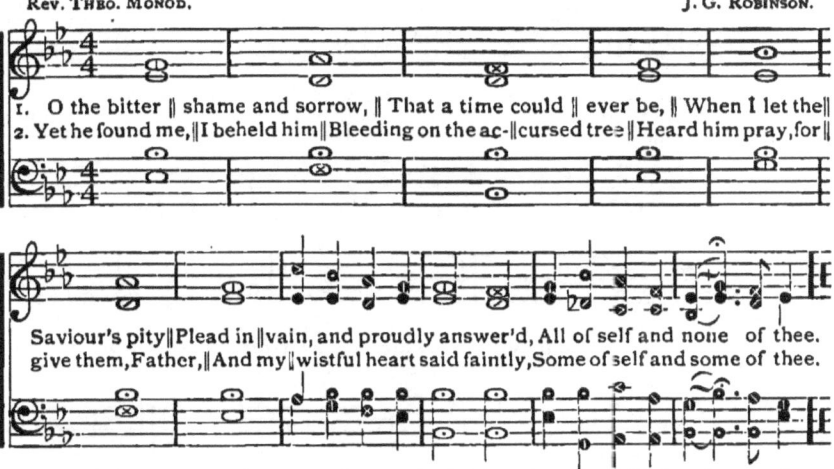

Rev. Theo. Monod. — J. G. Robinson.

1. O the bitter ‖ shame and sorrow, ‖ That a time could ‖ ever be, ‖ When I let the ‖
   Saviour's pity ‖ Plead in ‖ vain, and proudly answer'd, All of self and none of thee.
2. Yet he found me, ‖ I beheld him ‖ Bleeding on the ac- ‖ cursed tree ‖ Heard him pray, for ‖
   give them, Father, ‖ And my ‖ wistful heart said faintly, Some of self and some of thee.

3 Day by day his ‖ tender mercy, ‖
   Healing, helping, ‖ full and free, ‖
   Sweet, and strong, ‖ and, oh, so patient, ‖
   Brought me ‖ lower while I whispered,
   Less of self and more of thee.

4 Higher than the ‖ highest heaven, ‖
   Deeper than the ‖ deepest sea. ‖
   Lord, thy love ‖ at last has conquer'd, ‖
   Grant me ‖ now my soul's desire,
   None of self and all of thee.

Copyright, 1885, by John J. Hood.

DO RE MI FA SO LA SI

121. He is Calling.

FABER.   Arr. by S. J. VAIL.

1. There's a wideness in God's mercy, Like the wideness of the sea;
   There's a kindness in his justice Which is more than li-ber-ty.

CHORUS.
He is call-ing, "Come to me!" Lord, I'll gladly haste to thee.

2 There is welcome for the sinner,
   And more graces for the good;
  There is mercy with the Saviour;
   There is healing in his blood.

3 For the love of God is broader
   Than the measure of man's mind;

And the heart of the Eternal
 Is most wonderful and kind.

4 If our love were but more simple,
   We should take him at his word;
  And our lives would be all sunshine
   In the sweetness of our Lord.

122. The Golden Key.

"Prayer is the key to unlock the door, and the bolt to shut in the night."   J. R. S.

1. Prayer is the key For the bending knee To open the morn's first hours;
   See the incense rise To the star-ry skies, Like per-fume from the flow'rs.
2. Not a soul so sad, Nor a heart so glad, When cometh the shades of night,
   But the daybreak song Will the joy prolong, And some darkness turn to light.
3. Take the golden key In your hand and see, As the night tide drifts away,
   How its blessed hold Is a crown of gold, Thro' the weary hours of day.

4 When the shadows fall,
   And the vesper call
  Is sobbing its low refrain,
   'Tis a garland sweet
   To the toil dent feet,
  And an antidote for pain.

5 Soon the year's dark door
   Shall be shut no more:
  Life's tears shall be wiped away
   As the pearl gates swing,
   And the gold harps ring,
  And the sun unsheathe for aye.

From "Goodly Pearls," by per.   DO RE MI FA SO LA SI

123. Stay, Sinner, stay!

W. KENNEY.   Arr. by W. J. K.

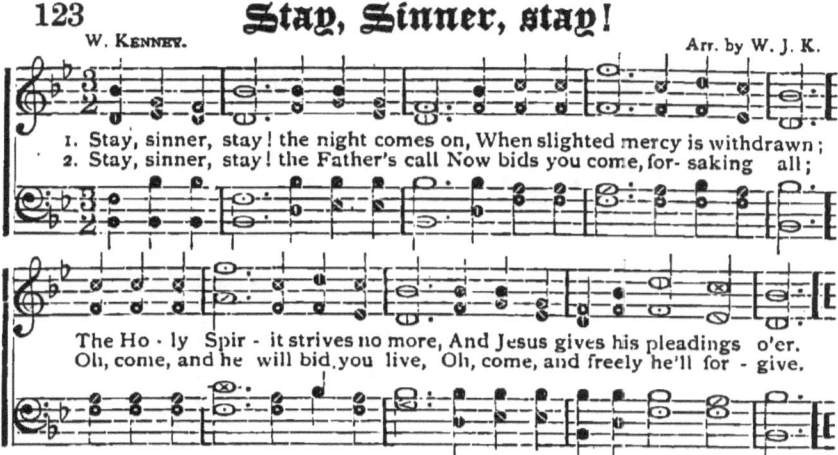

1. Stay, sinner, stay! the night comes on, When slighted mercy is withdrawn;
2. Stay, sinner, stay! the Father's call Now bids you come, for-saking all;

The Ho-ly Spir-it strives no more, And Jesus gives his pleadings o'er.
Oh, come, and he will bid you live, Oh, come, and freely he'll for-give.

3 Stay, sinner, stay! 'tis Jesus pleads,
For you he weeps, for you he bleeds;
Oh, let his love your heart constrain,
Nor let him weep and bleed in vain.

4 Stay, sinner, stay! the Spirit cries,
Awake, and from the dead arise;
Arise and plead for mercy now,
And at the cross repenting bow.

5 Come, sinner, come! though guilty now,
At Jesus' feet submissive bow,
And freely all shall be forgiven;—
Oh, come, and taste the joys of heaven.

6 See, sinner, see! where loved ones stand,
All saved in heaven—a happy band;
Oh, come, and join them on that shore,
Where death and parting are no more.

124. A Sinner like Me.

C. J. B.   CHAS. J. BUTLER.

1. I was once far away from the Saviour, And as vile as a sinner could be,
I wondered if Christ the Redeemer, Could save a poor sinner like me.

2 I wandered on in the darkness,
Not a ray of light could I see,
And the thought filled my heart with sad-
There's no hope for a sinner like me. [ness,

3 I then fully trusted in Jesus,
And oh, what a joy came to me;
My heart was filled with his praises,
For saving a sinner like me.

4 No longer in darkness I'm walking,
For the light is now shining on me,
And now unto others I'm telling,
How he saved a poor sinner like me.

5 And when life's journey is over,
And I the dear Saviour shall see,
I'll praise him forever and ever,
For saving a sinner like me.

Copyright, 1881, by JOHN J. HOOD.

125. Cleansing Wave.

Mrs. J. F. Knapp.

1 Oh, now I see the cleansing wave!
  The fountain deep and wide;
Jesus, my Lord, mighty to save,
  Points to his wounded side.
Cho.—The cleansing stream, I see, I see!
  I plunge, and oh, it cleanseth me!
  Oh, praise the Lord! it cleanseth me;
  It cleanseth me—yes, cleanseth me.

2 I rise to walk in heaven's own light,
  Above the world of sin, [white,
With heart made pure and garments
  And Christ enthroned within.

3 Amazing grace! 'tis heaven below
  To feel the blood applied;
And Jesus, only Jesus, know,
  My Jesus crucified.

1 There is a fountain filled with blood,
  Drawn from Immanuel's veins,
And sinners, plunged beneath that flood,
  Lose all their guilty stains.

2 Dear dying Lamb, thy precious blood
  Shall never lose its power,
Till all the ransomed Church of God
  Are saved to sin no more.

3 E'er since, by faith, I saw the stream
  Thy flowing wounds supply,
Redeeming love has been my theme,
  And shall be till I die.

4 Then in a nobler, sweeter song,
  I'll sing thy power to save,
When this poor lisping, stammering
  Lies silent in the grave. [tongue

126. The New Name.

J. E. H. J. E. Hall.

1. We shall have a new name in that land, In that land, that sunny, sunny land,
2. We'll receive it in a pure white stone, And no one will know the name therein;
3. Don't you wonder what that name will be, Sweeter far than aught on earth can be,

Cho.—We shall have a new name in that land, In that land, that sunny, sunny land,

When we meet the bright angelic band, In that sunny land.   A new name, a
Only unto him who hath 'tis known, When we're free from sin. A white stone, a
We will be quite satisfied when we Shall that new name know. I won-der, I

When we meet the bright angelic band, In that sunny land.

Copyright, 1878, by John J. Hood.

1 HOVER o'er me, Holy Spirit;
  Bathe my trembling heart and brow;
  Fill me with thy hallowed presence,
  Come, oh, come and fill me now.

2 Thou can'st fill me, gracious Spirit,
  Though I cannot tell thee how;
  But I need thee, greatly need thee;
  Come, oh, come and fill me now.

3 I am weakness, full of weakness;
  At thy sacred feet I bow;
  Blest, divine, eternal Spirit,
  Fill with power, and fill me.

4 Cleanse and comfort, bless and save me;
  Bathe, oh, bathe my heart and brow;
  Thou art comforting and saving,
  Thou art sweetly filling now.

1 COME, thou fount of every blessing,
  Tune my heart to sing thy grace;
  Streams of mercy never ceasing,
  Call for songs of loudest praise.

2 Teach me some melodious sonnet,
  Sung by flaming tongues above;
  Praise the mount—I'm fixed upon it—
  Mount of thy redeeming love!

3 Here I'll raise mine Ebenezer;
  Hither by thy help I'm come;
  And I hope by thy good pleasure,
  Safely to arrive at home,

4 Jesus sought me when a stranger,
  Wandering from the fold of God;
  He, to rescue me from danger,
  Interposed his precious blood.

Copyright, 1879, by JOHN J. HOOD.

130. Sun of My Soul.

JOHN KEBLE.
Tune, HURSLEY. L.M.

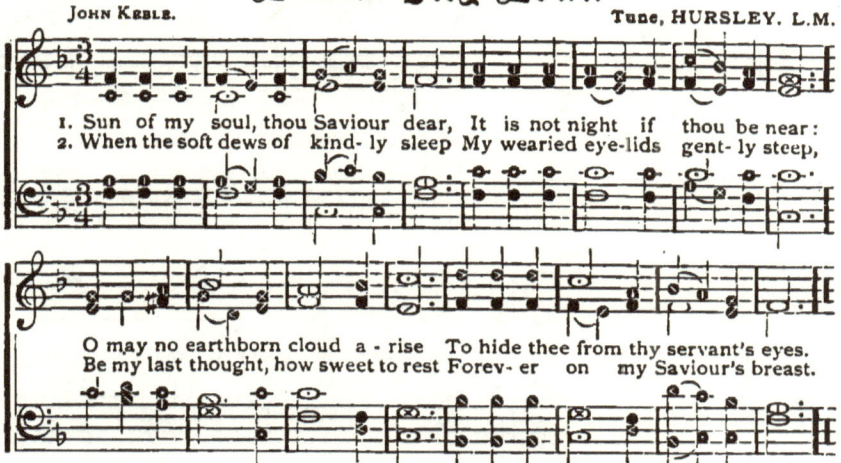

1. Sun of my soul, thou Saviour dear, It is not night if thou be near:
O may no earthborn cloud a-rise To hide thee from thy servant's eyes.

2. When the soft dews of kindly sleep My wearied eye-lids gently steep,
Be my last thought, how sweet to rest Forever on my Saviour's breast.

3 Abide with me from morn till eve,
For without thee I cannot live;
Abide with me when night is nigh,
For without thee I dare not die.

4 If some poor wandering child of thine
Have spurned to-day the voice divine,
Now, Lord, the gracious work begin;
Let him no more lie down in sin.

5 Watch by the sick; enrich the poor
With blessings from thy boundless store;
Be every mourner's sleep to-night,
Like infant's slumbers, pure and light.

6 Come near and bless us when we wake,
Ere through the world our way we take;
Till in the ocean of thy love,
We lose ourselves in heaven above.

131. Of Him who did Salvation.

Tr. by A. W. BOEHM.
Tune, ROCKINGHAM. L.M.

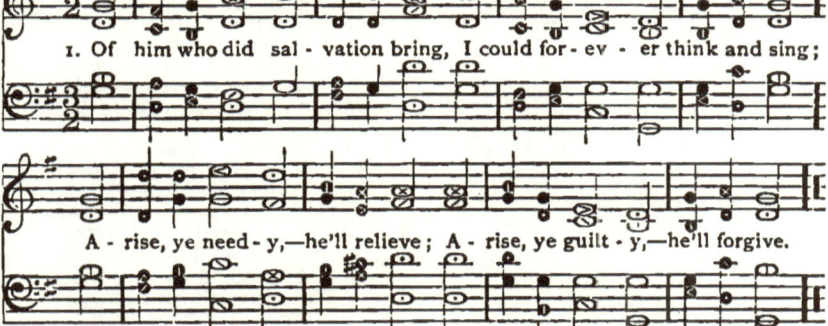

1. Of him who did salvation bring, I could forever think and sing;
A-rise, ye needy,—he'll relieve; A-rise, ye guilty,—he'll forgive.

2 Ask but his grace, and lo, 'tis given;
Ask, and he turns your hell to heaven:
Though sin and sorrow wound my soul,
Jesus, thy balm will make it whole.

3 To shame our sins he blushed in blood;
He closed his eyes to show us God:
Let all the world fall down and know
That none but God such love can show.

4 'Tis thee I love, for thee alone
I shed my tears and make my moan;
Where'er I am, where'er I move,
I meet the object of my love.

5 Insatiate to this spring I fly;
I drink, and yet am ever dry;
Ah! who against thy charms is proof?
Ah! who that loves, can love enough?

132. Doxology.

Words arr. by B. M. A.   Melody by J. R. S.   Harmony by W. J. K.

Slow, with dignity.

Glo - ry be to the FA - THER, Glo - ry be to the SON,
Glo - ry be to the HO - LY GHOST; As it was in the be - ginning,
Is now, and ev - er shall be, World without end. A - men, a - men.

1. I LOVE to tell the Story
   Of unseen things above,
   Of Jesus and his glory,
   Of Jesus and his love!
   I love to tell the Story!
   Because I know it's true;
   It satisfies my longings,
   As nothing else would do.

Cho.—I love to tell the Story!
   'Twill be my theme in glory,
   To tell the Old, Old Story
   Of Jesus and his love.

2. I love to tell the Story!
   More wonderful it seems,
   Than all the golden fancies
   Of all our golden dreams.
   I love to tell the Story!
   It did so much for me!
   And that is just the reason,
   I tell it now to thee.

3. I love to tell the Story!
   For those who know it best
   Seem hungering and thirsting
   To hear it, like the rest.
   And when, in scenes of glory,
   I sing the NEW, NEW SONG,
   'Twill be—the OLD, OLD STORY
   That I have loved so long.

1. STAND up, stand up for Jesus,
   Ye soldiers of the cross;
   Lift high his royal banner,
   It must not suffer loss:
   From victory unto victory
   His army shall he lead,
   Till every foe is vanquished
   And Christ is Lord indeed.

2. Stand up, stand up for Jesus,
   Stand in his strength alone;
   The arm of flesh will fail you;
   Ye dare not trust your own:
   Put on the gospel armor,
   Each piece put on with prayer;
   Where duty calls, or danger,
   Be never wanting there.

3. Stand up, stand up for Jesus,
   The strife will not be long;
   This day the noise of battle,
   The next the victor's song:
   To him that overcometh,
   A crown of life shall be;
   He with the King of glory
   Shall reign eternally.

PRAISE God, from whom all blessings flow;
Praise him, all creatures here below;
Praise him above, ye heavenly host;
Praise Father, Son, and Holy Ghost.

52
HYMNS OF THE HEART

SELECTED BY

C. C. McCABE,

PREFACE.

HOW shall our church music be improved? This is an unsettled question. From the meaningless chords played by the organist at the beginning of the service till the congregation rises to sing the doxology the music is unsatisfactory, almost everywhere. Why? Because it lacks heart. It lacks enthusiasm. It lacks volume. It lacks the joyful spirit of praise. Try an experiment,—Give out from the Church Hymnal, as part of the Sabbath-school lesson, "How firm a foundation, ye saints of the Lord." Let every member of the Sabbath-school learn it *by heart*. Let the pastor announce it as one of his hymns on Sabbath morning. Request the organist to omit all flourishes,—all *preludes* and *interludes*. Let not the leader be over anxious about the time. The people will sing much better with *heart* beat than with *hand* beat or *baton* beat. One blast on the organ to get the pitch. Then let choir, congregation, and Sabbath-school "sing unto the Lord." The question is answered at last. The music is majestic. The holy tide of song bears the congregation heavenward. Watch the old saints. Long ago they hung their harps on the willows. They are all singing now. Such music will attract sinners. It will help to fill up the empty pews. It will help you to preach. Try another hymn in the same way, till you have packed fifty-two of the grand old hymns of Zion into the memories of the children,—and after while you will have a singing church.

C. C. McCabe.

52
HYMNS OF THE HEART.

1 **Soldiers of the Cross.**

J. B. WATERBURY.   Tune, CALEDONIA. 7, 7, 7, 6.

1. Sol-diers of the cross, a-rise! Lo! your Lead-er from the skies
Waves be-fore you glo-ry's prize, The prize of vic-tor-y.
Seize your ar-mor, gird it on; Now the bat-tle will be won;
See, the strife will soon be done; Then struggle man-ful-ly.

2. Now the fight of faith be-gin, Be no more the slaves of sin.
Strive the vic-tor's palm to win, Trust-ing in the Lord:
Gird ye on the ar-mor bright, Warriors of the King of Light,
Nev-er yield, nor lose by flight Your di-vine re-ward.

3 Jesus conquered when he fell,
Met and vanquished earth and hell;
Now he leads you on to swell
   The triumphs of his cross.
Though all earth and hell appear,
Who will doubt, or who can fear?
God, our strength and shield, is near;
   We cannot lose our cause.

4 Onward, then, ye hosts of God!
Jesus points the victor's rod;
Follow where your Leader trod;
   You soon shall see his face.
Soon, your enemies all slain,
Crowns of glory you shall gain,
Soon you'll join that glorious train
   Who shout their Saviour's praise.

Copyright, 1882, by JOHN J. HOOD.

3. Jesus Shall Reign.

Isaac Watts.   Tune, MIGDOL. L. M.

1. Jesus shall reign where'er the sun Does his suc- ces - sive journeys run;
2. From north to south the princes meet, To pay their homage at his feet;

His kingdom spread from shore to shore, Till moons shall wax and wane no more.
While western empires own their Lord, And savage tribes attend his word.

3 To him shall endless prayer be made,
And endless praises crown his head;
His name like sweet perfume shall rise
With every morning sacrifice.

4 People and realms of every tongue
Dwell on his love with sweetest song,
And infant voices shall proclaim
Their early blessings on his name.

4. Just as I Am.

Charlotte Elliott.   Tune, HAMBURG. L. M.

1. Just as I am, with-out one plea, But that thy blood was shed for me,
2. Just as I am, and wait-ing not To rid my soul of one dark blot,

And that thou bids't me come to thee, O Lamb of God, I come! I come!
To thee whose blood can cleanse each spot, O Lamb of God, I come! I come!

3 Just as I am, though tossed about
With many a conflict, many a doubt,
Fightings within, and fears without,
O Lamb of God, I come! I come!

4 Just as I am—poor, wretched, blind;
Sight, riches, healing of the mind,
Yea, all I need, in thee to find,
O Lamb of God, I come! I come!

5 Just as I am—thou wilt receive,
Wilt welcome, pardon, cleanse, relieve;
Because thy promise I believe,
O Lamb of God, I come! I come!

6 Just as I am—thy love unknown
Hath broken every barrier down;
Now, to be thine, yea, thine alone,
O Lamb of God, I come! I come!

5. The Morning Light.

SAMUEL F. SMITH. Tune, WEBB. 7, 6.

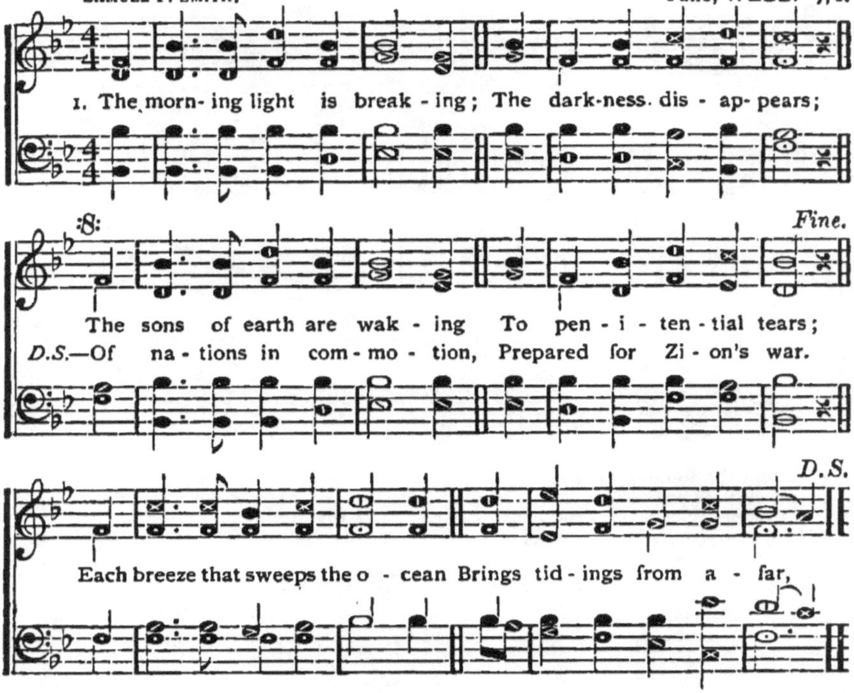

1. The morn-ing light is break-ing; The dark-ness dis-ap-pears;
The sons of earth are wak-ing To pen-i-ten-tial tears;
D.S.—Of na-tions in com-mo-tion, Prepared for Zi-on's war.
Each breeze that sweeps the o-cean Brings tid-ings from a-far,

2 See heathen nations bending
   Before the God we love,
  And thousand hearts ascending
   In gratitude above;
  While sinners, now confessing,
   The gospel call obey,
  And seek the Saviour's blessing,
   A nation in a day.

3 Blest river of salvation,
   Pursue thine onward way;
  Flow thou to every nation,
   Nor in thy richness stay:
  Stay not till all the lowly
   Triumphant reach their home:
  Stay not till all the holy
   Proclaim, "The Lord is come!"

6. STAND UP FOR JESUS. 7, 6.

1 Stand up, stand up for Jesus,
   Ye soldiers of the cross;
  Lift high his royal banner,
   It must not suffer loss:
  From victory unto victory
   His army shall he lead,
  Till every foe is vanquished
   And Christ is Lord indeed.

2 Stand up, stand up for Jesus,
   The trumpet call obey;
  Forth to the mighty conflict,
   In this his glorious day:
  "Ye that are men, now serve him,"
   Against unnumbered foes;
  Your courage rise with danger,
   And strength to strength oppose.

3 Stand up, stand up for Jesus,
   Stand in his strength alone;
  The arm of flesh will fail you;
   Ye dare not trust your own:
  Put on the gospel armor,
   Each piece put on with prayer:
  Where duty calls, or danger,
   Be never wanting there.

4 Stand up, stand up for Jesus,
   The strife will not be long;
  This day the noise of battle,
   The next the victor's song:
  To him that overcometh,
   A crown of life shall be;
  He with the King of glory
   Shall reign eternally.

7. Of Him who did Salvation.

Tr. by A. W. Boehm. Tune, ROCKINGHAM. L. M.

1. Of him who did sal-vation bring, I could forev-er think and sing; A-rise, ye need-y,—he'll relieve; A-rise, ye guilt-y,—he'll forgive.

2 Ask but his grace, and lo, 'tis given;
Ask, and he turns your hell to heaven:
Though sin and sorrow wound my soul,
Jesus, thy balm will make it whole.

3 To shame our sins he blushed in blood;
He closed his eyes to show us God:
Let all the world fall down and know
That none but God such love can show.

4 'Tis thee I love, for thee alone
I shed my tears and make my moan;
Where'er I am, where'er I move,
I meet the object of my love.

5 Insatiate to this spring I fly;
I drink, and yet am ever dry:
Ah! who against thy charms is proof?
Ah! who that loves, can love enough?

8. Come, O my Soul.

Thomas Blacklock. Tune, LUTON. L. M.

1. Come, O my soul, in sacred lays, Attempt thy great Crea-tor's praise:
2. Enthroned amid the radiant spheres, He glory, like a gar-ment, wears;
But oh! what tongue can speak his fame? What mortal verse can reach the theme?
To form a robe of light di-vine, Ten thousand suns around him shine.

3 In all our Maker's grand designs,
Omnipotence, with wisdom, shines;
His works, thro' all this wondrous frame,
Declare the glory of his name.

4 Raised on devotion's lofty wing,
Do thou, my soul, his glories sing;
And let his praise employ thy tongue,
Till listening worlds shall join the song.

9. And can it Be?

C. Wesley. — Tune, FILLMORE. L. M.

1. And can it be that I should gain An interest in the Saviour's blood?
Died he for me, who caused his pain? For me, who him to death pursued?

D.C.—A-mazing love! how can it be That thou, my Lord, shouldst die for me?

2 'Tis mystery all! the immortal dies!
  Who can explore his strange design?
In vain the first-born seraph tries
  To sound the depths of love divine;
'Tis mercy all! let earth adore!
  Let angel minds inquire no more.

3 He left his Father's throne above,—
  So free, so infinite his grace!—
Emptied himself of all but love,
  And bled for Adam's helpless race;
'Tis mercy all, immense and free,
  For, O my God, it found out me!

4 Long my imprisoned spirit lay,
  Fast bound in sin and nature's night;
Thine eye diffused a quickening ray,
  I woke, the dungeon flamed with light:
My chains fell off, my heart was free,
  I rose, went forth, and followed thee.

5 No condemnation now I dread,
  Jesus, with all in him, is mine;
Alive in him, my living Head,
  And clothed in righteousness divine,
Bold I approach the eternal throne,
  And claim the crown, thro' Christ, my own.

10. O Thou to whose.

Tr. by J. Wesley. — Tune, STONEFIELD. L. M.

1. O thou, to whose all-search-ing sight The dark-ness shin-eth as the light, Search, prove my heart, it
2. Wash out its stains, re-fine its dross, Nail my af-fec-tions to the cross; Hal-low each thought; let

132

O Thou to whose.—CONCLUDED.

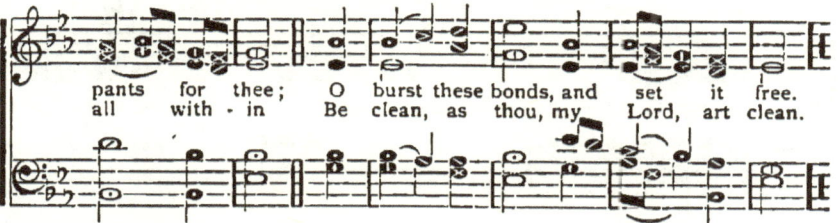

pants for thee; O burst these bonds, and set it free.
all with-in Be clean, as thou, my Lord, art clean.

3 If in this darksome wild I stray,
Be thou my light, be thou my way:
No foes, no violence I fear,
No fraud, while thou, my God, art near.

4 When rising floods my soul o'erflow,
When sinks my heart in waves of woe,
Jesus, thy timely aid impart,
And raise my head, and cheer my heart.

5 Saviour, where'er thy steps I see,
Dauntless, untired, I follow thee;
O let thy hand support me still,
And lead me to thy holy hill.

6 If rough and thorny be the way,
My strength proportion to my day;
Till toil, and grief, and pain shall cease,
Where all is calm, and joy, and peace.

11 O that My Load.

C. WESLEY. Tune, FOREST. L. M.

1. O that my load of sin were gone! O that I could at last sub-mit
At Je-sus' feet to lay it down—To lay my soul at Je-sus' feet!

2 Rest for my soul I long to find:
Saviour of all, if mine thou art,
Give me thy meek and lowly mind,
And stamp thine image on my heart.

3 Break off the yoke of inbred sin,
And fully set my spirit free;
I cannot rest till pure within,
Till I am wholly lost in thee.

4 Fain would I learn of thee, my God,
Thy light and easy burden prove,
The cross all stained with hallowed blood,
The labor of thy dying love.

5 I would, but thou must give the power;
My heart from every sin release;
Bring near, bring near the joyful hour,
And fill me with thy perfect peace.

12   O LORD, THY HEAVENLY GRACE.   L. M.

1 O Lord, thy heavenly grace impart,
And fix my frail, inconstant heart;
Henceforth my chief desire shall be
To dedicate myself to thee.

2 Whate'er pursuits my time employ,
One thought shall fill my soul with joy:
That silent, secret thought shall be,
That all my hopes are fixed on thee.

3 Thy glorious eye pervadeth space;
Thy presence, Lord, fills every place;
And wheresoe'er my lot may be,
Still shall my spirit cleave to thee.

4 Renouncing every worldly thing,
And safe beneath thy spreading wing,
My sweetest thought henceforth shall be,
That all I want I find in thee.

13. Jesus, Thou Joy.

Tr. by R. Palmer. Tune, WELTON. L. M.

1. Jesus, thou Joy of loving hearts! Thou Fount of life! thou Light of men!
From the best bliss that earth imparts, We turn un-filled to thee a-gain.

2 Thy truth unchanged hath ever stood;
Thou savest those that on thee call;
To them that seek thee, thou art good,
To them that find thee, all in all.

3 We taste thee, O thou Living Bread,
And long to feast upon thee still;
We drink of thee, the Fountain Head,
And thirst our souls from thee to fill!

4 Our restless spirits yearn for thee,
Where'er our changeful lot is cast;
Glad, when thy gracious smile we see,
Blest, when our faith can hold thee fast.

5 O Jesus, ever with us stay;
Make all our moments calm and bright;
Chase the dark night of sin away,
Shed o'er the world thy holy light!

14. From Every Stormy Wind.

H. Stowell. Tune, RETREAT. L. M.

1. From ev'ry storm-y wind that blows, From ev'ry swelling tide of woes,
There is a calm, a sure retreat: 'Tis found be-neath the mer-cy-seat.

2 There is a scene where Jesus sheds
The oil of gladness on our heads;
A place than all besides more sweet:
It is the blood-bought mercy-seat.

3 There is a place where spirits blend,
Where friend holds fellowship with friend:
Though sundered far, by faith they meet
Around one common mercy-seat.

4 Ah! whither could we flee for aid,
When tempted, desolate, dismayed?
Or how the hosts of hell defeat,
Had suffering saints no mercy-seat?

5 There, there on eagle wings we soar,
And sin and sense molest no more;
And heaven comes down our souls to greet,
While glory crowns the mercy-seat.

15 Jesus, the Name.

C. Wesley. Tune, CORONATION. C. M.

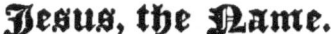

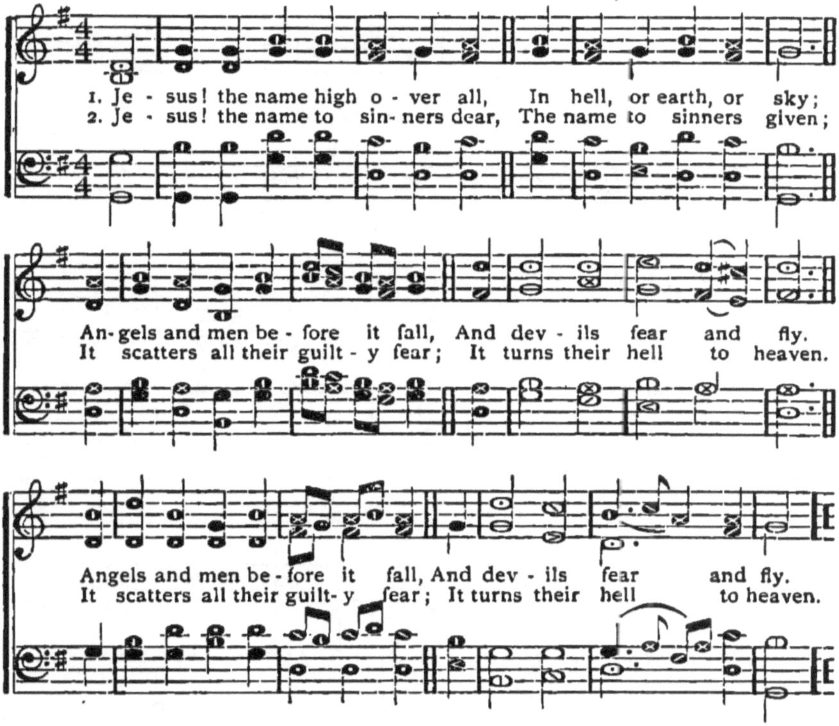
1. Je - sus! the name high o - ver all, In hell, or earth, or sky;
2. Je - sus! the name to sin- ners dear, The name to sinners given;
An- gels and men be - fore it fall, And dev - ils fear and fly.
It scatters all their guilt - y fear; It turns their hell to heaven.
Angels and men be - fore it fall, And dev - ils fear and fly.
It scatters all their guilt- y fear; It turns their hell to heaven.

3 Jesus the prisoner's fetters breaks,
And bruises Satan's head;
Power into strengthless souls he speaks,
And life into the dead.

4 O that the world might taste and see
The riches of his grace!
The arms of love that compass me
Would all mankind embrace.

5 His only righteousness I show,
His saving truth proclaim:
'Tis all my business here below,
To cry, "Behold the Lamb!"

6 Happy, if with my latest breath
I may but gasp his name;
Preach him to all, and cry in death,
"Behold, behold the Lamb!"

16 CROWN HIM LORD OF ALL. C. M.

1 All hail the power of Jesus' name!
Let angels prostrate fall;
Bring forth the royal diadem,
And crown him Lord of all.

2 Crown him, ye morning stars of light,
Who fixed this earthly ball;
Now hail the strength of Israel's might,
And crown him Lord of all.

3 Ye chosen seed of Israel's race,
Ye ransomed from the fall,
Hail him who saves you by his grace,
And crown him Lord of all.

4 Sinners, whose love can ne'er forget
The wormwood and the gall,
Go, spread your trophies at his feet,
And crown him Lord of all.

5 Let every kindred, every tribe,
On this terrestrial ball,
To him all majesty ascribe,
And crown him Lord of all.

6 O that with yonder sacred throng
We at his feet may fall!
We'll join the everlasting song,
And crown him Lord of all.

17. O Friend of Souls.

W. C. Dessler.   [Music by J. R. S.]   Tune, ROCKWELL. C. M.

1. O Friend of souls! how blest the time When in thy love I rest,
When from my wea-ri-ness I climb E'en to thy ten-der breast!
The night of sor-row end-eth there, Thy rays outshine the sun,
And in thy par-don and thy care The heaven of heavens is won.

2 The world may call itself my foe,
   Or flatter and allure :
I care not for the world ; I go
   To this tried Friend and sure.
And when life's fiercest storms are sent
   Upon life's wildest sea,
My little bark is confident,
   Because it holdeth thee.

3 To others death seems dark and grim,
   But not, O Lord, to me :
I know thou ne'er forsakest him
   Who puts his trust in thee.
Nay, rather, with a joyful heart
   I welcome the release
From this dark desert, and depart
   To thy eternal peace.

Copyright, 1882, by JOHN J. HOOD.

18 Father, whate'er.

Anne Steele.   Tune, NAOMI. C. M.

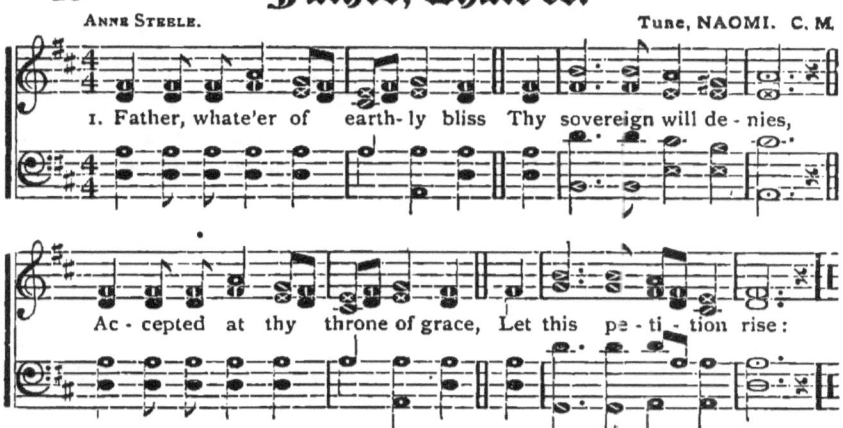

1. Father, whate'er of earth-ly bliss Thy sovereign will de-nies,
Ac-cepted at thy throne of grace, Let this pe-ti-tion rise:

2 Give me a calm, a thankful heart,
From every murmur free;
The blessings of thy grace impart,
And make me live to thee.

3 Let the sweet hope that thou art mine
My life and death attend;
Thy presence through my journey shine,
And crown my journey's end.

19 My Saviour, my almighty Friend.

Tune, EMMONS. C. M.

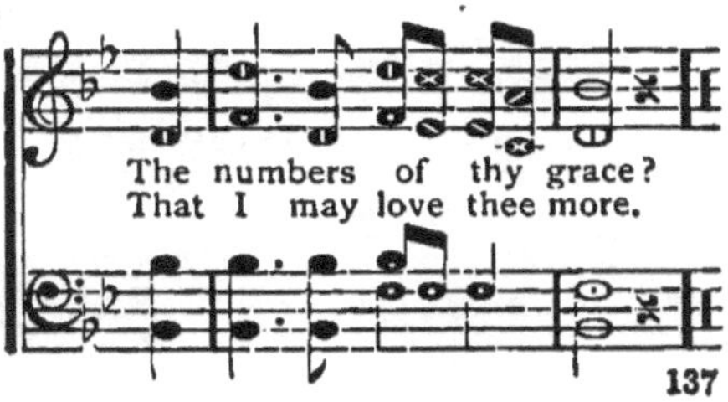

1. My Saviour, my al-mighty Friend, When I be-gin thy praise,
2. I trust in thy e-ter-nal word; Thy goodness I a-dore:

Where will the grow-ing numbers end, The numbers of thy grace,
Send down thy grace, O blessed Lord, That I may love thee more,

The numbers of thy grace?
That I may love thee more.

3 My feet shall travel all the length
Of the celestial road;
And march, with courage in thy strength,
To see the Lord my God.

4 Awake! awake! my tuneful powers,
With this delightful song;
And entertain the darkest hours,
Nor think the season long.

20 Eternal Father, Thou.

R. Palmer.   Tune, ROLLAND. L. M.

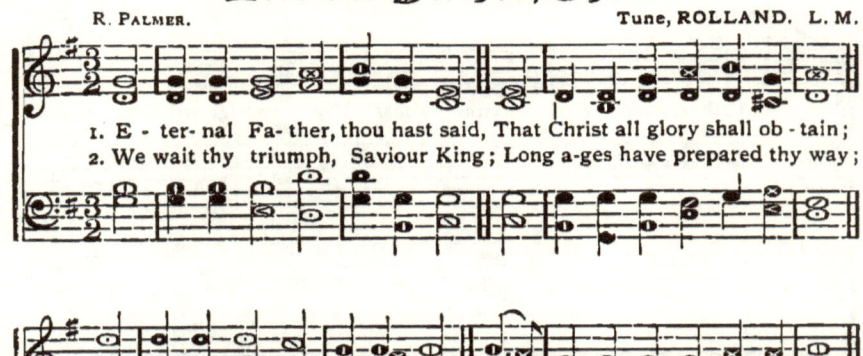

1. E - ter - nal Fa- ther, thou hast said, That Christ all glory shall ob - tain;
That he who once a sufferer bled Shall o'er the world a conqueror reign.

2. We wait thy triumph, Saviour King; Long a-ges have prepared thy way;
Now all a- broad thy banner fling, Set time's great battle in ar - ray,

Shall o'er the world a conqueror reign.
Set time's great battle in ar-ray.

3 Thy hosts are mustered to the field;
"The Cross! the Cross!" the battle-call;
The old grim towers of darkness yield,
And soon shall totter to their fall.

4 On mountain tops the watch-fires glow,
Where scattered wide the watchmen stand;
Voice echoes voice, and onward flow
The joyous shouts from land to land.

5 O fill thy Church with faith and power,
Bid her long night of weeping cease;
To groaning nations haste the hour
Of life and freedom, light and peace.

6 Come, Spirit, make thy wonders known,
Fulfil the Father's high decree;
Then earth, the might of hell o'erthrown,
Shall keep her last great jubilee.

21 The Solid Rock.

E. Mote.   Wm. B. Bradbury, by per.

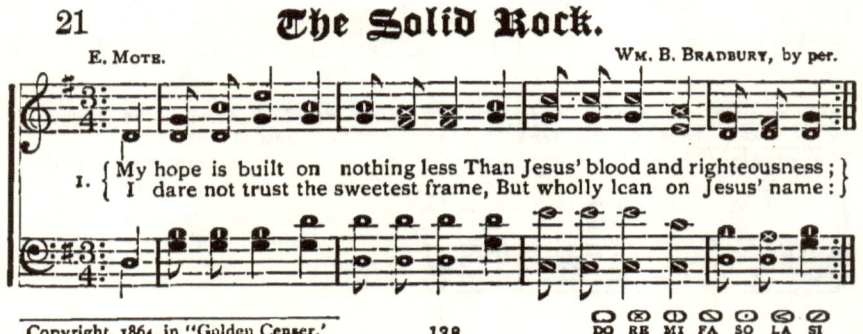

1. { My hope is built on nothing less Than Jesus' blood and righteousness;
   { I dare not trust the sweetest frame, But wholly lean on Jesus' name:

Copyright, 1864, in "Golden Censer."

DO RE MI FA SO LA SI

The Solid Rock.—CONCLUDED.

On Christ, the Sol-id Rock, I stand; All oth-er ground is sinking sand,

All oth-er ground is sinking sand.

2 When darkness seems to veil his face,
I rest on his unchanging grace;
In every high and stormy gale,
My anchor holds within the vale.

3 His oath, his covenant, and blood,
Support me in the whelming flood:
When all around my soul gives way,
He then is all my hope and stay.

22 He Dies! the Friend.

ISAAC WATTS. Tune, DUANE STREET. L. M. d.

1. He dies! the Friend of sinners dies! Lo! Salem's daughters weep around; A sol-emn darkness veils the skies, A sudden trembling shakes the ground.

D.S.—shed a thousand drops for you,—A thousand drops of rich-er blood.

Come, saints, and drop a tear or two For him who groaned beneath your load; He

2 Here's love and grief beyond degree,
The Lord of glory dies for man!
But lo! what sudden joys we see,
Jesus, the dead, revives again!
The rising God forsakes the tomb;
In vain the tomb forbids his rise;
Cherubic legions guard him home,
And shout him welcome to the skies.

3 Break off your tears, ye saints, and tell
How high your great Deliverer reigns;
Sing how he spoiled the hosts of hell
And led the monster Death in chains:
Say, "Live forever, wondrous King!
Born to redeem, and strong to save;"
Then ask the monster, Where's thy sting?
And, Where's thy vict'ry, boasting grave?

23. How Firm a Foundation.

Tune, PORTUGUESE.

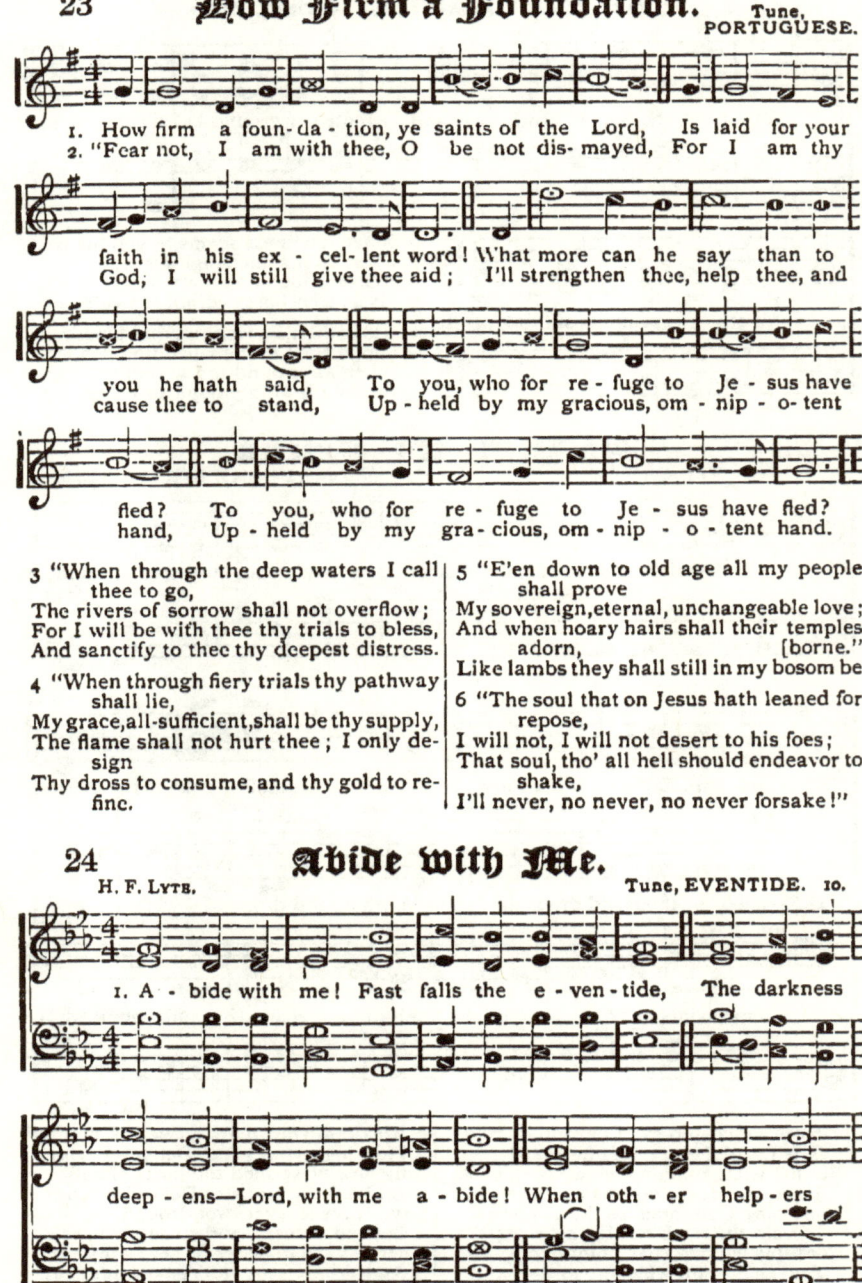

1. How firm a foun-da-tion, ye saints of the Lord, Is laid for your faith in his ex-cel-lent word! What more can he say than to you he hath said, To you, who for re-fuge to Je-sus have fled? To you, who for re-fuge to Je-sus have fled?

2. "Fear not, I am with thee, O be not dis-mayed, For I am thy God; I will still give thee aid; I'll strengthen thee, help thee, and cause thee to stand, Up-held by my gracious, om-nip-o-tent hand, Up-held by my gra-cious, om-nip-o-tent hand.

3 "When through the deep waters I call thee to go,
The rivers of sorrow shall not overflow;
For I will be with thee thy trials to bless,
And sanctify to thee thy deepest distress.

4 "When through fiery trials thy pathway shall lie,
My grace, all-sufficient, shall be thy supply,
The flame shall not hurt thee; I only design
Thy dross to consume, and thy gold to refine.

5 "E'en down to old age all my people shall prove
My sovereign, eternal, unchangeable love;
And when hoary hairs shall their temples adorn,
Like lambs they shall still in my bosom be borne."

6 "The soul that on Jesus hath leaned for repose,
I will not, I will not desert to his foes;
That soul, tho' all hell should endeavor to shake,
I'll never, no never, no never forsake!"

24. Abide with Me.

H. F. LYTE. Tune, EVENTIDE. 10.

1. A-bide with me! Fast falls the e-ven-tide, The darkness deep-ens—Lord, with me a-bide! When oth-er help-ers

Abide with Me.—CONCLUDED.

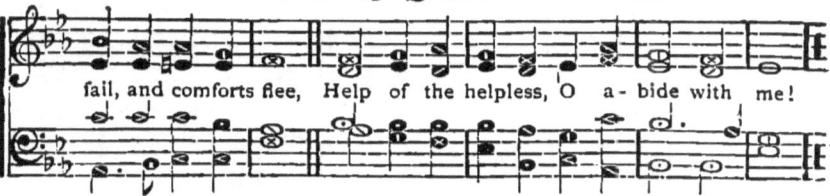

fail, and comforts flee, Help of the helpless, O a-bide with me!

2 Swift to its close ebbs out life's little day;
Earth's joys grow dim, its glories pass away;
Change and decay in all around I see;
O thou, who changest not, abide with me!

3 I need thy presence every passing hour;
What but thy grace can foil the tempter's power?
Who, like thyself, my guide and stay can be?
Through cloud and sunshine, Lord, abide with me!

4 I fear no foe, with thee at hand to bless;
Ills have no weight, and tears no bitterness;
Where is death's sting? where grave, thy victory?
I triumph still, if thou abide with me!

5 Hold thou thy cross before my closing eyes;
Shine through the gloom and point me to the skies; [shadows flee;
Heaven's morning breaks, and earth's vain
In life, in death, O Lord, abide with me!

25 My Times are in Thy Hand.

W. F. LLOYD.   Tune, SELVIN. S. M.

1. "My times are in thy hand:" My God, I wish them there;
My life, my friends, my soul, I leave En-tire-ly to thy care,
My life, my friends, my soul, I leave En-tire-ly to thy care.

2 "My times are in thy hand,"
Whatever they may be;
Pleasing or painful, dark or bright,
As best may seem to thee.

3 "My times are in thy hand;"
Why should I doubt or fear?
My Father's hand will never cause
His child a needless tear.

4 "My times are in thy hand,"
Jesus, the crucified!
The hand my cruel sins had pierced
Is now my guard and guide.

5 "My times are in thy hand;"
I'll always trust in thee;
And, after death, at thy right hand
I shall forever be

26. Jesus, the Very Thought.

Tr. by E. Caswall. Tune, EVAN. C. M.

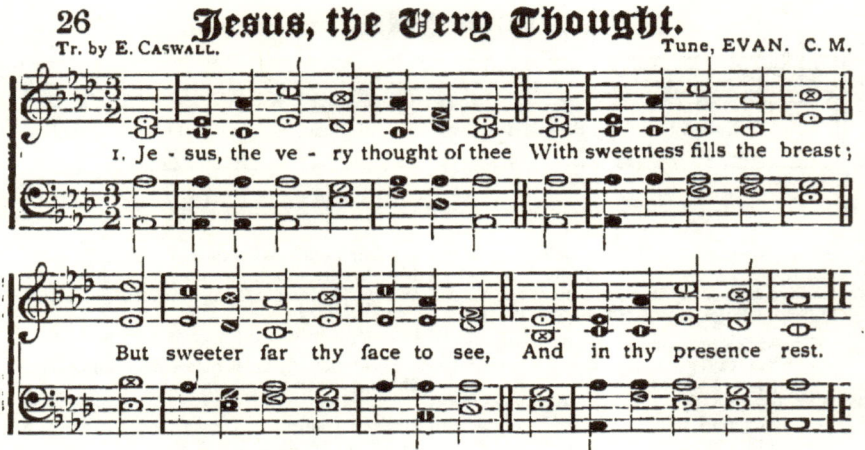

1. Jesus, the very thought of thee
With sweetness fills the breast;
But sweeter far thy face to see,
And in thy presence rest.

2 No voice can sing, no heart can frame,
Nor can the memory find
A sweeter sound than Jesus' name,
The Saviour of mankind.

3 O Hope of every contrite heart,
O Joy of all the meek,
To those who ask, how kind thou art!
How good, to those who seek!

4 But what to those who find? Ah, this
Nor tongue nor pen can show:
The love of Jesus, what it is,
None but his loved ones know.

5 Jesus, our only joy be thou,
As thou our prize wilt be;
In thee be all our glory now,
And through eternity.

27. O for a Heart.

C. Wesley. Tune, AVON. C. M.

1. O for a heart to praise my God,
A heart from sin set free!
A heart that always feels thy blood,
So freely spilt for me!

2 A heart resigned, submissive, meek,
My great Redeemer's throne;
Where only Christ is heard to speak,
Where Jesus reigns alone.

3 O for a lowly, contrite heart,
Believing, true, and clean,
Which neither life nor death can part
From him that dwells within!

4 A heart in every thought renewed,
And full of love divine;
Perfect, and right, and pure, and good,
A copy, Lord, of thine.

5 Thy nature, gracious Lord, impart;
Come quickly from above;
Write thy new name upon my heart,
Thy new, best name of Love.

28. My God, the Spring.

ISAAC WATTS.   Tune, PEORIA. C. M.

1. My God, the Spring of all my joys, The life of my delights, The glo-ry of my bright-est days, And com-fort of my nights!

2 In darkest shades, if thou appear,
  My dawning is begun;
Thou art my soul's bright morning star,
  And thou my rising sun.

3 The opening heavens around me shine
  With beams of sacred bliss,
If Jesus shows his mercy mine,
  And whispers I am his.

4 My soul would leave this heavy clay
  At that transporting word,
Run up with joy the shining way,
  To see and praise my Lord.

5 Fearless of hell and ghastly death,
  I'd break through every foe;
The wings of love and arms of faith
  Would bear me conqueror through.

29. While Thee I Seek.

H. M. WILLIAMS.   Tune, CADDO. C. M.

1. While thee I seek, pro-tect-ing Power, Be my vain wish-es stilled; And may this con-se-cra-ted hour With bet-ter hopes be filled.
2. Thy love the power of thought bestowed; To thee my thoughts would soar: Thy mer-cy o'er my life has flowed; That mer-cy I a-dore.

3 In each event of life, how clear
  Thy ruling hand I see!
Each blessing to my soul more dear,
  Because conferred by thee.

4 In every joy that crowns my days,
  In every pain I bear,
My heart shall find delight in praise,
  Or seek relief in prayer.

5 When gladness wings my favored hour,
  Thy love my thoughts shall fill;
Resigned, when storms of sorrow lower,
  My soul shall meet thy will.

6 My lifted eye, without a tear,
  The gathering storm shall see:
My steadfast heart shall know no fear;
  That heart will rest on thee.

Copyright, 1853, 1881, in "The Shawm."

30. I Will Praise Thee.

T. Olivers. C. C. Converse. By per.

1. O thou God of my salvation, My Redeemer from all sin;
Moved by thy divine compassion, Who hast died my heart to win,
D.S.—I will praise thee, I will praise thee; Where shall I thy praise begin?

2. Tho' unseen, I love the Saviour; He hath brought salvation near;
Manifests his pardoning favor; And when Jesus doth appear,
Soul and body, soul and body Shall his glorious image bear?

3 While the angel choirs are crying,
"Glory to the great I AM,"
I with them will still be vying—
Glory! glory to the Lamb!
O how precious
Is the sound of Jesus' name!

4 Angels now are hovering round us,
Unperceived amid the throng;
Wondering at the love that crowned us,
Glad to join the holy song:
Hallelujah,
Love and praise to Christ belong!

31 NEARER, MY GOD, TO THEE! 6, 4, 6

1 Nearer, my God, to thee!
Nearer to thee,
E'en though it be a cross
That raiseth me;
Still all my song shall be,
Nearer, my God, to thee,
Nearer to thee!

2 Though like the wanderer,
The sun gone down,
Darkness be over me,
My rest a stone,
Yet in my dreams I'd be
Nearer, my God, to thee,
Nearer to thee!

3 There let the way appear,
Steps unto heaven;
All that thou sendest me,
In mercy given;
Angels to beckon me
Nearer, my God, to thee,
Nearer to thee!

4 Then, with my waking thoughts
Bright with thy praise,
Out of my stony griefs
Bethel I'll raise;
So by my woes to be
Nearer, my God, to thee,
Nearer to thee!

5 Or if, on joyful wing
Cleaving the sky,
Sun, moon, and stars forgot,
Upward I fly,
Still all my song shall be,
Nearer, my God, to thee,
Nearer to thee!

32. What a Friend.

H. Bonar.   C. C. Converse. By per.

1. What a Friend we have in Jesus, All our sins and griefs to bear! What a privilege to carry Ev'rything to God in prayer!
   D.S.—All because we do not carry Ev'rything to God in prayer!
   O what peace we often forfeit, O what needless pain we bear,

2 Have we trials and temptations?
   Is there trouble anywhere?
   We should never be discouraged,
   Take it to the Lord in prayer.
   Can we find a friend so faithful
   Who will all our sorrows share?
   Jesus knows our every weakness,
   Take it to the Lord in prayer.

3 Are we weak and heavy laden,
   Cumbered with a load of care?—
   Precious Saviour, still our refuge,—
   Take it to the Lord in prayer.
   Do thy friends despise, forsake thee?
   Take it to the Lord in prayer;
   In his arms he'll take and shield thee,
   Thou wilt find a solace there.

33. O for a Closer Walk.

C. Wesley.   Tune, ORTONVILLE.

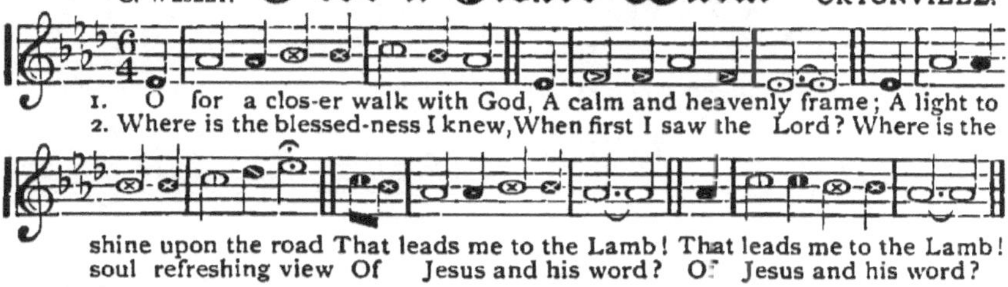

1. O for a closer walk with God, A calm and heavenly frame; A light to shine upon the road That leads me to the Lamb! That leads me to the Lamb!
2. Where is the blessedness I knew, When first I saw the Lord? Where is the soul refreshing view Of Jesus and his word? Of Jesus and his word?

3 What peaceful hours I once enjoyed!
   How sweet their memory still!
   But they have left an aching void
   The world can never fill.

4 Return, O holy Dove, return,
   Sweet messenger of rest;
   I hate the sins that made thee mourn,
   And drove thee from my breast.

5 The dearest idol I have known,
   Whate'er that idol be,
   Help me to tear it from thy throne,
   And worship only thee.

6 So shall my walk be close with God,
   Calm and serene my frame;
   So purer light shall mark the road
   That leads me to the Lamb.

34. Sun of My Soul.

JOHN KEBLE. Tune, HURSLEY. L.M.

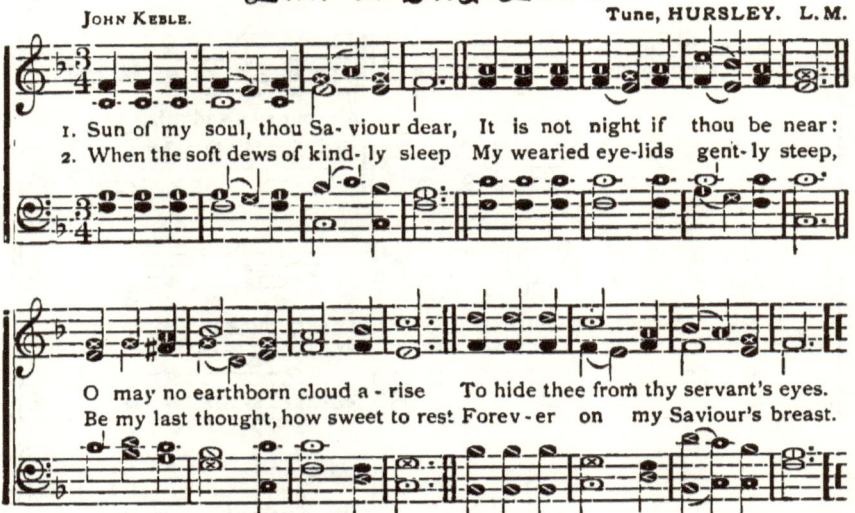

1. Sun of my soul, thou Sa-viour dear, It is not night if thou be near:
O may no earthborn cloud a-rise To hide thee from thy servant's eyes.

2. When the soft dews of kind-ly sleep My wearied eye-lids gent-ly steep,
Be my last thought, how sweet to rest Forev-er on my Saviour's breast.

3 Abide with me from morn till eve,
For without thee I cannot live;
Abide with me when night is nigh,
For without thee I dare not die.

4 If some poor wandering child of thine
Have spurned to-day the voice divine,
Now, Lord, the gracious work begin;
Let him no more lie down in sin.

5 Watch by the sick; enrich the poor
With blessings from thy boundless store;
Be every mourner's sleep to-night,
Like infant's slumbers, pure and light.

6 Come near and bless us when we wake,
Ere through the world our way we take;
Till in the ocean of thy love,
We lose ourselves in heaven above.

35. Great God, Attend.

ISAAC WATTS. Tune, BRIDGEWATER. L.M.

1. Great God, attend, while Zi-on sings The joy that from thy presence springs;
To spend one day, To spend one day with thee on earth, To
To spend one day with thee on earth, To spend one day with

Great God, Attend.—CONCLUDED.

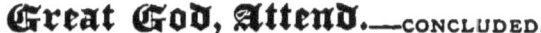

spend one day with thee on earth Exceeds a thousand days of mirth.
thee on earth Ex - ceeds . . . a thou - - - - sand days of mirth.

2 Might I enjoy the meanest place
Within thy house, O God of grace,
Not tents of ease, nor thrones of power,
Should tempt my feet to leave thy door.

3 God is our sun, he makes our day,
God is our shield, he guards our way
From all assaults of hell and sin,
From foes without, and foes within.

4 All needful grace will God bestow,
And crown that grace with glory too;
He gives us all things, and withholds
No real good from upright souls.

5 O God, our King whose sovereign sway
The glorious hosts of heaven obey,
And devils at thy presence flee;
Blest is the man that trusts in thee.

36 Glorying in the Cross.

Isaac Watts. Tune, EUCHARIST. L. M.

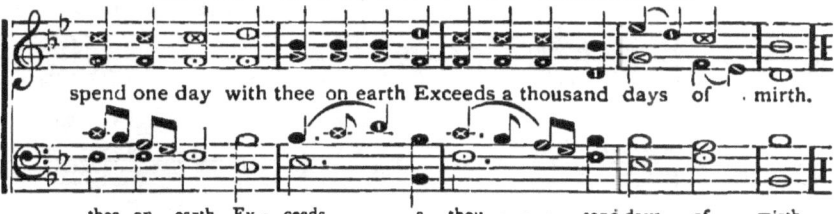

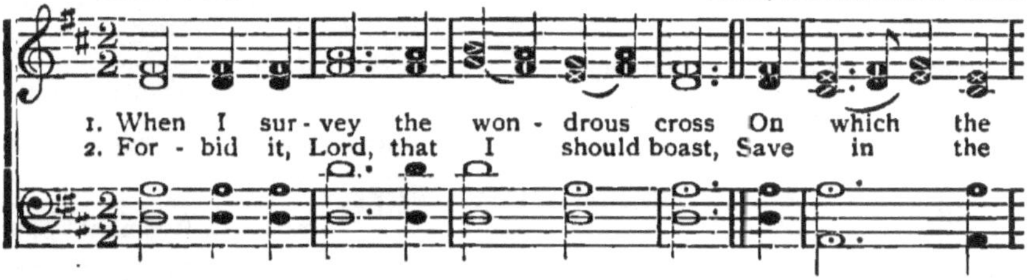

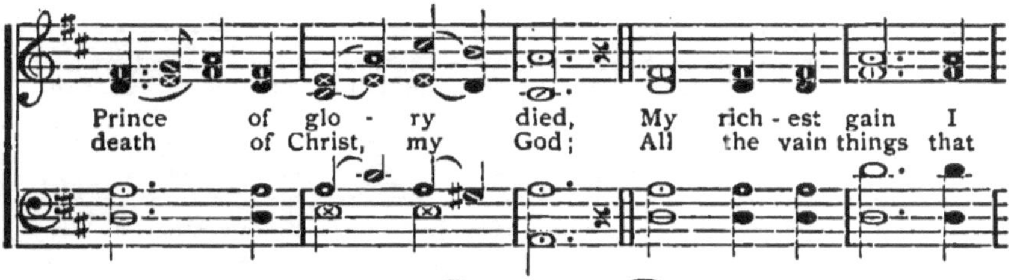

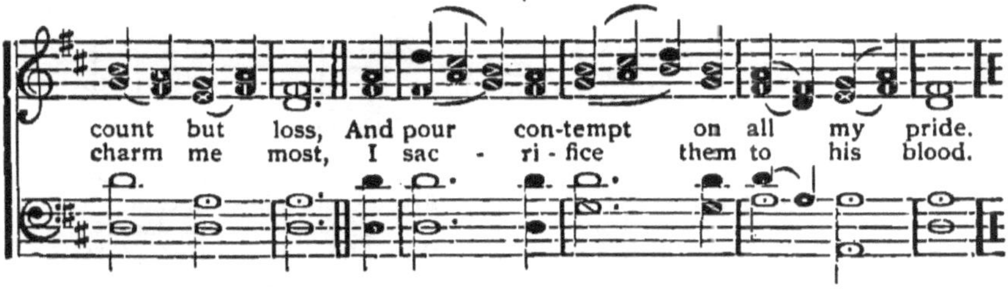

1. When I sur - vey the won - drous cross On which the
2. For - bid it, Lord, that I should boast, Save in the

Prince of glo - ry died, My rich - est gain I
death of Christ, my God; All the vain things that

count but loss, And pour con-tempt on all my pride.
charm me most, I sac - ri - fice them to his blood.

3 See, from his head, his hands, his feet,
Sorrow and love flow mingled down:
Did e'er such love and sorrow meet,
Or thorns compose so rich a crown?

4 Were the whole realm of nature mine,
That were a present far too small;
Love so amazing, so divine,
Demands my soul, my life, my all.

37. In the Cross of Christ.

Sir. J. Bowring.   Tune, RATHBUN. 8,7.

1. In the cross of Christ I glory, Tow'ring o'er the wrecks of time; All the light of sacred story Gathers round its head sublime.

2 When the woes of life o'ertake me,
   Hopes deceive, and fears annoy,
Never shall the cross forsake me;
   Lo! it glows with peace and joy.

3 When the sun of bliss is beaming
   Light and love upon my way,
From the cross the radiance streaming
   Adds more lustre to the day.

4 Bane and blessing, pain and pleasure,
   By the cross are sanctified;
Peace is there, that knows no measure,
   Joys that through all time abide.

5 In the cross of Christ I glory,
   Towering o'er the wrecks of time;
All the light of sacred story
   Gathers round its head sublime.

38. O Happy Day.

P. Doddridge.   Tune, HAPPY DAY. L. M.

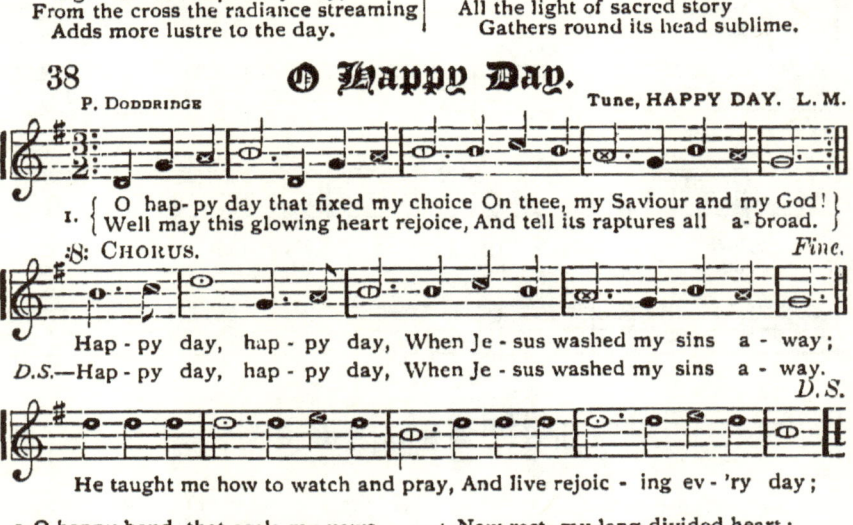

1. { O happy day that fixed my choice On thee, my Saviour and my God! Well may this glowing heart rejoice, And tell its raptures all abroad. }

CHORUS.
Happy day, happy day, When Jesus washed my sins away;
D.S.—Happy day, happy day, When Jesus washed my sins away.

He taught me how to watch and pray, And live rejoicing ev'ry day;

2 O happy bond, that seals my vows
   To him who merits all my love!
Let cheerful anthems fill his house,
   While to that sacred shrine I move.

3 'Tis done, the great transaction's done;
   I am my Lord's, and he is mine;
He drew me, and I followed on,
   Charmed to confess the voice divine.

4 Now rest, my long-divided heart;
   Fixed on this blissful center, rest;
Nor ever from thy Lord depart,
   With him of every good possessed.

5 High Heaven, that heard the solemn vow,
   That vow renewed shall daily hear,
Till in life's latest hour I bow,
   And bless in death a bond so dear.

39. Rock of Ages

Tune, TOPLADY. 7.

1. Rock of ages, cleft for me,
Let me hide myself in thee;
Let the water and the blood,
From thy wounded side which flowed,
Be of sin the double cure,
Save from wrath and make me pure.

2 Could my tears forever flow,
Could my zeal no languor know,
These for sin could not atone;
Thou must save, and thou alone:
In my hand no price I bring;
Simply to thy cross I cling.

3 While I draw this fleeting breath,
When my eyes shall close in death,
When I rise to worlds unknown,
And behold thee on thy throne,
Rock of ages, cleft for me,
Let me hide myself in thee.

40. Vain, Delusive World.

Tune, PENITENCE.

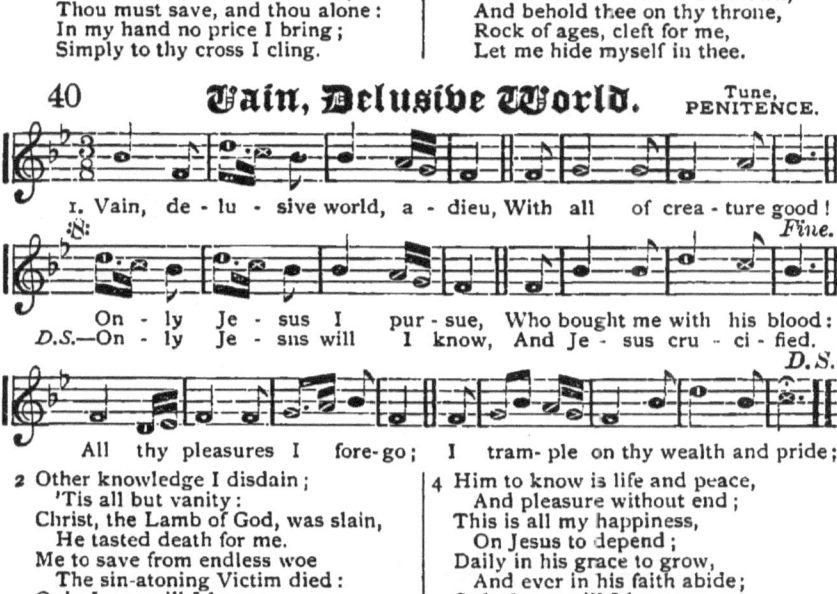

1. Vain, delusive world, adieu,
With all of creature good!
Only Jesus I pursue,
Who bought me with his blood:
All thy pleasures I forego;
I trample on thy wealth and pride;
Only Jesus will I know,
And Jesus crucified.

2 Other knowledge I disdain;
'Tis all but vanity:
Christ, the Lamb of God, was slain,
He tasted death for me.
Me to save from endless woe
The sin-atoning Victim died:
Only Jesus will I know,
And Jesus crucified.

3 Here will I set up my rest;
My fluctuating heart
From the haven of his breast
Shall never more depart:
Whither should a sinner go?
His wounds for me stand open wide;
Only Jesus will I know,
And Jesus crucified.

4 Him to know is life and peace,
And pleasure without end;
This is all my happiness,
On Jesus to depend;
Daily in his grace to grow,
And ever in his faith abide;
Only Jesus will I know,
And Jesus crucified.

5 O that I could all invite,
This saving truth to prove;
Show the length, the breadth, the height,
And depth of Jesus' love!
Fain I would to sinners show
The blood by faith alone applied;
Only Jesus will I know,
And Jesus crucified.

41. Come, Said Jesus.

Mrs. A. L. Barbauld.   Tune, HORTON. 7.

1. Come, said Jesus' sacred voice, Come, and make my path your choice;
I will guide you to your home; Weary pilgrim, hither come.

2. Thou who, houseless, sole, forlorn, Long hast borne the proud world's scorn,
Long hast roamed the barren waste, Weary pilgrim, hither haste.

3. Ye who, tossed on beds of pain,
Seek for ease, but seek in vain;
Ye, by fiercer anguish torn,
In remorse for guilt who mourn;

4. Hither come, for here is found
Balm that flows for every wound,
Peace that ever shall endure,
Rest eternal, sacred, sure.

42. Come, My Soul.

John Newton.   Tune, HENDON. 7.

1. Come, my soul, thy suit prepare, Jesus loves to answer prayer;
He himself invites thee near, Bids thee ask him, waits to hear.

2. Lord, I come to thee for rest; Take possession of my breast;
There thy blood-bought right maintain, And without a rival reign.

3. While I am a pilgrim here,
Let thy love my spirit cheer;
As my guide, my guard, my friend,
Lead me to my journey's end.

4. Show me what I have to do;
Every hour my strength renew;
Let me live a life of faith,
Let me die thy people's death.

43. Jesus, Lover of my Soul.

C. Wesley. Tune, MARTYN. 7.

1. Jesus, Lover of my soul, Let me to thy bosom fly,
While the nearer waters roll, While the tempest still is high!
D.C.—Safe into the haven guide, O receive my soul at last!

Hide me, O my Saviour, hide,
Till the storm of life is past;

2 Other refuge have I none;
Hangs my helpless soul on thee:
Leave, O leave me not alone,
Still support and comfort me;
All my trust on thee is stayed,
All my help from thee I bring;
Cover my defenseless head
With the shadow of thy wing!

3 Thou, O Christ, art all I want;
More than all in thee I find;
Raise the fallen, cheer the faint,
Heal the sick, and lead the blind.
Just and holy is thy name,
I am all unrighteousness:
False and full of sin I am,
Thou art full of truth and grace.

4 Plenteous grace with thee is found,
Grace to cover all my sin:
Let the healing streams abound;
Make and keep me pure within.
Thou of life the fountain art,
Freely let me take of thee;
Spring thou up within my heart,
Rise to all eternity.

44. Come unto Me.

Tune, HENLEY. 11, 10.

1. Come unto me when shadows darkly gather, When the sad heart is weary and distressed, Seeking for comfort from your heavenly Father,
D.S.—Come unto me, and I will give you rest.

2 Large are the mansions in thy Father's dwelling,
Glad are the homes that sorrows never [dim;
Sweet are the harps in holy music swelling,
Soft are the tones which raise the heav- [enly hymn.

3 There, like an Eden blossoming in gladness,
Bloom the fair flowers the earth too rude- [ly pressed;
Come unto me, all ye who droop in sadness,
Come unto me, and I will give you rest.

45. Let Earth and Heaven Agree.

C. WESLEY.　　　　　　　　　　　Tune, CARMARTHEN. H. M.

1. Let earth and heav'n agree, Angels and men be joined, To cel-ebrate with me The Saviour of mankind: To a-dore the all a-ton-ing Lamb, And bless the sound of Je-sus' name, And bless the sound of Je-sus' name.

2. Jesus! transporting sound! The joy of earth and heav'n; No oth-er help is found, No oth-er name is given, By which we can sal-va-tion have; But Je-sus came the world to save, But Je-sus came the world to save.

3 Jesus! harmonious name!
　It charms the hosts above;
They evermore proclaim
　And wonder at his love:
'Tis all their happiness to gaze,—
'Tis heaven to see our Jesus' face.

4 His name the sinner hears,
　And is from sin set free;
'Tis music in his ears;
　'Tis life and victory;
New songs do now his lips employ,
And dances his glad heart with joy.

5 O unexampled love!
　O all-redeeming grace!
How swiftly didst thou move
　To save a fallen race!
What shall I do to make it known,
What thou for all mankind hast done?

6 O for a trumpet voice,
　On all the world to call,
To bid their hearts rejoice
　In him who died for all!
For all my Lord was crucified;
For all, for all, my Saviour died.

46. My Jesus, as Thou Wilt.

Tr. by Miss J. BORTHWICK.　　　　　　　Tune, JEWETT. 6.

1. My Je-sus, as thou wilt: O may thy will be mine; In-to thy hand of love I would my all re-sign. Thro' sor-row or thro' joy,

2. My Je-sus, as thou wilt: Tho' seen thro' many a tear, Let not my star of hope Grow dim or dis-ap-pear. Since thou on earth hast wept

3. My Je-sus, as thou wilt: All shall be well for me; Each changing fu-ture scene I gladly trust with thee. Straight to my home a-bove,

My Jesus, as Thou wilt.—CONCLUDED.

Conduct me as thine own, And help me still to say, "My Lord, thy will be done."
And sorrowed oft alone, If I must weep with thee, My Lord, thy will be done.
I travel calmly on, And sing in life or death, "My Lord, thy will be done."

47 O Day of Rest and Gladness

C. WORDSWORTH.   Tune, MENDEBRAS. 7, 6.

1. O day of rest and gladness, O day of joy and light,
   O balm of care and sadness, Most beautiful, most bright:
2. On thee, at the creation, The light first had its birth;
   On thee, for our salvation, Christ rose from depths of earth;

On thee, the high and lowly, Through ages joined in tune,
On thee, our Lord, victorious, The Spirit sent from heaven;

Sing "Holy, holy, holy," To the great God Triune.
And thus on thee, most glorious, A triple light was given.

3 To-day on weary nations
　The heavenly manna falls;
To holy convocations
　The silver trumpet calls,
Where gospel light is glowing
　With pure and radiant beams,
And living water flowing
　With soul-refreshing streams

4 New graces ever gaining
　From this our day of rest,
We reach the rest remaining
　To spirits of the blest;
To Holy Ghost be praises,
　To Father, and to Son;
The Church her voice upraises
　To thee, blest Three in One.

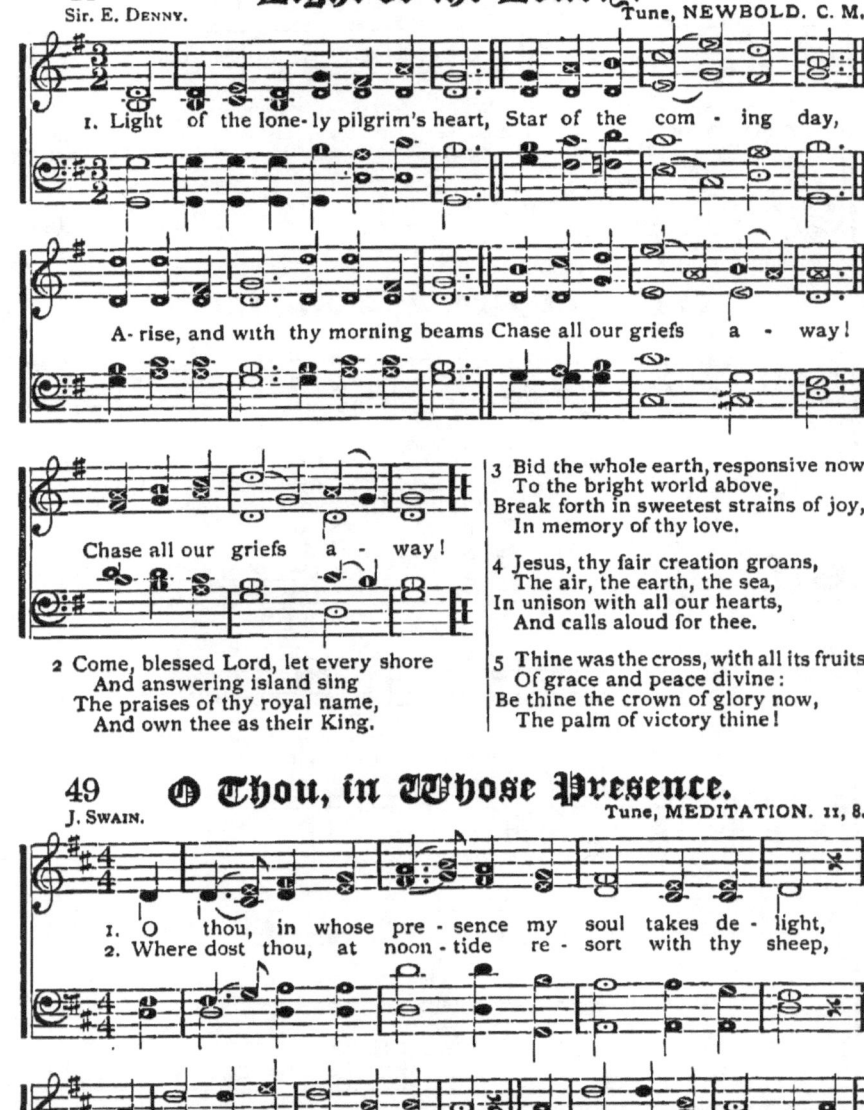

48. Light of the Lonely.

Sir. E. Denny.   Tune, NEWBOLD. C. M.

1. Light of the lonely pilgrim's heart, Star of the coming day,
Arise, and with thy morning beams Chase all our griefs away!

2 Come, blessed Lord, let every shore
And answering island sing
The praises of thy royal name,
And own thee as their King.

3 Bid the whole earth, responsive now
To the bright world above,
Break forth in sweetest strains of joy,
In memory of thy love.

4 Jesus, thy fair creation groans,
The air, the earth, the sea,
In unison with all our hearts,
And calls aloud for thee.

5 Thine was the cross, with all its fruits
Of grace and peace divine:
Be thine the crown of glory now,
The palm of victory thine!

49. O Thou, in Whose Presence.

J. Swain.   Tune, MEDITATION. 11, 8.

1. O thou, in whose presence my soul takes delight,
On whom in affliction I call, My comfort by day, and my

2. Where dost thou, at noontide resort with thy sheep,
To feed them in pastures of love? Say, why in the valley of

O Thou, in Whose, etc.—CONCLUDED.

song in the night, My hope, my sal-va-tion, my all!
death should I weep, Or alone in this wil-der-ness rove?

3 O why should I wander an alien from
Or cry in the desert for bread? [thee,
Thy foes will rejoice when my sorrows
   they see,
And smile at the tears I have shed.

4 Ye daughters of Zion, declare, have you
The star that on Israel shone? [seen
Say, if in your tents my Beloved has been,
And where with his flocks he is gone.

5 His voice, as the sound of the dulcimer
   sweet,
Is heard 'mid the shadows of death;
The cedars of Lebanon bow at his feet;
The air is perfumed with his breath.

6 He looks! and ten thousands of angels
And myriads wait for his word: [rejoice,
He speaks! and eternity, filled with his
Re-echoes the praise of the Lord. [voice,

50 Awake, My Soul.

MEDLEY. Tune, LOVING-KINDNESS. L.M.

1. Awake, my soul, in joyful lays, And sing thy great Redeemer's praise;
2. He saw me ru-ined in the fall, Yet loved me not-withstanding all;

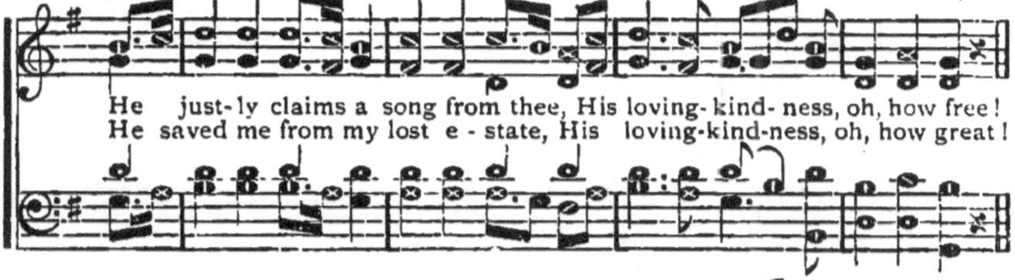

He just-ly claims a song from thee, His loving-kind-ness, oh, how free!
He saved me from my lost e-state, His loving-kind-ness, oh, how great!

Lov-ing-kindness, lov-ing-kindness, His lov-ing-kind-ness, oh, how free!
Lov-ing-kindness, lov-ing-kindness, His lov-ing-kind-ness, oh, how great!

3 Though num'rous hosts of mighty foes,
Though earth and hell my way oppose,
He safely leads my soul along,
His loving-kindness, oh, how strong!

4 When trouble, like a gloomy cloud,
Has gathered thick, and thundered loud,
He near my soul has always stood,
His loving-kindness, oh, how good!

51. All-victorious Love.

ISAAC WATTS. Tune, ST. MARTIN'S. C. M.

1. Je - sus, thine all - vic - to - rious love Shed in my heart a-broad: Then shall my feet no long - er rove,
2. O that in me the sa - cred fire Might now be-gin to glow, Burn up the dross of base de - sire
3. O that it now from heaven might fall, And all my sins consume! Come, Ho - ly Ghost, for thee I call;

Root-ed and fixed in God.
And make the mountains flow!
Spir-it of burn-ing, come!

4 Refining fire, go through my heart;
  Illuminate my soul;
  Scatter thy life through every part,
  And sanctify the whole.

5 My steadfast soul, from falling free,
  Shall then no longer move,
  While Christ is all the world to me,
  And all my heart is love.

52. Come, Ye Disconsolate.

T. MOORE. 11, 10.

1. Come, ye dis-con-so-late, where'er ye lan-guish; Come to the mercy-seat, fer - vently kneel; Here bring your wounded hearts, here tell your anguish; Earth has no sorrow that Heav'n cannot heal.

2 Joy of the desolate, light of the straying,
  Hope of the penitent, fadeless and pure,
  Here speaks the Comforter, tenderly saying,
  "Earth has no sorrow that Heaven cannot cure."

3 Here see the bread of life; see waters flowing
  Forth from the throne of God, pure from above
  Come to the feast of love; come, ever knowing
  Earth has no sorrow but Heaven can remove.

INDEX.

FIRST LINES in roman; TITLES in capitals; METRICAL TUNES in italic.
H indicates 52 HYMNS OF THE HEART.

A		HYMN.
Abide with me, fast falls the even-	*H.*	24
ABIDING,		35
All hail the power of Jesus' name,	*H.*	16
ALWAYS WITH US,		61
And can it be that I should gain,	*H.*	9
ARE YOU READY?		19
Are you ready for the Bridegroom?		58
Are you weary, are you heavy-hearted?		28
ARISE AND SHINE,		94
A SINNER LIKE ME,		124
At the sounding of the trumpet,		68
Avon, C. M.,	*H.*	27
Awake! awake! our festive day is dawn-		97
Awake! awake! the Master now is call-		96
Awake, my soul, in joyful lays,	*H.*	50

B		
Beautiful day, lovely thy light,		18
BEHOLD THE BRIDEGROOM,		58
Behold the Lamb of God,		43
Bridgewater, L. M.,	*H.*	35
BRINGING IN THE SHEAVES,		78

C		
Caddo, C. M.,	*H.*	29
Caledonia, 7, 6,	*H.*	1
Called to the feast by the King are we,		110
Carmarthen, H. M.,	*H.*	45
CHURCH OF GOD, AWAKE,		80
CHURCH RALLYING SONG,		96
CLEANSING WAVE,		125
CLEFT FOR ME,		71
Come, my soul, thy suit prepare,	*H.*	42
Come, oh, come to the ark of rest,		117
Come, O my soul, in sacred lays,	*H.*	8
Come, said Jesus' sacred voice,	*H.*	41
COME, SINNER, COME,		70
Come, thou Bright and Morning Star,		44
Come, thou fount of every blessing,		127

		HYMN.
Come unto me,—in measured tones,		91
Come unto me when shadows,	*H.*	44
Come unto me when shadows darkly		51
Come, ye disconsolate,	*H.*	52
COMING TO JESUS,		22
Coronation,	*H.*	15

D		
DAYSPRING,		44
Down in the valley, among the sweet		6
Down at the cross, where my Saviour		27
Duane Street, L. M.,	*H.*	22

E		
Each cooing dove and sighing bough,		75
Emmons, C. M.,	*H.*	19
Enthroned is Jesus now,	*H.*	2
Eternal Father, thou hast said,	*H.*	20
Eternity is dawning,		64
Eucharist, L. M.,	*H.*	36
Evan, C. M.,	*H.*	26
EVEN ME,		52
Eventide, 10,	*H.*	24
EVERMORE,		60

F		
Father, whate'er of earthly bliss,	*H.*	18
FILL ME NOW,		127
Fillmore, L. M.,	*H.*	9
FLING DOWN YOUR GOLD FOR JESUS,		64
FOLLOW ME,		15
Forest, L. M.,	*H.*	11
Forever here my rest shall be,		93
FOR YOU AND FOR ME,		10
FREELY FOR ME,		54
FREELY SPEAK FOR JESUS,		23
FREELY TO ALL,		38
From ev'ry stormy wind that	*H.*	14
From mountain top and dewy vale,		34

157

GENERAL INDEX.

G

GATHERING HOME,	66
Gentle Saviour mine, oh, the joy divine,	108
GIVE ME JESUS,	48
Give me thy heart, the sweet words	65
GIVE TO JESUS GLORY,	34
GLORIOUS FOUNTAIN,	25
Glory be to the Father,	128
GLORY TO HIS NAME,	27
GOING HOME REJOICING,	42
Great God, attend, while Zion sings, *H.*	35

H

Hamburg, L. M.,	*H.*	4
HAPPY IN THEE,		108
HAPPY TIDINGS,		33
Hark the song of holy rapture,		92
Have you heard of those heavenly		9
Hear the footsteps of Jesus,		72
Hear you not the Saviour calling?		15
He dies! the Friend of sinners dies!	*H.*	22
He has come! He has come!		112
HE INVITES YOU TO-DAY,		116
HE IS CALLING,		121
Hendon, 7,	*H.*	42
Henley, 11, 10,	*H.*	44
HE WAITS TO ANSWER PRAYER,		45
Ho! ev'ry one that thirsteth,		63
HOME AT LAST,		92
HOME OF THE RANSOMED,		56
Horton, 7,	*H.*	41
Hover o'er me, Holy Spirit,		127
How firm a foundation, ye saints,	*H.*	23
How sweet the sacred rest it brings,		111
Hursley, L. M.,	*H.*	34

I

I am bowed at the cross,	104
I am dwelling on the mountain,	31
I am saved, the Lord hath saved me,	84
I COME TO THEE,	47
I have laid my burden down where	39
I love to tell the story,	128
I'M REDEEMED,	20
In Christian love united,	45
In some way or other the Lord will	119
IN THE CLEFT OF THE ROCK,	13
In the cross of Christ I glory, *H.*	37
In the dark and cloudy day,	114
In the Rock that is higher than I,	13
IN THY HAND,	114
I saw a happy pilgrim,	81
IS MY NAME WRITTEN THERE?	32
IS NOT THIS THE LAND OF BEULAH?	31
I take my pilgrim staff anew,	114
IT REACHES ME,	102
I was once far away from the Saviour,	124
I WILL GIVE YOU REST,	51
I WILL PRAISE THEE, *H.*	30
I WILL TRUST IN THE BLOOD,	93

J

JESUS COMES,		95
Jesus, lover of my soul,		118
Jesus, lover of my soul,	*H.*	43
Jesus loves the little ones,		115
Jesus, my Lord, to thee I cry,		79
Jesus my Saviour, thou Lamb of God,		54
Jesus now offers forgiveness of sin,		38
JESUS SAVES,		85
Jesus shall reign where'er the sun,	*H.*	3
Jesus, the name high over all,	*H.*	15
Jesus, the very thought of thee,	*H.*	26
Jesus, thine all-victorious love,	*H.*	51
Jesus, thou joy of loving hearts,	*H.*	13
JESUS WILL GIVE YOU REST,		21
JESUS WILL SAVE YOU NOW,		117
Jewett, 6,	*H.*	46
JOY COMETH IN THE MORNING,		99
JOY IN HEAVEN,		103
Just as a little tired child,		47
Just as I am, without one plea,		79
Just as I am, without one plea,	*H.*	4

L

LAND OF THE BLESSED,		74
Let earth and heaven agree,	*H.*	45
LET ME CLING TO THEE,		90
Light of the lonely pilgrim's heart,	*H.*	48
Lord, I care not for riches,		32
Lord, I hear of showers of blessing,		52
Loving-kindness, L. M.,	*H.*	50
Luton, L. M.,	*H.*	8

M

MARCHING ONWARD,		26
Martyn, 7,	*H.*	43
Meditation, 11, 8,	*H.*	49
MEMORIES OF GALILEE,		75
Mendebras, 7, 6,	*H.*	47
Migdol, L. M.,	*H.*	3
Mighty Rock, whose tow'ring form,		71
My Father is rich in houses and lands,		57
MY FATHER-LAND,		29
My God, the spring of all my joys,	*H.*	28
My hope is built on nothing less,	*H.*	21
My Jesus, as thou wilt,	*H.*	46
My Saviour, my Almighty Friend,	*H.*	19
MY SHEPHERD,		82
My soul for light and love had earnest		35
My times are in thy hand,	*H.*	25

N

Naomi,	*H.*	18
NEARER HOME,		87
Nearer, my God, to thee,	*H.*	31
Newbold, C. M.,	*H.*	48
NO NIGHT IN HEAVEN,		53
Now the sowing and the weeping,		59

GENERAL INDEX.

O

O, bless the Lord, our souls and all	46
O day of rest and gladness, *H.*	47
Of him who did salvation bring, *H.*	7
O Friend of souls, how blest the *H.*	17
O for a closer walk with God, *H.*	33
O for a heart to praise my God,	27
O happy day that fixed my choice, *H.*	38
Oh, freely speak for Jesus,	23
Oh, land of the blessed, thy shadowless	74
Oh, let me cling to thee,	90
Oh, now I see the cleansing wave,	125
Oh, pray for the wretched and perish-.	50
Oh, sometimes the shadows are deep,	86
Oh, the song of the soul shall not die	4
Oh, this uttermost salvation,	102
OH, 'TIS GLORY IN MY SOUL,	69
Oh, weary pilgrim, lift your head,	99
O Lord, thy heavenly grace impart, *H.*	12
Once for all the Saviour died,	11
One by one, our loved ones slowly	67
One sweetly solemn thought,	87
ON THE LORD'S SIDE,	100
Ortonville, C. M., *H.*	33
O, sing of Jesus, Lamb of God,	20
O that my load of sin were gone, *H.*	11
O, the bitter shame and sorrow,	120
O thou God of my salvation, *H.*	30
O thou in whose presence my soul *H.*	49
O thou, to whose all-searching sight, *H.*	10
OUR WAY OF DUTY,	113
Out of darkness into light,	94
OUTSIDE THE GATE,	17

P

Peace in believing the words of my	106
Penitence, 7, 6, *H.*	40
Peoria, C. M.,	28
Poor, starving soul, there's room for	17
Portuguese, 11, *H.*	23
Praise God, from whom all blessings	128
Prayer is the key,	122
PRAY FOR THEM NOW,	50

R

Rathbun, 8, 7, *H.*	37
Redeemed! how I love to proclaim it,	7
REDEEMING LOVE,	3
Rejoice with me, the lost is found,	73
REJOICING EVERMORE,	30
RESTING AT THE CROSS,	14
Retreat, L. M., *H.*	14
Rockingham, L. M., *H.*	7
Rock of Ages, cleft for me,	39
Rockwell, C. M., *H.*	17
Rolland, L. M., *H.*	20

S

SACRED REST,	111
SAVIOUR, COMFORT ME,	114
Saviour, though long I have slighted	98
SAY, ARE YOU READY?	37
Selvin, S. M., *H.*	25
Should the death angel knock at thy	37
Should the summons, quickly flying,	19
Sinner, come, will you come?	116
SIN NO MORE?	55
S. Martins, *H.*	51
Softly and tenderly Jesus is calling,	10
Softly fades the twilight ray,	62
Soldiers of the cross, arise, *H.*	1
Soldiers of th'-eternal King,	101
Sowing in the morning, sowing seeds	78
Speak to me Jesus, I'm far from thy	8
Stand up, stand up for Jesus,	128
Stand up, stand up for Jesus, *H.*	6
Stay, sinner, stay! the night comes on,	123
Stonefield, L M., *H.*	10
Sun of my soul, thou Saviour dear, *H.*	34

T

TAKE ME AS I AM,	79
Take the world, but give me Jesus,	48
Tell it out among the heathen,	88
TELL IT TO JESUS,	28
Tell me the story of Jesus,	107
THE ALTERED MOTTO,	120
The beautiful river, the life-giving river,	40
THE BELOVED,	6
THE CHILD OF A KING,	57
THE GOLDEN KEY,	122
THE GREAT JUDGMENT DAY,	24
THE HAPPY PILGRIM,	81
The home where changes never come,	12
The Lord is my Shepherd,	82
THE LORD WILL PROVIDE,	19
The morning light is breaking, *H.*	5
THE NEW NAME,	126
THE RANSOMED SINGERS,	41
There is a fountain filled with blood,	25, 125
There is a place where the angels,	29
There is joy, there is joy,	103
THERE'S A BLESSING AT THE CROSS,	39
There's a bright land of promise for	56
There's a wideness in God's mercy,	121
THE ROCK THAT IS HIGHER THAN I,	86
THE SOLID ROCK, *H.*	21
THE SONG OF THE SOUL,	4
They are coming with songs, the	41
They are looking down upon us from	60
This is not my place of resting,	105
Though my sins were once like crimson.	5
Though troubles assail, and dangers	30
THY PRECIOUS, PRECIOUS FOLD,	98
Tidings, happy tidings,	33
Toplady, 7, *H.*	39
To the cross of Christ, my Saviour,	14
To the shadow of the Rock, in a thirsty,	16
To thy cross, dear Christ, I'm clinging,	69

U

Up to the bountiful Giver of life,	.	66

V

Vain, delusive world, adieu,	. *H.*	40

W

WAIT AND MURMUR NOT, . . .		12
Walking with Jesus, my Saviour divine,		109
WASHED IN THE BLOOD, . . .		104
WASHED WHITE AS SNOW, . .		5
Watch, ye saints, with eyelids waking, .		95
We are going home rejoicing, . .		42
We are marching, marching onward, .		26
Webb, 7, 6, ... *H.*		5
We have each our work to do, . .		113
We have heard a joyful sound, . .		85
Welton, L. M., ... *H.*		13
We shall have a new name, . .		126
WE SHALL KNOW, ...		76
What a Friend we have in Jesus, *H.*		32
WHAT A GATH'RING THAT WILL BE,		68
WHAT A REFUGE, ...		16
What of the future, my brother? . .		49
Whatso'er our sowing be, . . .		36
When did ever words so tender, . .		55
When I survey the wondrous cross, *H.*		36
WHEN THE KING COMES IN, . .		110
When the mists have rolled in splendor,		76
While Jesus whispers to you, . .		70
While thee I seek, protecting power, *H.*		29
Who is on the Lord's side? . . .		100
Will you come, will you come? . .		21
WILT THOU BE MADE WHOLE? .		72
With my sin-wounded soul, . .		22
With us when we toil in sadness, .		61

Y

You are under condemnation, careless.	42

www.ingramcontent.com/pod-product-compliance
Lightning Source LLC
Chambersburg PA
CBHW031945230426
43672CB00010B/2058